"Herrick's book proposes a st
sion of our freedoms—includi.. g
thinkers, scientists, artists and writers are among the first to suffer
from any loss of freedom, the artistic community should pay attention
to Herrick's book and support his proposal for a 2nd constitutional
convention."
—Kenneth Herlihy, sculptor and former mutual fund manager

"… I do agree that conservatives and liberals must join together to
reform our federal government. Herrick makes a strong case for a 2nd
constitutional convention."
—Emil Franzi, Libertarian and Republican campaign manager

"Neal Herrick has made an admirable attempt to reflect on the unique
history of the United States and has generated proposals that could
cast a broader and brighter light on our contemporary dilemmas."
—Dick Howard, author of *The Primacy of the Political.*
*A History of Political Thought from the Greeks to the French
and American Revolutions.* Dick Howard.com

"I couldn't put it down …Herrick takes us along a hard path, coaxing
us to muster the energy and courage to press on. First, for me, it was
fascination; the scholarship and writing is so crisp and engaging. Then
it was *incredulity*, I thought his stunning critique of our governance,
past and present, vis-à-vis the Constitution, must surely be unwarrant-
ed. Yet Herrick is overwhelmingly persuasive. As he points out, the
framers were the original authors of his thesis! Then, I felt *embarrass-
ment*, that —as a citizen—I had so thoroughly and mindlessly colluded
with the corruption of the heart and soul of our Constitution. Then
outrage, that so magnificent a document could have been stolen from
the people, for whom it was written, and in whose hands lays the
responsibility for expanding, deepening and correcting it. Finally, I
felt *enlistment*, a readiness to find my place in the strategic plan that
Herrick so meticulously profiles. As one who looks at politics through
the lens of the message and movement of Jesus and the prophets, it
occurs to me how precisely the same sequence of feelings might arise
in reading Jeremiah or Isaiah, surely Micah or Amos, certainly Jesus!"
—Rev. Dr. Howard E. Friend, pastor, professor,
social activist and author of *Recovering the Sacred Center*

Reversing America's Decline
Jefferson's Remedy

Neal Q. Herrick

History Publishing Company
Palisades, New York

Copyright © 2013 by Neal Q. Herrick
Neal Q. Herrick
LCCN: 2013947674
ISBN: 9781933909592 (QP)
        1933909595
ISBN: 9781933909943 (eBook)
        1933909943
SAN: 850-5942

Herrick, Neal Q.

    Reversing America's decline : Jefferson's remedy / by Neal Herrick. --
1st ed. -- Palisades, NY : History Publishing Co., c2013.

    p. ; cm.

    ISBN: 978-1-933909-59-2 ; 978-1-933909-94-3
(ebook)
    Includes bibliographical references and index.
    Summary: Thomas Jefferson held that the
Federalist Papers contain the "genuine meaning" of the Constitution.
The author focuses on the "manifest tenor," the general principles,
 structural principles and operational principles as they are stated and
implied in the Declaration of Independence and shows how Jefferson's
interpretation could be applied to today's government to reverse
national decline.--Publisher.

    1. United States--Politics and government--17th
century. 2. United States--Politics and
government--21st century. 3. Constitutional
history--United States. 4. Political culture--
United States. 5. Jefferson, Thomas, 1743-1826--
Political and social views. 6. United States.
Declaration of Independence. 7. Federalist.
I. Title.

                                                    2013947674
                                                       1309

Published in the United States of America by
History Publishing Company, LLC
Palisades, New York

Printed in the United States on acid-free paper

First Edition

CONTENTS

PREFACE

*Every constitution . . . naturally expires at the end of nineteen years
. . . the earth belongs to the living and not to the dead.*
—Thomas Jefferson in his letter to James Madison
dated Sept. 6, 1789

America is in a state of crisis. It is declining politically, economically and morally. The messages of this book are, first, that America's decline is not part of an inevitable cycle. It could have been avoided and it can be reversed. Second, the present strategy for reforming the US government and reversing America's decline is futile. Reformers complain about our government, protest its policies and actions, hold rallies, petition Congress to pass laws or propose constitutional amendments and "occupy" it. This strategy is nonsensical and ironic. It is nonsensical because federal civil officers have neither the inclination nor the power to reform our government. It is ironic because the reformers have both the motivation and the power. Third, there are several ways the American people can exercise this power in an orderly, peaceful and constitutional manner.

America is a miracle. It is a miracle that was made possible by an unlikely combination of circumstances. Political philosophers met with statesmen to draft the Constitution. It was also a time of crisis. Shays' rebellion and the prospect of anarchy moved the delegates to accept the necessities for compromise and for acting quickly and in concert. Their recent experience with a monarchy moved them to act on new and radical principles. In this context, they created a government "of, by and for" the people rather than "of, by and for" its civil officers. The Constitution upon which our government is based has changed the world for the better. As Hamilton predicted in *Federalist 9*, it has served as the foundation for other "edifices no less magnificent." British philosopher Lord Action was still able to write, in 1907, that the plain ideas of America "burst forth . . . upon the world they were destined to transform."

Yet the US Constitution was and is seriously flawed. Its framers realized and acknowledged this.[1] They relied on future generations to correct its flaws. However, its most serious flaw prevented this from happening. While the Declaration of Independence, the structure of the Constitution and its "genuine meaning" (as interpreted by the *Federalist Papers*)[2] all give the people the power and the duty to alter the Constitution as they deem necessary, Article V neglects to "mark out the road"[3] by which they can do so. It fails even to mention us. Thus our only direct check upon the federal government was negated by simple neglect—perhaps combined with a desire to placate the states.[4] At any rate, we (the American people) have never found a way to do our duty by the Constitution and the country. All twenty seven of the amendments to the Constitution were proposed by the federal government and all but one were rat-

---

[1] See Hamilton in *Federalist 65* and *85* and Madison in *37* and *49*.
[2] Jefferson expressed his opinion that the *Federalist Papers* were the authority on the "genuine meaning" of the Constitution in a letter to Madison of Nov. 18, 1788.
[3] See Madison in *Federalist 49*.
[4] Article V provides the state legislatures with a clear road for their use in altering the Constitution. It also makes it possible for state conventions to ratify proposed amendments, but leaves this possibility to be chosen or declined at the discretion of the state and federal governments.

ified by our state legislatures rather than by state conventions.

The events of US history tell the story behind the country's decline. This decline was (and is) not inevitable. There is no mysterious law of nature that requires empires to decline. They decline for specific causes, some of which can be eliminated. One of the great virtues of the democratic form of government is its potential flexibility. It can, if properly crafted, give its people "a clearly marked road" to use in correcting and updating their constitution. In this way, they can periodically rejuvenate their government, thus preventing their country's decline. In the present case, since there is no Article V road "marked out" Americans must mark one out for themselves. Part III of this book proposes several possible approaches that might be used to alter the Constitution.

THANK YOU THOMAS JEFFERSON

We learn from our Declaration of Independence that we have the right to alter or abolish our Constitution.[5] We learn from Madison that we are the only "legitimate fountain of power"[6] and that the Constitution is "established" by us and "unalterable" by the government.[7] These abstractions are very well, but Jefferson gets down to "brass tacks." We learn from him that we should exercise our power at least once each nineteen years. To exercise our power in any rational way we must have a constitutional convention. Over two centuries have passed, however, and Congress has yet to call a second convention. As a result, the Constitution's principles have been violated, altered and torn to shreds by all three branches of the federal government. It is time for the American people to require Congress to call a second constitutional convention. In addition to serving as a reminder of Jefferson's advice, this book raises

[5] See *Federalist 78.*
[6] See *Federalist 49.*
[7] See *Federalist and 53.*

issues that should be discussed at a second convention and suggests a strategy for seeing that Congress calls one. This Preface places these issues and this strategy in context.

OUR POTENTIAL VERSUS OUR PERFORMANCE

1947 was the best of years—and the worst of years for America. It was the best of years because the US gave the world the Marshall Plan. This Plan extended the hand of friendship to our enemies and established the US as a moral and peaceful nation. The Marshall Plan led the world toward democracy, not by "nation building," but by example. 1947 was also the "worst of years." It produced the Taft-Hartley Act, thereby weakening US labor unions and helping make this country a nation of "haves and have-nots"—a nation with the greatest gap between the rich and the poor of any developed country in the world.[8] 1947 was also the "worst of years" because it laid the groundwork for the US to become a nation of invasions, air strikes, missile attacks and a world-wide military presence. It did this with the National Security Act. This Act effectively transferred the power to declare war from Congress to the presidency. But these are only three of the many historical events that can shed light on our present predicament. There are many other historical events and historical figures that are worth attention. This book discusses and comments on a few of them.

THE ROAD THAT IS LEADING US TO TYRANNY

Recent abridgements of our freedom have not come about as a result of violence. Our own representatives, senators, presidents and justices have "gradually" imposed them. Taft-Hartley and the National Security Act are examples of how the stage was set for the gradual encroachment of our freedoms. The Patriot Act of 2001 is also a case in point. The process of abridging the

---

[8] "Income gap between rich and poor the widest ever," *CBS News*, Sept. 28, 2010.

freedom of Americans has been silent, if not gradual.[9] It has been made possible by two larger processes: the accumulation of governmental powers in the hands of the executive and the increasing responsiveness of Congress to corporations and other special interest groups.

THE ACCUMULATION OF POWER IN THE EXECUTIVE BRANCH

Over the years the executive branch has become less and less a servant of the people and more and more the dominant branch of government. The power of initiating hostilities, which the Constitution reserves to Congress, has migrated to the presidency. This is especially striking since the framers explicitly expressed their desire that presidents have nothing to do with "commencing, continuing or ending"[10] wars. Further, when presidents disagree with a legislative provision, they attach a "signing statement" to it. These statements, in effect, amend the law by declining to carry out certain of its provisions. This violates Article I, Section 1 of the Constitution, which assigns all legislative powers to Congress. The Constitution assigns presidents the routine aspects of treaty negotiation (with the substantive aspects reserved to the Senate). Yet our presidency now has virtually total control of foreign policy. At the same time, the two-party system has enabled presidents to increase their influence over judiciary appointments. As Madison wrote, in *Federalist 47*, "The accumulation of all powers, legislative and judiciary, in the same hands . . . may justly be pronounced the very definition of tyranny."

---

[9]Madison replied to Patrick Henry on June 6, 1788 in the Virginia Convention, "Since the general civilization of mankind, I believe there are more instances of the abridgement of the freedom of the people, by gradual and silent encroachments of those in power than by violent and sudden usurpations." Bailyn, Vol. II, p. 612.

[10]Madison quoted in Louis Fisher, *Presidential War Power*, 1st ed. p. 9.

THE INCREASING CONTROL OF GOVERNMENT BY BIG MONEY

Jefferson predicted in an 1816 letter to George Logan, that corporations would "challenge our government in a trial of strength." They have not, however, challenged our government. They have found it more convenient to co-opt it. This co-option was legalized in January of 2010 when the US Supreme Court decided that the "freedom of speech" guarantee in our 1st Amendment allows special interests groups to contribute to federal election campaigns.[11] This decision increases the influence exerted by "big money" in the legislative process. Under the influence of special interest groups, laws are written or changed so as to make questionable (illegal) activities legal. Laws are also written so as to place the main burden of financing government (including a defense budget that in 2010 amounted to 663.8 billion dollars) on middle and lower income Americans. The increasing influence of "big money" on our quality-of-life is suggested by the ever-widening gap between our rich and our poor and our ever-increasing national debt. It is also significant that the US was ranked 6th among developed nations in the 2008 Legatum Prosperity Index—but dropped to 9th in 2009 and 10th in 2010. The Census Bureau reported the "widest income gap ever" in 2010. The ratio between the dollars received by the top-earning 20 percent and those below the poverty line had increased from 7.7 in 1968 to 14.5.[12] According to the most recent GINI index, the US has the widest gap of any developed country. It used to be said that what was good for General Motors was good for the country. That may no longer be the case.

WE HAVE MET THE ENEMY AND HE IS US

Walt Kelley put these words in the mouth of his comic strip

[11]*Citizens United v. Federal Election Commission*, 558 U.S. 08-205 (2010).
[12]See"Income gap," *CBS News*, Sept. 28, 2010.

character, Pogo. They fit our present predicament. US courts are not responsible for our decline. Presidents are not responsible. Congress is not responsible. We ordinary people have no cause for complaint. The Declaration of Independence gives us the power and the Constitution, ratified by our forefathers in 1789, gives us the responsibility. It gives us both the responsibility and the means (however vague and confusing) for carrying it out.

THE PEOPLE'S ROLE IN GOVERNMENT

Hamilton wrote, in *Federalist 78*, that "the fundamental principle of republican government admits the right of the people to alter or abolish the established constitution whenever they find it inconsistent with their happiness." In *Federalist 49*, Madison wrote that the people should be "recurred to . . . when it may be necessary to enlarge, diminish, or new-model the powers of government..." John Stevens, Jr. wrote, in the *New York Daily Advertiser* on Jan. 21, 1788, "Should these restraints (the checks and balances) prove insufficient, it then rests with the people to restore the Constitution to its wonted vigor." Our checks and balances have indeed proved insufficient. Since genuine governmental reform requires constitutional amendments, it is clear that, as regards governmental reform, the "buck stops with us." Complaining to the civil officers of the federal government is "whistling into the wind."

WHAT "WE THE PEOPLE" HAVE DONE SO FAR

So far, we have contented ourselves with three futile exercises. First, we periodically replace one set of lawless civil officers with another set. Second, we make contributions to our many non-governmental organizations (NGO's) and rely on them to negotiate incremental changes with our federal government. Third, we protest against corruption in our federal government and ask it to reform itself (for example, the Tea Party and

Occupy movements) forgetting that the government has neither the motivation nor the power to do so. Our forefathers were willing to fight to gain their liberty. The question before us now is "What are we willing and able to do to retain ours and to stop America's decline?" This book discusses this question and proposes some possible answers.

WHAT AMERICANS COULD (AND SHOULD) DO

It is irrational for us to ask Congress to reform itself by statute or by proposing reform amendments to the Constitution. It is irrational because our present arrangements are so beneficial to the Members of Congress and to other civil officers. Further, it is not their job to reform government. They are our employees not our masters. Both the responsibility and the job belong to us. Since genuine reform requires constitutional amendments, we must act, not through Congress, but either directly[13] or through our state legislatures. Upon the application of two-thirds of these bodies, Congress must call a constitutional convention. This convention could propose reforms aimed at supporting America's claim to be a nation "of, by and for the people." For example, it could propose setting term limits for Congress, prohibiting the use of private money in federal elections, strengthening the impeachment provisions, granting employees and students an explicit right to organize and rewriting Article V to make this a true government "of, by and for the people." The time has also come for Americans to give serious consideration to instituting some forms of direct democracy at the national level. Granting ourselves the abilities to propose legislation, alter law and recall civil officers would help us regain control of our federal government.

[13] "Acting directly" means, for example, that we can compel Congress to call a convention by 1st Amendment petitions. While we clearly have the right to do so, exercising this right might involve the courts since it is not explicitly provided for in the Constitution. Four possible approaches to bringing about a convention are discussed in Part III.

The Conclusion to this book suggests a strategy and several tactics for bringing about a truly representative second constitutional convention. An essential element of this strategy is that rank-and-file conservatives and liberals (Tea Party members and Occupiers alike) join together to organize petitioning drives. This means, of course, that a 2nd constitutional convention must be limited to considering only amendments that bear on federal government reform (such as amendments dealing with impeachment, campaign finance, term limits and Article V). The petitions for the convention must specify that no social issues (on which liberal and conservative delegates are bound to disagree) may be discussed.

ACKNOWLEDGEMENTS

Thanks to my beloved wife, Zhang Yuan Yuan, who, along with her mother Yuan Min, elder brother Xiao Dong, son Yuan Hao, sister Man Xue and nieces Jing Han and Si Si, gave me a peaceful, harmonious home environment in which to work on this book. Thanks to my sister (Judith Herrick-Beard), my children (Peter, Ken, Julia and Liz) and my grandchildren (Jesse, Jacob, Virginia, Sam and Gus) for their love and support

Special thanks to my long-time friend, Ken Herlihy—one-time Harvard scholarship student, retired mutual fund manager and noted sculptor. Between our time in the military and our college days, Ken and I were charter members of United Auto Workers Local 422 at the Buick/Oldsmobile/Pontiac plant in Framingham, Massachusetts. During our daily drives to and from the BOP plant, Ken (who insisted that the car radio be tuned to classical music) instructed me and "Rocky" (the third member of our car pool) in philosophy, economics and political science. None of it meant much to me at the time but, in my riper years, Ken's lectures have stood me in good stead.

Thanks to the late Harold Sheppard who opened an important door for me when he invited me to be his co-author of *Where Have All the Robots Gone?* Thanks to Michael Maccoby and the late Eric Trist, who encouraged me to earn my PhD while in my forties—and served on my doctoral committee. Thanks to Eric's widow, Beulah Trist, for her life-long friendship and for her help with my writing.

Thanks also to Terry Mazany, John Simmons, Jon Showalter, Howard Friend, Bob Smith, Addison Kemath, Nelson Karp, Emil Franzi, J.L. (Joss) Morin, Lou Kochanek, Elin O'Hara Slavick and political philosopher Dick Howard for their encouragement and friendship.

A CAUTIONARY NOTE

This book is about lawlessness. More specifically, it is about the lawlessness of our federal government. This lawlessness is not the fault of our federal civil officers. It is rooted in constitutional flaws and is therefore our fault—the fault of "the people." We have the right and the duty to alter our Constitution when necessary but, for over two centuries, have not done so. The government, which has neither the right nor the duty to alter our Constitution, has (illegally) filled the vacuum created by our neglect.

The illegal actions (that is the lawlessness) attributed in this book to the US government are of three kinds. First, they involve violations of the Constitution. For example, a president is lawless when he invades another country without Congress having declared war—and when he attaches a signing statement to a bill declining to enforce one or more of its provisions. Congress is lawless when it abdicates its power to declare war or passes laws legitimizing its own illegal and unethical behaviors. The judiciary is lawless when a judge or a justice relies on case law in interpreting the Constitution—instead of on the Constitution itself. The first kind of lawlessness is, perhaps, the most serious.

The second kind, however, is the most insidious. It sometimes involves making statutes (or judicial decisions) that allow the passage of money from special interest groups to the civil officers of government. It comes into play whenever Congress makes a law favoring the strong over the weak or weakening the control of ordinary Americans over their government. This kind of lawlessness legitimizes actions that violate the tenor of our supreme law—the Constitution.

The third kind of governmental lawlessness occurs when a civil officer violates a statute to further his or her own interests over the interests of his or her employers—the people. This kind of lawlessness is probably far more common—and far less serious—than are constitutional violations. However, it can be traced to the same cause: our failure to pass constitutional provisions designed to encourage honesty and discourage dishonesty among our federal civil officers.

The reader will, perhaps, tire of the iteration and reiteration of the various forms of the word "lawless." The theme of the book, however, makes this recurrence unavoidable.

INTRODUCTION

*The interests of the man must be connected with the constitutional
rights of the place.*
—James Madison in *Federalist No. 51*

The "father" of our Constitution, James Madison, proposed to
his fellow-framers an astonishing and radical plan. He proposed
that they draw on the ideas of political philosophers to establish
a new and different kind of government. Previous governments
had been established to meet the needs and wishes of kings and
despots. The new American government would devote itself to
meeting the needs and wishes of its people.

This had been tried before. But this time the framers hoped
to accomplish it by taking a realistic view of human nature and
writing a constitution based on this view. That is, the framers
accepted as a given that human beings, in general, strive to further their own personal self-interests—and exert themselves on
behalf of others only when this advances their own goals. In a
monarchy, for example, its civil officers further their own interests by seeking to please the king. Thus the wheels of a monarchial government are kept turning by the love of human beings
for the titles and glory that are at the disposal of the king. In a

dictatorship, the civil officers exert themselves on behalf of their dictator in order to avoid torture and imprisonment. Fear keeps the wheels turning. Civil officers in a democracy cannot hope for titles or glory in return for honest service. Neither do they fear torture or death. Yet, in order to keep the wheels of our government turning, our civil officers must be motivated to serve their masters—the people. That is, democracies must either depend on human virtue to keep their wheels turning or they must create supplementary motivations. Our founding fathers gave a great deal of consideration to this inherent "weakness" of democracy[14] and designed a structure of what Hamilton called "new discoveries" to provide these "supplementary motivations." This structure consists of an independent judiciary, an elected legislature, a separation of governmental powers and a system of checks and balances. Impeachment was, in the minds of the framers, prominent among these checks and balances. However, the "new discoveries" proved to be imperfectly designed. The impeachment and amendment provisions, for example, were fatally flawed. Our civil officers now have little to gain by meeting our needs and little to fear from neglecting them. On the other hand, they have a great deal to gain by meeting the needs of corporations and other special interest groups and a great deal to fear from neglecting them. On Election Day we vote one group of rascals out and another group in.[15] This is futile. It does nothing to cure the flaws in our political system that foster lawlessness, corruption and an over responsiveness to corporations.

Of course, our federal civil officers are not really rascals. They

---

[14]Madison and his fellow-framers relied heavily on Charles-Louis de Montesquieu. In *The Spirit of the Laws*, Book III (1698), de Montesquieu called democracy's dependence of virtue its "weakness."

[15]This is not to say that all people are the same. It is true that we are all the same in that we are in accord with Jeremy Bentham's theory that we all seek pleasure and avoid pain. Some of us, however, get a great deal of pleasure from helping others. Some others of us get pleasure mainly from helping themselves.

are rational, well-meaning, human beings. However, they are not angels either. They do what gives them pleasure and avoid doing what brings them pain. They often do what brings them pleasure in the short run, even though it will, in the long run, make them miserable. In order to bring our country back from the brink of tyranny and create for ourselves a lawful and responsive government that does not spend more than it takes in, we must break this pattern. We must be willing to suffer the short-run pain and inconvenience of fighting for genuine governmental reform - in order to gain the long-term satisfaction of having done the right thing for ourselves and for future generations.

Our forefathers attempted to write a Constitution that aligned the personal interests of our civil officers with our interests. It is remarkable that they even attempted this feat. It is more remarkable that they came close to succeeding. They were designing a complex political experiment under great pressure. It is important to note that they did not expect the Constitution, as crafted, approved and ratified by them, to stand the test of time. Madison and Hamilton were explicit on this point. Jefferson went so far as to write that constitutions should be declared void after twenty years—and new ones made.[16] The framers made it the responsibility of future generations, informed by experience, to remedy their creation's flaws and adjust it to changing times. On the other hand, they did not intend that the government alter our Constitution. Article V purposefully withholds this power from the federal government. Our Declaration of Independence and the Constitution itself - as interpreted by the *Federalist Papers*, give this power (and responsibility) solely to the people. We (the people) have failed miserably to exercise this power and to carry out this responsibility. Had we not neglected this duty, our country might not be in crisis today.

---

[16] Thomas Jefferson wrote this on Sept. 6, 1789.

THE CONSTITUTION WAS INTENDED TO BE A WORK IN PROGRESS

The framers of our Constitution carried out a project that was new, large and incredibly complex. They knew they could not get it right with their first effort. A pioneering effort of such complexity was bound to involve a great deal of trial and error. This trial and error part of the project was to be carried out by future generations of Americans. In *Federalist 9*, Madison alluded to a time when "it may be necessary" (for the people) "to enlarge, diminish, or new-model the powers of government." Hamilton in *Federalist 65*, urged his fellow framers not to strive for perfection. He argued, in *Federalist 85*, that it would be far easier to amend the Constitution later than to make it perfect in 1787. Experience would shed light on issues that were then clouded. Jefferson proposed that constitutional conventions be held no less often than once each twenty years. In a letter to James Madison, he wrote, "every constitution expires at the end of nineteen years." He believed that constitutions should serve the needs and wishes of living populations, not the needs and wishes of their ancestors. Madison, in *Federalist 53*, alluded to our Constitution as "established by the people and unalterable by the government." Our founding fathers wished us to maintain a truly "living" constitution that would reflect the wishes and needs of each successive generation. We have not, however, heeded their wishes. Instead of holding periodic constitutional conventions, we have stood idly by while our courts, our Congresses and our presidents have (illegally) twisted and turned the original Constitution until it has become virtually meaningless. We can no longer take pride in being a nation ruled by law rather than by men and women. As Madison wrote in *Federalist 37*, "An irregular and mutable legislation is not more an evil in itself than it is odious to the people."

This book proposes that we no longer neglect the duty imposed on us by our forefathers. It is our responsibility to improve and adjust our Constitution.[17]   We should (1) correct the inevitable flaws in the original document and (2) make such changes as are necessary to accommodate the changes that have come about in our economy, our culture and our demographics. This requires periodic constitutional conventions. A 2nd convention would give us the means of complying with our Constitution's "rock bottom" principles (self-government and protecting the weak from the strong) and, at the same time, correct and adjust its flaws as necessary.

Statutes cannot remedy our difficulties. A convention is necessary for two reasons. First, there are flaws in the Constitution that cannot be corrected by statute. Second, Congress controls the making of statutes. The Constitution is the only law that can be made directly by the people. It is therefore, the only practicable means of achieving genuine governmental reform. It is a logical strategy because a vast majority of ordinary Americans (on the right and on the left) are in favor of genuine governmental reform. The major difficulty to be overcome in affecting this strategy will be the bringing together of the Tea Party, Occupy (and all the other groups that are funded by the small donations of ordinary Americans) together to jointly bring about a 2nd constitutional convention. The key to success will be to petition for a "limited" convention to discuss only amendments concerned with governmental reform. Social issues—on which the left and the right have genuine differences—must be kept "off the table" by prior agreement.

TWO PHILOSOPHERS WHOSE IDEAS INSPIRED THE FRAMERS

Some of the ideas about government that were current in the late 18th century came from France and England. de Montesquieu wrote about the structure of government. Bentham was an early utilitarian.

---

[17] It is also our duty to prevent our government from altering the Constitution.

BARON LOUIS DE MONTESQUIEU

The political philosophy of de Montesquieu (See Chapter 6) was influential among our founding fathers. Madison, in particular, was well familiar with the work of the French Baron. Not an enthusiastic supporter of democracy, de Montesquieu was, however, an advocate of the separation of powers. His comments on the various forms of government were of great use to Madison and his colleagues. He theorized that each form of government is dependent on a guiding principle. The principle on which monarchies are based, he said, is honor. The principle upon which totalitarian governments are based is fear. The principle on which democracies are based is virtue.

This, de Montesquieu believed, is a fundamental weakness of democracies. Unlike the love of honor and the fear of torture and death, the love of virtue (for its own sake) is neither pervasive nor remarkably strong among human beings. According to Montesquieu, the weakness of virtue (for its own sake) as a motivator is the main structural weakness of democracies. The civil officers in a monarchy are honored for doing the bidding of their king. The civil officers in a dictatorship must do the bidding of the dictator or suffer the consequences. Civil officers in a democracy, while we pay their salaries, sometimes seem to forget that they are accountable to us. They find it more pleasurable and less painful to do the bidding of corporations and special interest groups. This is not the fault of our civil officers. It is the fault of our Constitution—for which we, not our civil officers, are responsible.

It is, of course, true that many of us humans are strongly motivated by the pleasure we get from doing good to others. This is especially true when the others (to whom we do good) are appreciative. In a democracy, however, the people are rarely appreciative of a lawful and honest civil officer. Further, honors are awarded according to quite different criteria. For example, the late Gerald Ford received the Kennedy Profiles in Courage Award for 1974. The Kennedy committee chose Mr. Ford for this honor because he (illegally) pardoned the late President Nixon (See Chapter 2). Perhaps the most serious offense a president can commit is to violate the Constitution. The Constitution specifically prohibits presidential pardons in impeachment cases. Yet Mr. Ford's offense earned him one of the highest "honors" available to a civil officer in America. If we want an honest, lawful responsive government, we should not reward dishonest, lawless unresponsive behavior. Instead, we should impeach, remove and disqualify miscreant civil officers.

JEREMY BENTHAM

English philosopher Jeremy Bentham's *Fragment on Government* was published in 1776. While I have not found any evidence that the framers read Bentham, it seems likely that they did. In any event, they applied his theory to the problem they had in hand. This problem is suggested by the following two questions: "How can we overcome the weakness that Montesquieu says is inherent in democracy? How can we induce our civil officers to be 'virtuous' when human nature does not include a passionate love of virtue for its own sake?" One of Bentham's bold statements on human nature might have be useful in answering these questions. He wrote: ". . . the only consequences that men are at all interested in, what are they but pain and pleasure?" This statement suggests a more specific question "How can we structure the Constitution so that dishonesty and, lawlessness bring pain and honest, lawful behavior in pursuit of the 'good of the people' brings pleasure?" It would seem that the framers did ask themselves this question and acted upon their answers. They did not, however, expect their answers to be perfect.

THE IDEAS OF MADISON AND HIS FELLOW FRAMERS

An answer that evidently occurred to Madison was to make behavior that was good for the people also bring pleasure to the civil officer and to make behavior that was bad for the people bring pain to the civil officer. He commented in *Federalist 51* that "parchment" prohibitions would not motivate the civil officers of the three branches to maintain the separation of powers. Instead, the separation of powers must be made to rely on the natural desire of the civil officers of each branch to defend their branch from any usurpation by the other branches. In order to make this theory work, the civil officers must be given the means of repelling attempts at usurpation. Madison added that, where a branch is too weak it should be strengthened—and where a branch is too strong, it should be weakened. In this way, Madison thought to harness the civil officers' natural desire for power and prominence to further the public good. By protecting their own "turf" they would maintain the separation of powers and by doing so, protect the liberty of the people. As for producing pain as a response to lawlessness and corruption, the framers relied upon the impeachment provisions. James Monroe called these provisions the "mainspring of the great machine of government. It is the pivot on which it turns. If preserved in full vigor, and exercised with perfect integrity, every branch will perform its duty."[18]

HOW THEIR IDEAS WORKED OUT IN PRACTICE

The powers of government have not been kept separate. Madison's theory that the civil officers of each branch would defend their powers has proved invalid for Congress. Presidents, on the other hand, have not only defended their own powers. They have successfully usurped powers belonging to the other

---

[18] James Monroe, *The People, the Sovereigns*, James River Press, p. 16

branches. The substantial control of treaty-making and foreign policy, and the total control of decisions involving war and peace have migrated from the Congress to the presidency. Our recent presidents have also gained a significant control over the legislative process through the use of signing statements. These signing statements identify portions of the bill being signed that the president disagrees with and will not carry out.

While the war powers evidently provide the president with pleasure, the Members of Congress want no part of them. Congress does not preside over the dispensing of the new jobs and emoluments created by war.[19] Further, Congress lacks the strategic intelligence capability that is needed to make war and peace decisions. The individual members of Congress derive their pleasure from the money and favors provided by corporations and special interest groups and from the celebrity that goes along with the money and favors. The presidential signing statements do not materially interfere with this pleasure. The war powers, which Congress has abdicated, have no charms for its members. To Congress the war powers mean an increased vulnerability to voter criticism whereas voters, for a time at least, rally around a war president.

The impeachment provisions were neither preserved in full vigor nor exercised with integrity. They were doomed from the very beginning. At Hamilton's insistence the critical judicial power to try impeachments was assigned to a legislative body—the Senate. This violation of the separation of powers quickly led to the provisions becoming worthless as deterrents to lawless behavior. Of our 1,000 or so civil officers in the legislative, executive and judiciary branches, over the past 220 years only seven (all federal judges) have been impeached and convicted. One of

---

[19] Madison is quoted, in the 1st edition of Louis Fisher's *Presidential War Power* (p. 21) as writing, "War is, in fact, the true nurse of executive aggrandizement. . . In war, the public treasures are to be unlocked and it is the executive hand which is to dispense them."

the seven judges was not impeached until he had been indicted, convicted and imprisoned under criminal law. What James Monroe called the "pivot" of government has proved worthless. We relied upon it to make lawlessness so painful that civil officers would be scrupulously honest and would observe their oaths to protect the Constitution. But the pivot of our government was fatally flawed from the start. The framers, thinking little of the Supreme Court's potential, violated the separation of powers principle by assigning the power to try impeachments to a legislative body—the Senate. The Senate, of course, has been incapable of rendering impartial justice.

SUMMARY

On Nov. 15, 1777, the Continental Congress approved the thirteen Articles of Confederation. These articles brought the thirteen colonies through their war for independence. However, in the years immediately following the Revolution it became clear that amendments were needed. The existing Articles did not provide for a central government strong enough to prevent rebellions, negotiate commercial treaties and in other ways resolve problems of coordination among the thirteen colonies. In 1786, delegates from five colonies met in Annapolis to discuss problems of "trade and commerce." Thinking that the problems were too large and the representation too small, the delegates, led by Alexander Hamilton of New York and James Madison of Virginia, proposed that a convention be called, "to meet at Philadelphia on the second Monday in May next . . . to devise such further provisions as shall appear to them to be necessary to render the constitution of the federal government adequate to the exigencies of the Union."[20]

This convention was held in Philadelphia from May to September of 1787. It produced the extraordinary Constitution that is (with twenty seven amendments) still in effect today. The

[20]The University of Oklahoma College of Law: A chronology of US historical documents, accessed June 2, 2011.

framers of the document that, according to philosopher Lord Dalberg-Acton, "transformed" the world[21] were careful to tell us that their creation was not perfect. Madison emphasized the peoples' power (and responsibility) for amending it. For example, he wrote, in *Federalist 53*, that our Constitution is "established by the people and unalterable by the government." Hamilton, in *Federalist 85*, argued that the delegates should approve the Constitution, despite their disagreements and the document's flaws—on the grounds that it would be far easier to amend it in the future than to agree on changes during the Convention.

The founding fathers made it clear that "we, the people" should correct the acknowledged flaws in the Constitution and, in addition, up-date it frequently to assure that it continues to express our will. Instead, we have passively allowed our government to usurp this most crucial power. All twenty seven of our constitutional amendments have been initiated by the federal government. Rather than holding a convention each twenty years, as suggested by Jefferson, we have not held a single one since 1787.

THE PLAN OF THIS BOOK

The Preface and Introduction are intended to help the reader view our present predicament in an historical context. They introduce the idea that our many serious public policy problems are rooted in the lawlessness, corruption and lack of responsiveness of our federal government. Part I comments on a number of historical events and figures that, in some way, shed light on possibilities for governmental reform. Part II discusses some of the major problems that must be taken into account by any genuine effort at reform and rejuvenation. It also discusses some specific proposals that should be considered by any reform

---

[21]John Bartlett. *Familiar Quotations*, fourth ed., p. 750.

movement and suggests language for use (as a starting point) in altering our Constitution. Part III lists some conclusions regarding reform and proposes a strategy and tactics for re-forming our federal government. The most important problem discussed by this book is that, while the Constitution denies the federal government the power to change it, the government is routinely and illegally exercising that power. There is a potential solution: the people can exercise their power to alter the Constitution legally so as to correct the flaws that have tempted government to alter it illegally. We have the power, the duty and the motivation to correct these flaws, but have failed, during the first two centuries of the country's existence, to either exercise this power or acknowledge our duty. It is crucial that all Americans from the non-wealthy ninety per cent (90%), what-ever their partisan views, join together to retake control of the country. Our present predicament arises, in large part, from the difficulty of persuading ordinary Americans of all parties to join together in bringing about a convention. It is clear that a con-vention aimed at governmental reform must exclude social issues such as gun control and abortion and be limited to amend-ments bearing on governmental reform.

PART I

LEARNING FROM US HISTORY

The charm of history and its enigmatic lesson consist in the fact that, from age to age, nothing changes and yet everything is completely different.
—Aldous Huxley, 1894-1963, British novelist and critic

This Part describes twenty seven historical events and six historical figures. These are just a few of the events and figures in US history that have lessons to teach. But first, here are the thoughts of a few political philosophers on learning from history.

WHAT SOME POLITICAL PHILOSOPHERS SAY ABOUT HISTORY

The above quote from Huxley challenges us to distinguish between the things that do not change and the things that are completely different. Georg Hegel wrote, ". . . people and governments never have learned anything from history, or acted on principles deduced from it."[22]   Santayana wrote, "Those who cannot learn from the past are doomed to repeat it."[23] In short, if we were to believe all three philosophers, we would believe that only principles stay the same over time, people and governments have never learned from history, and we are, therefore, doomed to repeat the past. I don't think we are doomed, but I do think we have something to learn from these three philosophers.

HUXLEY

Huxley's message is, perhaps, the most important of the three. He suggested that our first step in "learning from history" should be to distinguish between principles (which do not change) and the means of giving these principles efficacy.[24] Our constitutional principles are discussed below, under Learning from our own history.

HEGEL

Hegel's words suggest that people and governments have succeeded in deducing some principles from their consideration of history, but have not acted on them. To Hegel this lack of action suggests that people and governments have not really learned. The quote leads us to ask ourselves why neither people nor governments have acted on the principles deduced from

---

[22] German philosopher Georg Hegel in *Philosophy of History*, II Reflective History, 2. Pragmatical History, Para 8 (1803).
[23] George Santayana in *The Life of Reason*, Vol. .I, 1905.
[24] "Efficacy" is a word employed by Alexander Hamilton in Federalist 80.

history. In our present day, there are, no doubt, many reasons we Americans have not learned from history. For example, most of us are busy with our individual concerns. Further, we tend to rely on elections and on the efforts of our non-governmental organizations (NGO'S) to do what can be done to correct governmental violations of widely-held principles. The main reason for our inactivity, however, is the lack of effective means by which we might alter our government so that it acts upon sound principles. As for our present government voluntarily taking actions based on sound governmental principles, why should it? Why, for example, should our civil officers "shoot themselves in the foot" by adopting term limits? This would deprive them of their status and comfortable life style. Why should they require public financing of federal elections? This would build a firewall between them and corporate money.

SANTAYANA

Santayana tells us we are bound to repeat history if we do not learn from it. We should regard this as an understatement of our situation. Each year that we allow to go by without a constitutional convention we are repeating history. We are ignoring the intent of the framers and continuing to live with a flawed Constitution. Our failure to bring about a 2nd constitutional convention is leading us closer and closer to a manipulated tyranny.

WHAT WE CAN LEARN FROM OUR CONSTITUTION AND OUR HISTORY

Three lenses through which we can profitably look at events in US history are our Declaration of Independence, our Constitution, and the *Federalist Papers*. We should learn from the Declaration of Independence that we ordinary Americans have the right and the duty to alter our Constitution whenever we feel alteration is needed. Our Constitution has been the prime mover of these events and the *Federalist Papers*, according to Thomas Jefferson, contain the "genuine meaning" of the Constitution.[25] The following are the writer's ideas of the "manifest tenor," general principles, structural principles and operational principles as they are stated and implied in the Declaration, the Constitution and the *Federalist Papers*. They are presented here so that the reader can conveniently relate them to the historical events and figures discussed in Chapters 1-6.

OUR CONSTITUTION'S MANIFEST TENOR (OR FIRST PRINCIPLES)

First, "we the people" possess the supreme power." Judging from the structure and text of the Constitution and from the *Federalist Papers*, it is the manifest tenor of our Constitution that we should be self governed and that we should govern ourselves so as to protect the weak from the strong.

OUR CONSTITUTION'S THREE GENERAL PRINCIPLES

Article V seems to have been intended to give this principle "efficacy." This Article, however, is seriously flawed. Article I gives us the power to make our own laws through our elected representatives. This Article has also failed in practice and needs updating.

Second, the Constitution is our supreme law. The *Federalist Papers* support this view. For example, Hamilton (in No. 78) wrote that it is the duty of the courts to find "all acts contrary to the manifest tenor of the Constitution void." The facts that the

---

[25] Jefferson expressed this view in a letter to Madison of Nov. 18, 1788. See also the Minutes of the Board of Visitors of the University of Virginia for March 4, 1825.

[26] This sub-principle is explicitly stressed by both Hamilton and Madison in at least seven parts of the *Federalist Papers*.

Constitution is "established by the people" and cannot be altered by the federal government verify the "supreme" power of the people.

Third, impartial justice is our supreme end. This principle is given "efficacy" by Article III, which makes members of the judiciary independent by giving them life tenure. Recent developments suggest that some further check upon judicial bias may be necessary. Congress has failed to provide the courts with the "strict rules"[27] that could strengthen the enforcement of this principle.

OUR CONSTITUTION'S STRUCTURAL PRINCIPLES

The structural features the framers designed to translate these principles into action are:
(1) The governmental powers should be kept separate.
(2) Our system of checks and balances should be maintained.
(3) Our judiciary should be kept independent.
(4) Congressional seats should be filled by civil officers elected to represent us.

SOME OF ITS OPERATIONAL PRINCIPLES

Some of the many operational rules that can be gleaned from the *Federalist Papers* are:
(1) No one should be judge in his or her own case, (*Federalist 10* and *80*),
(2) The people and the government must abide by the Constitution until it is amended, (*Federalist 78*),
(3) Impeachment and trial should be swift and certain, (*Federalist 65*),

---

[27] Hamilton, in *Federalist 78*, calls "strict rules and precedents" indispensable. Our judiciary's reliance on precedents without strict rules has resulted in a mutable Constitution. Hamilton makes it clear, in *Federalist 81*, that it is Congress's responsibility to provide these strict rules.

(4) Constitutional provisions should be given efficacy, (*Federalist 80*),

(5) Principle should always trump expediency (*Federalist 80*),

(6) Congress (or the people) should establish strict rules to guide the courts. (*Federalist 78* and *81*),

(7) Rules providing for the personal security of impeachment defendants (that is, 5th Amendment due process rules) are prohibited. (*Federalist 65*),

(8) No civil officer should be allowed to decide the extent of his or her own constitutional power.

EVENTS AND HISTORICAL FIGURES FROM US HISTORY

The twenty-seven events and the six historical figures discussed in Chapters 1-6 are only a few of the events and figures that can be used to help us produce a true living Constitution and, ultimately, to create a lawful and responsive federal government dedicated to protecting the weak from the strong. These events and historical figures are discussed in the context of the tenor and principles set forth above.

CHAPTER 1

SIX HISTORICAL EVENTS (2001-2010)

- The Gulf oil spill (2010) illustrates the consequences of big business's disproportionate influence with Congress.

- *Citizens United v. FEC* (2010) is a landmark case that has facilitated the transfer of money from the corporate world to Congress—thus aiding the strong at the expense of the weak.

- The clearing of Lt. Col. Jordan (2008) symbolizes the breakdown of our country's moral values.

- The Afghanistan address (2009) shows how completely our war powers have illegally migrated from Congress to the presidency.

- *Doe v. Bush* (2003) is an example of the judiciary's reluctance to deal with abdications and usurpations of power.

- The Patriot Act (2001) suggests the extent to which our civil rights are being eroded during the present period of permanent war.

Some of these events are milestones on our slide towards tyranny. All of them relate to our government's lawlessness and have implications for the future.

THE GULF OIL SPILL (2010)

The people are the only legitimate fountain of power, and it is from them that the constitutional charter . . . is derived.
—James Madison in *Federalist 49*

Two months after the Gulf Spill, President Obama called it the "worst environmental disaster America has ever faced." Justin Gillis (*New York Times*, June 18) interviewed a number of environmental historians and found support for other disasters such as the Johnstown, PA Flood of 1889, the Dust Bowl of the early 20th Century, and the 1910 oil spill in Kern County, CA. The Dust Bowl was caused by poor farming methods that stripped away native vegetation. The Johnstown Flood and the Kern County oil spill might have been prevented by better construction and maintenance. Recent scientific assessments of the damage done by the BP spill (see "After the BP Spill," in the Jan. 21, 2011 issue of *The Nation*" and the Sept.—Oct., 2010 issue of *Mother Jones*), seem to support Mr. Obama's initial reaction.

Is "business" to blame?

Were the farmers to blame for the Dust Bowl?" Were the builders, operators and maintainers of the Johnston dam and the Kern County oil rigs to blame? Are the executives and employees of BP to blame for our present predicament? These farmers, builders and executives acted with varying degrees of awareness.

Certainly the farmers who settled the mid-west could not have been expected to give much thought to the preservation of native grasses. The builders and maintainers of the Johnstown Dam and of the Lakeview and BP oil rigs were no doubt, more culpable.

However, builders and maintainers are human—like the rest of us. They do those things that are in their personal self-interests and avoid doing those things that are not. It follows that they attempt to maximize their profits by taking as few precautions as lax government standards let them get away with. To expect them to erode their profits by doing more is unrealistic.

Is government to blame?

Congress and state legislatures are responsible for making laws containing minimum standards governing the construction, operation and maintenance of dams and oil rigs. Presidents and governors are responsible for enforcing these laws and for establishing detailed regulations and standards. The courts issue decisions that motivate corporations to either abide by the laws and standards or to ignore them. In the case of the BP oil spill, it appears that the laws and standards were inadequate and, further, that—despite their inadequacy—the federal executive granted BP exemptions from certain of their provisions. Our political system makes it in the personal self-interests of our civil officers to respond more to corporate money than to the long-term needs and interests of average Americans. To expect them to be more conscientious than the law requires on these matters is unrealistic.

If BP and the government are not to blame, who is?

As Madison pointed out, we (the people) are the only legitimate source of power in America.[28] Along with our power goes responsibility. We have no basis for complaining about BP executives or about the civil officers of our federal government. They acted (and continue to act) in accordance with their self-interests. We have the power, the means and the responsibility for acting in accordance with our self interests and the interests of our children and grandchildren. Instead, we do nothing but complain and protest.

If we had exercised our power and met our responsibility, our government would have been obliged to do its job. If our government had done its job properly, it would have set, enforced, and issued adequate standards and handed down court decisions supporting these standards. This would have made it in the best interests of BP to have complied with these standards. It would not have drilled with sub-standard equipment. It would have constructed auxiliary wells. It would have prepared and rehearsed a written disaster plan. If we had done our job, the Gulf oil spill would not have happened. We are to blame for the Gulf Oil Spill.

What can we learn from the Gulf Oil Spill?

First, we should learn that disasters such as the Gulf Oil spill can be caused by activities that are, while corrupt, in accordance with our statutory law. It is "legal" for corporations to make donations to candidates for office. It is "legal" for civil officers to make laws that are not strict enough to prevent disasters. It is "legal" for civil officers to set standards that are inadequate and to grant inappropriate exceptions to these standards. Whether or not these activities are consistent with our constitutional tenor and principles is a question to be discussed later.

---

[28] See *Federalist 49*.

Second, we should learn that these legal misdeeds cannot be cured by, "throwing the rascals out." This is our default response to governmental wrongdoing. Our Congress failed to make laws assuring that oil rigs are designed, constructed and operated so as to prevent oil spills. For this and other shortcomings, we went to our polling places in late 2010 and made substantial changes in the make-up of Congress. This, of course was "love's labor lost." It is true that congressional law-making may have been influenced by the oil lobby, but this is a systemic fault. It cannot be remedied, or even ameliorated, by changing the cast of characters.

Third, we should learn that people act rationally. That is, we do that which brings us pleasure and avoid doing that which brings us pain. Writing ineffective federal laws and standards and failing to enforce even these inadequate safeguards was a major factor in causing the Gulf Oil Spill. Members of Congress and civil officers of the executive are people just like us. It is foolish, for example, to expect new senators and representatives to join a Congress that has already come to terms with a culture of "big money" influence and act contrary to the prevailing culture. As Hamilton tells us in *Federalist 61*, "There is a contagion in example which few men have the strength to resist." We should learn that free elections are not enough to protect us from legal wrongdoing.

We should also learn that, given the tattered state of our political and economic systems, our non-governmental organizations (NGO's) can bring about only incremental improvements in the making and enforcing of laws and standards. Many of us turned to our pocketbooks as a means of preventing future disasters. We wrote checks made out to one or more of the NGO's devoted to environmental and/or anti-corruption concerns. These organizations do fine work and deserve our support. However, their influence, while positive, is ameliorative.

They can influence our federal government, but only within a fairly narrow range of options. Further, most of them accept the root problem (an unresponsive government) as a given. Even the few that attempt to deal with this root problem rather than with symptoms (such as the BP oil spill) try to convince the federal government to reform itself. For example, they call on Congress to propose a constitutional amendment preventing future court decisions like *Citizens United v. FEC*. Why should federal civil officers take an action that might stop the flow of funds from corporations and special interest groups to themselves? Would this be a rational thing for them to do? The answer to this question is "No." Like "reform" statutes, an amendment proposed by Congress would be ameliorative—if that. We should learn the futility of spending our energy and our money attempting to persuade the fox to guard the chicken coop. This approach didn't produce the effective laws, standards and enforcement that might have prevented the Gulf Oil Spill and it will not produce the means of preventing future disasters.

In short, we can learn that Congress does not make adequate laws to protect us from unsafe corporate practices that endanger our environment. Instead Congress, influenced by corporate campaign donations, makes lax and inadequate laws. We can also learn that both parties to this arrangement are acting in accordance with statutory law. Further, we can learn that the executive branch, influenced by corporate power, makes weak safety standards, grants exceptions to these standards, and fails to vigorously enforce the inadequate laws made by Congress.

The Gulf Oil Spill and our Constitution.

The actions of our government in the matter of the Gulf Oil Spill were not, however, consistent with the tenor and principles of our Constitution. They did not adequately protect the weak from the strong. Our elected representatives were influenced more by the needs of oil companies than by our needs. BP failed to take the necessary precautions and we, especially those of us that live on the Gulf coast, must suffer. All this, however, was neither the fault of BP nor of our government. It was our fault.

In America, the supreme power and the responsibility lie with the people. We did not exercise this supreme power nor meet our responsibility. We could have reformed our government so that it would have been capable of protecting us. Until we exercise our power and meet our responsibility to bring about genuine reform—we have no grounds for complaint.

CITIZENS UNITED v. THE FEDERAL ELECTIONS COMMISSION (2010)

I hope we shall take warning . . . and crush in its birth the aristocracy of our monied (sic) corporations which dare already to challenge our government to a trial of strength and bid.
—Thomas Jefferson in a letter to George Logan, 1816

The *Citizens United v. FEC* decision is tearing down the last vestiges of the "fire wall" that once hindered the passage of money from special interests to Congress. Over the years Jefferson's hopes have been dashed to an extent he could hardly have imagined. Our corporations, far from having been "crushed" are now so powerful they have no need to challenge the government. They have co-opted it instead. The Citizens United decision facilitated congressional access to corporate money. However, as with most storm clouds, it may have a silver lining. Its extreme nature may energize us to call a constitutional convention aimed at reforming our corrupt federal government. We should now consider the obstacles we must deal with in bringing about a constitutional convention.

First, we are not united.

In America we rely on our member-funded non-governmental organizations to fight our battles for us with the federal government. On many specialized issues, our reliance is justified. As regards governmental reform, we must find another way. Common Cause is reacting to the United Citizens decision by pressing Congress to pass the Fair Elections Now Act. The Public Citizen group is reacting by lobbying Congress to pass a constitutional amendment. The Move On group supports amending the Constitution, passing the Fair Elections Now Bill and writing an anti-lobbyist bill. The "99% Declaration" attempts to persuade our federal government to reform itself. These leading NGO's should agree on a single reform strategy aimed at bringing about a representative 2nd constitutional convention. They should then lead a reform coalition made up of our tens of thousands of member-funded NGO's to pursue this single strategy.

Second, our present strategies have serious flaws.

These leading NGO's propose to lobby the federal government to either pass reform statutes or propose an anti-corruption amendment. Two considerations make these strategies nonsensical. First, history shows that laws passed by Congress to reform itself are palliative only. To suppose that the Members of Congress might make a genuine reform bill is unrealistic. To do so would shut off their supply of corporate money, give up the comforts of their present life style (such as first and business class air travel), and surrender their outrageous pensions. If you and I were in their places, we would laugh at the idea of genuine reform. Why do we insult their intelligence?

Further, constitutional amendments are our duty—not the

duty of Congress. Congress can influence amendments in only two ways. It can propose them to the states and it can "propose" to the state legislatures whether they vote on ratification themselves or call state conventions for this purpose. We, on the other hand, have the duty, the power and the motivation to propose and ratify genuine reform amendments to our Constitution. Acting through our state legislatures, we can require Congress to call a constitutional convention. We then have the power, acting through our state legislatures or through state conventions, to accept or reject amendments proposed by such a national convention. As Madison points out in *Federalist 53*, our Constitution is "established by us and is 'unalterable' by our government." By making it so, the framers gave us the power and the duty to keep our federal government honest. **It is in our self interest to exercise this power.** It would be Congress, the judiciary and a handful of executive branch presidential appointees—not us—who would be obliged to moderate their elitist life style. We would stand to gain an honest federal government.

There are long-term benefits of an honest, responsive federal government.

In the short term, there would be losers as well as winners. The losers would be the present group of 1,500 or so civil officers who have become accustomed to the incomes, status and lifestyles of celebrities. They would have to accustom themselves to doing without all the junkets and other favors that are now provided them by corporate and special interest groups. They would travel economy class with their constituents rather than business class or first class with the rich and powerful. This would enable them to exchange stories and concerns with ordinary people. Travel would educate them with regard to the frustrations and cares of ordinary people rather than with those of the rich and powerful.

Of course, they would not be troubled by these changes for any long period of time. The Members of Congress would soon serve their "term limits" and return to private life. They would be replaced by a new kind of representative and a new kind of senator. This new breed would be attracted, less by glory, status and wealth than by the honor, experience, reputation and satisfaction they would receive from serving a term with Congress. Congress would be famed throughout the world for the idealism and integrity of its members. Just as other nations emulated our innovations of 1787, they might emulate the improvements we can now make in our Constitution after two centuries of experience.

The change in the behavior expected of our civil officers would soon improve their reputation among the American people. This, in turn, would change the kind of people who would be attracted to serve as civil officers in government. They would be younger, more idealistic and would view their federal service not as a career but as a step on their actual career ladder. The time of the career politician would be over. Many more Americans would serve as federal civil officers and would, therefore, understand more fully the workings of our government. The pool of recruits eager to serve terms as federal civil officers would increase in both size and quality.

The benefits to the country of an honest, lawful, responsive federal government would be incalculable. Such a government would find ways to stimulate the private sector—at the same time reducing the gap between our rich and our poor. Congress, the courts and the presidency would abide by the rule of law. This would provide a more stable "playing field" for corporations, reduce the gap between the rich and the poor and tend to curb our militaristic tendencies. Most would agree that an honest, lawful federal government is desirable.

What we can learn from *Citizens United v. FEC?*

We can learn that our Supreme Court does not always render impartial justice based on the Constitution and its "genuine meaning"[29] as it is found in the *Federalist Papers.* The tenor of the Constitution requires that the weak be protected from the strong. The substantive intent of the framers of the 1st Amendment was to assure individual citizens the right to criticize their government without fear of retaliation. The Court interpreted its intent as being that that the strong should be permitted to oppress the weak by spending money to buy influence in Congress. We can also reflect that the Court should not be independent from the will of the people as this will is expressed by the Constitution. Congress should make our will explicit by making strict rules to guide the courts.[30]

OBAMA'S AFGHANISTAN ADDRESS (2009)

. . . every breach of the fundamental laws, though it be dictated by necessity, impairs that sacred reverence which ought to be maintained in the breast of rulers towards the Constitution . . .
—Alexander Hamilton in *Federalist 25*

On December 2, 1999 President Obama told us of his intentions regarding the war in Afghanistan. The decision he announced in his address (to escalate our military interventions in the Middle East) was a breach of our most fundamental law: the US Constitution. This breach could not even be defended on the grounds of necessity.

---

[29] Jefferson used this term in a letter to Madison of Nov. 18, 1788.
[30] In *Federalist 78*, Hamilton wrote that Congress should make "strict rules . . . to define and point out their" (the courts') "duty in every particular case that comes before them." He alluded to this congressional power again in *Federalist 81.*

What the Constitution says:

Article I, Sec. 8 of the Constitution assigns Congress the power to "declare war, grant letters of Marque, and reprisal, and make rules concerning captures on land and water." Section 8 goes on to give Congress all the specific powers associated with war and peace—except the conduct of a war once it is declared. Article I gives Congress the following powers:

- To define and punish piracies and felonies committed on the high seas, and offenses against the law of nations;
- To raise and support armies, but no appropriation of money to that use shall be for a longer term than two years;
- To provide and maintain a Navy;
- To make rules for the government and regulation of the land and naval forces;
- To provide for calling forth the militia to execute the laws of the Union, suppress insurrections and repel invasions;
- To provide for organizing, arming and disciplining the Militia and for governing such part of them as may be employed in the service of the United States.

Article II, on the other hand, says only that "The President shall be Commander-in-Chief of the Army and Navy of the United States and of the Militia of the several states when called into the actual service of the United States." The president's war powers, as Hamilton put it, ". . . amount to nothing more than the supreme command and direction of the military forces, as first general and admiral . . ."[31]

---

[31] See *Federalist 69.*

What the framers intended:

Madison, Pinckney, Hamilton and their fellow-framers made it clear that their intent was not simply to place decisions regarding war and peace in the hands of Congress. It was also to keep these decisions out of the hands of the presidency. Charles Pinckney, speaking in the 1787 debate on executive power, said that an elected president whose powers extended to decisions regarding "peace and war" was actually the "worst kind" of monarch. In his "Helvidius" essays, Madison called the Constitution's clause confiding "the question of war and peace to the legislature, and not to the executive" to be its "wisest part." Madison was explicit regarding the framers' reasons for wishing to keep decisions on war and peace out of any president's hands. He wrote, in Helvidius, "In war, the public treasures are to be unlocked, and it is the executive hand which is to dispense them. In war, the honours (sic) and emoluments of office are to be multiplied, and it is the executive patronage under which they are to be enjoyed." Yet Mr. Obama's address announcing his decision to send thirty thousand additional troops to Afghanistan does not even mention the US Congress.

What should be done?

A law which is ignored is a pernicious thing. It is soon disrespected and violated as a matter of course. A Constitution that is ignored is even more destructive of a nation's well-being. Hamilton wrote, in *Federalist 25*, ". . . every breach of the fundamental laws, though it be dictated by necessity, impairs that sacred reverence which ought to be maintained in the breast of rulers towards the Constitution of a country, and forms a precedent for other breaches." Madison wrote in *Federalist 37*, "An irregular and mutable legislation is not more an evil in itself than it is odious to the people." We should consider what has been the result of the presidential exercise of the war powers and decide whether it should be continued and, if so, to exactly what extent. We should then explicitly define this extent in the Constitution. We should also make specific provisions for the impeachment of any president who exceeds his constitutional powers.

This essay is no criticism of Mr. Obama alone.

It would be difficult for Mr. Obama to avoid breaching the Constitution. Congress abdicated the war powers, in effect, sixty-three years ago when the National Security Act gave the resources necessary to exercise them to the presidency. As a practical matter, a constitutional amendment is now required to transfer these resources (the strategic intelligence agencies) to their appropriate branch (Congress). US presidents, however, have no role as regards constitutional amendments. This makes Mr. Obama's position difficult. On the one hand he lacks the power to return the intelligence resources to Congress. On the other hand, his continued use of them is an impeachable offence.

The buck stops with us.

The Constitution, as Madison said, is "established by the people and unalterable by the government."[32] This is perhaps the most potentially significant statement made in the *Federalist Papers*. Our federal government has no decisive role in the ratification of federal amendments. This fact is the basis for Madison's claim in *Federalist 49* that we (the people) are America's "only legitimate fountain of power." We have, however, failed to exercise this power. For this reason it is our fault-

---

[32] See *Federalist 53*.

not the fault of Mr. Obama, Congress or the judiciary—that our powers of government are out-of-balance.

We have the power, not only to tell our presidents the extent and the limitations of their powers, but also to provide—in our Constitution—the resources and means of impeaching, removing and disqualifying presidents who exceed their powers. It is true that presidents already take oaths to "protect and defend" the Constitution. Unfortunately, however, they have all—in recent years—violated their oaths routinely. It is time we make their oaths more explicit and begin to call them to account for violations. It is our duty to amend the Constitution to clarify the presidential war powers and to provide the means of enforcing the exceeding of these powers. A constitutional convention is badly needed.

What we can learn from the Afghanistan address:

We can learn that our executive branch considers itself to have sole possession of the war powers. We can also learn that our President is in violation of Article I and therefore subject to impeachment. Most important we can learn that neither our elective system nor our impeachment provisions are adequate checks upon our executive branch.

THE "CLEARING" OF LT. COL. JORDAN (2008)

The degree of civilization in a society can be judged by entering its prisons.
—Fyodor Dostoyevsky

In January, 2008, reserve Maj. Gen. Richard J. Rowe, Commander of the Military District of Washington, announced that Lt. Col. Steven L. Jordan, former director of the Abu

Ghraib detention and interrogation facility in Iraq, was "cleared of any criminal wrongdoing" in connection with the torturing that occurred during his tenure at the facility.[33] Eleven enlisted personnel had already been convicted (nine were imprisoned) for their roles in the Abu Ghraib torturing. Jordan's acquittal meant, in effect, that none of the seven commissioned officers who were legally responsible for the torturing would be held accountable.[34] Rowe's announcement told our Army officers that they need not be concerned with the provisions of the Army Field Manual holding them "legally responsible" for the actions of personnel under their command.[35] It told enlisted personnel that the Uniform Code of Military Justice is far from "uniform." It told the world that, while we ratified the UN Convention on torture in 1994, we have no intention of observing it. It told the people of the Middle East that the US cares little about their human rights.

Slavery, child abuse, rape and torture are among the most heinous examples of man's continuing inhumanity to man. They all stem from the same fundamental evil: the granting to one human being (or group of human beings) absolute power over

[33] "Army tosses Abu Ghraib conviction," USA Today, Jan. 10, 2008
[34] The seven military officers in the chain of command were: Gen. Tommy Frank, Commander of the 10th Unified Combat Command, Lt. Gen. Ricardo S. Sanchez, Senior Commander in Iraq, Brig. Gen. Janis Karpinski, Commander of the 800th M.P. Brigade, Col. Thomas Pappas, Commander of the 205th M.I. Brigade, Lt. Col. Jerry Phillabaum, Commander of the 320th M.P. Battalion, Lt. Col. Stephen L. Jordan,, and Capt. Carolyn A. Wood, Commander of the M.P. Company at Abu Ghraib. This chain of command was ambiguous. No one at Abu Ghraib (or at any level below the 800th M.P. Brigade) was sure who was responsible for what. However, it is clear that the military "buck" stopped with Gen. Tommy Frank.
[35] Paragraph 501 of Army Field Manual 27-10 states that a commander is legally responsible "if he has actual knowledge, or should have knowledg . . . that troops or other persons subject to his control are about to commit or have committed a war crime and he fails to take the necessary and reasonable steps to insure compliance with the law of war or to punish violators thereof."

other human beings. Human progress can be described in terms of our success in eradicating this evil. The world's greatest political success may have been the ratification of the US Constitution in 1791 followed by our 13th Amendment in 1865. These two legislative actions set world precedents for reforming power relationships among human beings. Our country has also made incremental progress with its statutes aimed at child abuse and rape.

As regards torture, however, we have regressed, while other developed nations have advanced. The UN Convention against Torture and Other Cruel, Inhuman or Degrading Treatment or Punishment prohibits "any act by which severe pain or suffering, whether physical or mental that is intentionally inflicted on a person . . . when such pain is inflicted by or at the instigation of or with the consent or acquiescence of a public official." Countries ratifying the Convention agree to take "effective measures to prevent any act of torture in any territory under their jurisdiction." The Convention also prohibits rendition (the sending of detainees to other counties where torture is allowed). The US, instead of setting a positive example for other countries, has reneged on its promise to abide by the Convention against Torture.

It is true that, in addition to the "clearing" of Lt. Col. Jordan, there are other events that might have been selected to symbolize our endorsement of torture as morally acceptable. For example, in 2006 President Bush attached an unconstitutional "signing statement" to the Anti-Torture bill of that year saying that he reserved the right to torture when he thought it appropriate.[36] For another example, in August of 2009 Attorney General Eric Holder immunized from criminal investigation and prosecution (1) Bush officials who ordered torture (2) Bush lawyers

[36] Charlie Savage. "Bush could bypass new torture ban," *The Boston Globe*, Jan. 4, 2006.

who pronounced it legal and (3) those upper level officers in the CIA and the military that authorized torture within the limits permitted by the Bush officials. Only lower level CIA agents and military personnel who actually commit murder may now be "investigated."[37]

What happened at Abu Ghraib?

Abu Ghraib is the name of the town in Iraq where one of an undisclosed number of US detention and interrogation facilities is located. Abu Ghraib detains and interrogates Iraqis suspected of resisting the American occupation. Seymour Hersh wrote, in 2004, "Most of the prisoners (there were several thousand, including women and teen-agers) were civilians, many of whom had been picked up in random military sweeps and at highway checkpoints."[38] An investigative report written by Maj. Gen. Antonio M. Taguba, found that "sixty per cent (60%) of the civilian inmates at Abu Ghraib were deemed not to be a threat to society, which should have enabled them to be released."[39]

The events at Abu Ghraib are very likely only the "tip of an iceberg." Soldiers are reluctant to report abuses because they fear it will hurt their careers. The Army disciplines "whistle blowers" and does its best to keep conditions at its detention facilities from becoming public. After reading Gen. Taguba's investigative report, Hersh also wrote that the report indicated a "failure of Army leadership at the highest levels."[40] Yet the public became aware of the torturing at Abu Ghraib only because of the foolishness of the torturers in taking photos of themselves in the act of torturing and because of the heroism of Spec. Joseph M. Darby of Jenners, PA and Sgt. Samuel Provance of

---

[37] "Detainee abuse continues at Bagram," *Salon.com*. Sept. 21, 2009.
[38] Seymour Hersh, "Torture at Abu Ghraib," *The New Yorker*, May 10, 2004.
[39] Ibid.
[40] Ibid.

Uniontown, PA. In April of 2001, Darby, from the 372nd M.P. Company, gave testimony to the Criminal Investigation Division (CID) and provided it with some of the infamous Abu Ghraib photos. Sgt. Provance was the only Military Intelligence soldier to give testimony in General Taguba's 2002 investigation. He was later demoted for talking to ABC.[41] None of the other M.I. soldiers "broke ranks." Thus it was only through a combination of special circumstances that knowledge of the Abu Ghraib tortures became public. In order to fully appreciate the horror of the torture and sexual abuse that occurred at Abu Ghraib, the reader should go to *Salon.com* and view the 279 photos the torturers took of each other in the act of torturing. Gen, Taguba's investigative report also details the acts of sexual humiliation and brutalization that occurred at Abu Ghraib.[42]

Who was at fault?

President Bush said that the Abu Ghraib torturing was the work of a "few bad apples." However, it takes more than a few bad apples to produce torture on the scale that it existed (and, perhaps still exists) in some US detention and interrogation facilities. It takes authorization, either tacit or explicit. What the researchers who have studied Abu Ghraib term "administrative evil" has its roots in national policy. In order to gain a foothold among normal military personnel, torture must be authorized (explicitly or tacitly) by the chain of command.

The enlisted personnel who actually tortured the Abu Ghraib detainees were certainly at fault. They committed heinous crimes against humanity and were rightly (but lightly) punished. Nevertheless, in a very real sense most of them were

---

[41] JoAnn Wypijeuski. "The final act of Abu Ghraib," *Mother Jones*, March/April 2008.
[42] See "Article 15-6 Investigation of the 800th Military Police Brigade," pgs. 16-17.

victims as well as victimizers. Given the actions (and inactions) of the civil and military officers involved, the torturing was predictable—if not inevitable. We know from academic experiments that most people, when given absolute power over others and are instructed to inflict pain upon them will, in most cases, do as they are told.[43] A few will torture because they are sadistic by nature. A few will refuse to torture and a very few will attempt to stop it. Most of us will "go along" with authorized torture—and even participate in it.

A greater fault for the crimes at Abu Ghraib lies with the military officers who have legal responsibility for the actions of their subordinates. In the case of Abu Ghraib, the responsible lower ranking officers were "slapped on their wrists" with reprimands. None were court marshaled or imprisoned. The higher ranking military officers in the chain of command were responsible, not only for preventing tortures, but for maintaining a well-disciplined military force in the 10th Unified Combat Command. Gen. Tommy Franks, commander of the 10th UCC and Lt. Gen. Ricardo Sanchez, top commander in Iraq, were not even reprimanded.

A still greater fault lies with the two civil officers in the chain of command, the President and the Secretary of Defense. They were not even impeached. Neither were the Members of Congress punished for neglecting to instruct the military and civil officers regarding their responsibilities for preventing torture.[44] Even Congress does not, however, have the final responsibility.

The final responsibility is ours. In a representative democracy

[43]A bibliography of torture research is available on
http://torturerresearch.wordpress.com

[44]Article I, Sec. 8 of the Constitution says that it is a duty of Congress "to make rules for the government and regulation of the land and naval forces." It is also the duty of Congress to impeach and convict civil officers who fail to do their duty.

such as the United States, "we the people" are the only source of "legitimate power."[45] It is our duty to assure that Congress instructs the other branches of government in such a way that our will is carried out. Where Congress neglects this duty, it is our responsibility to intervene directly by calling a constitutional convention. The fundamental fault for tragedies such as Abu Ghraib is ours. We enjoy the benefits of living in a country that seeks to be "of, by and for the people." In order to preserve these benefits for ourselves and for future generations, we must perform the duties that go with them. In short, you and I and the rest of "ordinary America" are ultimately at fault for the torturing at Abu Ghraib and at other US detention and interrogation facilities.

What are the consequences of condoning torture?

- First, the people who are tortured suffer a degree of immediate pain that most of us have never experienced and can hardly imagine. Their pain and humiliation become a major factor in their lives for many years—perhaps forever. Many become embittered and some seek revenge. Our detention and interrogation facilities may be the most valuable recruiting tool available to terrorist organizations.

- Second, some experienced interrogators and most academics agree that the information obtained through "enhanced" interrogations is often worthless. Former CID agent Willie J. Rowell believes that the use of force or humiliation is always counterproductive. He told Hersh, "They'll tell you what you want to hear, truth or no truth . . . You don't get righteous information."[46] Scientific research supports Rowell's view. Summarizing a 2009 study

---

[45] Madison in *Federalist 49*.
[46] Seymour Hersh. See above.

by Metin Basoglu, Oxford neuroscientist Kathleen Taylor writes, "Torture is best at breaking the innocent and uninvolved civilians caught in the system by mistake—and may fail to work against its real targets. It's also . . . good at radicalizing victims, thereby storing up future problems for the torturing regime." [47]

• Third, since US torturers (and authorizers of torture) are, for the most part, normal men and women, they must live with guilt and remorse for the rest of their lives.

• Fourth, US taxpayers are paying billions of dollars each year for intelligence which is often faulty and misleading.

• Fifth, our detention and interrogation facilities are radicalizing many of the tens of thousands of Iraqi and Afghanistan civilians who pass through them each year.

• Sixth, their knowledge of our mistreatment and torture makes it difficult for us to "win the hearts and minds" of Iraqis and Afghans—whether or not they have ever been detained.

• Seventh, while we are at a point in time when we should be leading other countries toward a "new world order" based on peace, cooperation and the rule of law, our willingness to torture has contributed to the erosion of our credibility with the international community.

Finally, we—"the people"—are tearing down the moral fab-

---

[47] See Metin Basoglu, "A multivariate contextual analysis of torture," *American Journal of Orthopsychiatry*, 79(2), pp. 135-145 (2009).

ric of our own country by failing to take action. It is our duty to stop our government from authorizing and ordering the torture and mistreatment of detainees and other Middle Eastern civilians. Our priority goal in the Middle East should be to make friends and admirers, not enemies. As Lewis Gallantièr wrote in 1950, " . . . when a nation . . . attains to world leadership, it preserves that rank only so long as its culture—which is to say not only its achievements in the humanities but also its manners and beliefs and civil institutions— commands respect and some degree of emulation." [48]

What should be done and who should do it?

One obvious conclusion to be drawn from all this is that the US Army cannot be trusted to disciple its commissioned officers. None of the commissioned officers in positions of responsibility for the Abu Ghraib tortures was convicted or imprisoned. We are already bound by our ratification of the Geneva Convention on Torture to prevent its occurrence and, certainly, to cease its actual performance. We need to find a way to exercise our rightful control over our federal government. This raises two crucial questions.

First, if our military cannot be trusted to discipline its officers, who should be entrusted with this responsibility? Crimes committed by military officers against the human rights of detainees and other civilian foreign nationals could best be investigated, prosecuted and tried by independent agencies of government that have no association with the executive branch. An appropriate agency for investigating and prosecuting such crimes is the General Accountability Office. This independent agency is loosely associated with Congress. Without such an

---

[48] Lewis Gallantièr, "America Today," *Foreign Affairs*, July, 1950.

independent agency dedicated to the prevention of human rights offenses against the civilians of other countries, torture and mistreatment will continue. These offenses could be tried by our federal judiciary.

Second, while it is clear that a transfer of the powers to investigate, prosecute and try human rights offenses is critical to our national interests, it is also clear that such a transfer would be opposed by what the late President Eisenhower called the military-industrial-complex. Since Congress, although authorized to do so, is unlikely to pass legislation effecting such a transfer, we must effect it ourselves. This, and other badly-needed reforms, can best be accomplished by calling a constitutional convention. We have the power to call such a convention and, for the first time, we should use this power.

DOE v. BUSH (2003)

The judicial power shall extend to all cases, in law and equity, arising under this Constitution.

Article III, Section 1 of the Constitution

The judicial power does not extend, in practice, to all cases arising under the Constitution. It extends only to those cases that courts choose to decide. Congress, however, has not provided the courts with any rules to guide them in making these choices.

The *Doe v. Bush* complaint:

On February 13, 2003, three unnamed US soldiers, ("John Does") and five parents of US soldiers filed a complaint against President Bush and Secretary of Defense Rumsfeld. The plaintiffs were joined by six Members of Congress. The complaint challenged the authority of the President and Secretary of Defense to "wage war against Iraq" and enjoined them from doing so "without a congressional declaration of war." The plaintiffs alleged that the Iraq Resolution of October, 2002, "...unconstitutionally cedes to the President the power to decide whether or not to send the nation into war." The complaint charged that war with Iraq would cause harm to the soldiers and their parents. It would also deny the Members of Congress their right to vote on whether or not to declare war.

Actions of the District and Circuit Courts:

The Massachusetts District Court chose not to decide the case. Its reason for dismissal was that *Doe v. Bush* was a "political" case. It should, therefore, be decided by the two political branches of government rather than by the judiciary. The plaintiffs appealed but, on March 13, 2003, the US Court of Appeals for the First Circuit affirmed the district court's dismissal. It did so, however, for a different reason. It said that the case was "not suitable for judicial review because there is not a ripe dispute" between the President and Congress. Neither court responded to the plaintiff's allegation regarding the unconstitutionality of the Iraq Resolution.

The "political case" issue:

Baker v. Carr (1962) found that the case at hand did not involve a "political question." However, it established a number of criteria for identifying one. Prominent among these criteria are: Does the case involve a "textually demonstrable constitutional commitment of the issue to a coordinate political department" and, does the case involve "a lack of judicially discoverable and manageable standards for resolving it?" While the First Circuit found a different reason for dismissing *Doe v. Bush*, the "political question" rational is worthy of note here because it has been used by the courts to avoid deciding other war powers cases.

The "ripe dispute" issue:

The First Circuit dismissed *Doe v. Bush* because it did not involve a "ripe dispute" between the President and Congress. In its dismissal, it quotes Justice Powell (*Goldwater v. Carter*, 1979), who wrote that courts should decline, on ripeness grounds, to decide "issues affecting the allocation between the President and Congress until the political branches reach a constitutional impasse." This rule is flawed both generally and as regards its application to *Doe v. Bush*. It is flawed generally because it makes the judiciary impotent as regards abdications of constitutional powers. In effect, it allows the branches of government to amend the Constitution. It is flawed in its application to *Doe v. Bush* because *Doe v. Bush* does not rest its case upon any controversy between Congress and the President. The plaintiffs in *Doe v. Bush* claim a controversy between themselves (as private individuals) and the executive arm of government. The soldiers and their families claim that they would suffer "irreparable harm" from an illegal war. The Members of Congress claim they would be denied their constitutional right to vote for or against a declaration of war. The Court's "ripeness" theory dealt with a controversy that was not claimed and ignored the controversy that was.

The Iraq Resolution issue:

The plaintiffs alleged that the Iraq Resolution was unconstitutional because it "cedes to the President the power to decide whether or not to send this nation into war." This is, far and away, the most serious issue raised by the *Doe v. Bush* Complaint.

The ceding or transfer of power among the branches of our government can be legally accomplished only be an amendment to our Constitution. Article V pointedly omits giving the federal government any role in the approval of constitutional amendments. The Circuit Court rejected the plaintiffs' claim that the Iraq Resolution is unconstitutional, claiming that the notion that "power must be either in, or only in, Congress or the President . . . (is a) rigid, mechanical view." It also said that the power to decide on war versus peace is a "shared congressional and presidential responsibility," and cited a number of court cases to support this opinion.

The Court denied the plaintiffs in *Doe v. Bush* their request to have their case heard. It rationalized its denial by pretending that the plaintiffs were claiming a controversy between Congress and the presidency. Having created this "straw man," they proceeded to knock it down. In this way, the Court deprived the plaintiffs of their right to seek judicial remedies for injuries done them by their government.

The Circuit Court also avoided deciding the central issue in *Doe v. Bush*. A major power of government was "officially" transferred (by the Iraq Resolution) from Congress to the presidency. This illegal transfer of power destroyed the feature of our Constitution that is most critical to the preservation of our freedom—the feature that makes it "unalterable" by government. The war powers themselves are critical and there is ample evidence that the framers did not wish Congress to "share" them with the president.[49] It is even more critical to our freedom,

---

[49] For example, Madison wrote that those who are to "conduct a war" are "not proper judges" of whether it should be "commenced, continued or concluded." He also wrote that the wisest provisions of the Constitution were those that confided questions of war and peace to Congress rather than to the president. He added that presidents had strong personal reasons for favoring war, (6 *The Writings of James Madison* 148, as quoted in Louis Fisher, pp. 9.and 21). Washington refused state requests that he take action against the Creek Nation—saying that such actions were the province of Congress.

however, that the federal government not be allowed to usurp the most important constitutional power of the people: the power to alter the Constitution.

Remedies:

Hamilton wrote, in *Federalist 81* that "A legislature, without exceeding its province, cannot reverse a determination made in a particular case; though it may prescribe a new rule for future cases." If Congress should prescribe a new rule requiring the courts to interpret the Constitution only in the light of its intent as indicated by its text and by the *Federalist Papers*, errors such as those made in *Doe v. Bush* would not be likely to occur. For a court to rely on case law in interpreting the Constitution simply compounds and magnifies errors made by previous courts. On the other hand, the *Federalist Papers* are a reflection of the meaning of the Constitution as understood by its framers and the people who ratified it.[50]

What we can learn from *Doe v. Bush*?

We can learn that we cannot trust the justices of our Supreme Court to place principle above expediency. The principle at stake in *Doe v. Bush* was America's dedication to impartial justice without regard to what courts believe would be best for the country. We can learn that a court's refusal to decide cases involving the boundaries between branches can cost billions of dollars and tens of thousands of human lives. We can learn that Congress has neglected its duty to set "strict rules . . . which serve to define and point out their duty in every particular case that comes before them."[51] We might also learn to ask ourselves

[50] See Jefferson as quoted in Clinton Rossiter's Introduction to the Mentor Books 1999 edition of *The Federalist Papers*.
[51] Hamilton in *Federalist 77*.

whether all the various war resolutions are unconstitutional and, if so, what should be done about it and who should do it. Finally, we might ask ourselves whether the *Doe v. Bush* courts acted in a manner consistent with constitutional tenor and principles.

THE PATRIOT ACT (2001)

Our country! In her intercourse with foreign nations, may she always be in the right; but our country, right or wrong.
—Stephan Decatur, Commodore, United States Navy, 1816

The actions of our government are oftentimes contrary to our own ideas of right and wrong. Framer John Iredell differed from Decatur in his ideas about the relationship between us and our federal government. He said "Let them" (the people) "be watchful over their rulers."[52] Decatur's and Iredell's different opinions raise an important question: Is it more patriotic to support or to oppose our country when we believe it to be wrong?

Patriotism:

Merriam-Webster defines patriotism as "love for or devotion to one's country." The question becomes: Can we best express our love or devotion to our country by supporting it when we believe it to be wrong or by taking action to correct its wrongdoings? There are, of course, different ways of taking action. Protesting is not one of these ways. It assumes that our government, not us, is the responsible party. On the other hand, Henry David Thoreau took action when he refused to pay taxes to a government that condoned slavery. Franklin McCain, Ezell Blair, Joe McNeil and David Richmond took action when they "sat in" at the Woolworth's lunch counter in Greensboro, NC. Ernest

---

[52] Bernard Bailyn (ed.) *The Debate on the Constitution*, Part II, p. 874.

Gruening (D-AK) and Wayne Morse (D-OR) took action when they voted against the 1964 Tonkin Gulf Resolution. All of these actions were taken in opposition to the US government and most of us would agree that they were all patriotic.

In a different era, Thomas Jefferson endorsed violence as a means of keeping government honest and responsive. When commenting on Shays' Rebellion in Massachusetts, he wrote that it "was honorably conducted" and that "the tree of liberty must be refreshed from time to time with the blood of patriots & tyrants." [53] This book neither proposes nor condones violent revolutions. They are dangerous and destructive and America has no need for them. When we wish to reform or change our government, our Declaration of Independence and our Constitution gives us the power and the means to do so. Decatur's notion that we should support our country "right or wrong" is at odds with our Constitution, which (as interpreted by the *Federalist Papers*), makes us, "the only legitimate fountain of power" in America. It is our duty to exercise this power by remedying wrongs done by our government.

The Patriot Act:

The Patriot Act was an immediate response to the terrorist attacks of Sept. 11, 2001. It was signed into law on Oct. 26 of that year. It expresses its love and devotion to our country by seeking to protect us from acts of terrorism. It does this by reducing restrictions on accessing telephone calls, e-mail com- munications, medical, financial, and other records; by easing restrictions on foreign intelligence gathering within the United States; by expanding the government's authority to regulate financial transactions; by easing restrictions on the detaining and

---

[53] Thomas Jefferson in a letter to William Smith dated Nov. 13, 1787.

deporting of immigrants; and by expanding the definition of terrorism to include "homegrown" attacks.

The American Civil Liberties Union has challenged the constitutionality of a number of Patriot Act provisions in court—with mixed results. The ACLU report titled *Reclaiming Patriotism* reads, in part, "The Patriot Act vastly—and unconstitutionally—expanded the government's authority to pry into people's private lives" As Justice David Davis wrote in deciding Ex Parte Milligan (1866), "No doctrine involving more pernicious consequences was even invented by the wit of man than that any of its (the Constitution's) provisions can be suspended during any of the great exigencies of government."

Who is responsible for national wrongdoing?

To the extent the Patriot Act is unconstitutional, it is certainly wrong. Congress passed it in landslide votes and the president signed it just forty-five days after 9/11. The fact that it is the law of the land does not make it right. It makes our country wrong. We must now ask ourselves, "Who is responsible when our country is wrong?" The answer is that we, the people, are responsible. We elected the members of Congress who acted hastily and, by seeking to protect our country, degraded it instead. We are not only responsible. We have the power and the means of correcting our government's wrongdoing. While statutes are the province of our government, the Constitution—which prevails over all statutes—is our province. It is made and amended by us and is, as Madison put it in *Federalist 53*, "unalterable by the government." The buck stops with us. When our government acts wrongly, it is up to us to remedy the wrong. As Daniel Webster put it, we are a country "made for the people, made by the people, and answerable to the people."[54]

---

[54] John Bartlett, *Familiar Quotations*, p. 547.

What we can learn from the Patriot Act?

We can learn that very few of our civil officers have been strong enough to reject the doctrine Justice Davis characterized as "most pernicious" in *Ex Parte* Merryman (1861—See Chapter 4). Their suspension of constitutional principles in the Patriot Act may or may not have saved American lives. But it has almost certainly injured our faith in our government, our international reputation and our relations with the people who live in the Middle Eastern countries. We can also learn that our present methods of influencing our representatives in Congress need strengthening.

CHAPTER 2

FIVE HISTORICAL EVENTS (1964-2000)

- Bush v. Gore (2000) is both a milestone and an illustration of the problems caused by our judiciary's reliance on case law to decide constitutional issues.

- The Lawless 106th Senate (1999) shows how necessary it is that the power to try executive and legislative impeachments be transferred to the judiciary.

- The El-Shifa missile strike (1993) is a disheartening example of the arbitrary and lawless violence that has cost us the world's good opinion.

- Ford's Pardon of Nixon (1974) shows how blatantly our civil officers can violate our Constitution with impunity (and, in Ford's case) win an ironic honor by doing so.

- The Gulf of Tonkin Resolution (1964) defied our Constitution by transferring the power to declare war from Congress to the executive without recourse to Article V.

BUSH v. GORE (2000)

. . . there is no liberty if the power of judgment (the judiciary) be not separated from the legislative and the executive powers . . . liberty . . . would have everything to fear from its union with either of the other departments.
—Alexander Hamilton in *Federalist 78*

With the evolution of our two-party system in the first half of the 19th century, the groundwork was laid for the "union" of the judiciary and the executive departments. Of course, this union is not yet complete—but, with the Clinton acquittal, *Gore v. Bush* and *Citizens United v. Federal Election Commission*, the handwriting is on the wall. The presidential dual role as head of the executive department and leader of a political party has encouraged this union. Presidents now have the power to endorse candidates for Congressional seats and to influence the allocation of party campaign funds. These powers strengthen the influence of presidents on the appointment of justices to the Supreme Court. They may fail with their first choices. They may even fail with their 2nd choices. But there are inexhaustible supplies of both conservative and liberal candidates. The framers were attempting to create an appointment process that would give an equal influence over appointments to the legislative and executive branches—with the desired result being an impartial, non-partisan court. That is not the way it has worked out.

Today's version of the separation of powers:

Vincent Bugliosi writes, "In terms, then, of natural law and justice—these five justices (Rehnquist, O'Connor, Kennedy, Scalia and Thomas) are criminals in every 'true' sense of the word, and in a fair and just world, belong behind prison bars."[55] The purpose of this small essay is to discuss (1) the 2000 Florida election, (2) the law the five justices violated (3) why they violated it (4) the danger of the judiciary's union with the executive branch, and (5) what we can do to prevent future courts from breaking our laws. Of course, there are other judicial miscarriages of justice that would serve our purpose almost as well. For example, the disgraceful 1999 acquittal of former President Clinton would do nicely. According to their own statements, some members of the Clinton Court believed him guilty but voted him not guilty.

Florida and the 2,000 election: [56]

Mr. Gore received 543,895 more votes than Mr. Bush in the 2000 election. Nevertheless, Mr. Bush won the presidency. Florida was the key state. Bush appeared to have won the state by 1, 784 votes (1/2 a percentage point.) On Nov. 26, the Florida Election Canvassing Commission declared him the winner of Florida's 25 electoral votes. These votes were enough for Bush to win in the electoral college on Dec. 20, despite Gore's national plurality. However, in mid-December it began to look like the key 25 votes might not hold firm. The Florida Supreme Court, hearing a suit by Mr. Gore, first consulted earlier manual recounts (in Palm Beach and Miami-Dade counties) and reduced his deficit from 1,784 to 1,401 votes. It then ordered a manual recount of 9,000 ballots in Miami-Dade County. Since Miami-Dade County had a confusing ballot and a predominantly Democratic voting population, it appeared for a day or two

---

[55] *The Betrayal of America*, p. 49.
[56] The reader can consult the majority opinion in *Bush v. Gore* for a more lengthy and detailed description of the events in Florida in late 2000. All four dissenters also wrote opinions.

that Mr. Gore might become our 43rd President. But this was not to be. Mr. Bush filed a suit aimed at stopping the recount. The Florida Supreme Court denied his suit, but the US Supreme Court agreed to hear the case on appeal and, on Dec. 12, ordered the recount stopped. Some Miami-Dade voters interviewed later said they left their polling places in November thinking they had voted for Gore, but—in talking to other voters—discovered they had voted for Bush by mistake. It now appears that the US Supreme Court's Dec. 12 decision not only appointed Mr. Bush President of the United States against the wishes of a majority of voting Americans—but also may have appointed him against the wishes of most Floridians.

The gist of the ruling:

The five justices ruled, in effect, that the "equal protection under the law" clause of the 14th Amendment required that all Florida voters be given an equal chance of having their votes counted. Should the ballots in Miami-Dade be recounted by hand, this would result in the voters in other counties having a lesser chance of having their votes counted—compared to the voters in Miami-Dade. Therefore, the justices decided that they would stop the recount. This effectively gave the presidency to Mr. Bush. A number of factors suggested that either completing the Miami-Dade recount or extending the recount to other counties would have favored Mr. Gore.

The law the five justices violated:

It appears to me that the five justices violated our Constitution and at least one of the statutes made pursuant to it. It is certainly open to doubt whether they were acting impartially when they voted to stop the Miami-Dade recount. On January

11, 2001, over 500 professors from 137 law schools placed an ad in the *New York Times* that read, in part, "By stopping the vote count in Florida, the US Supreme Court used its power to act as political partisans . . ." Yet, Article VI of our Constitution requires all judicial officers of the US to be bound by "oath or affirmation to support the Constitution." The heart of our Constitution is the rule of law and the essence of the rule of law is the rendering of impartial justice. In fact, according to Title 28, Chapter I, Part 453 of the United States Code, each Supreme Court Justice must swear or affirm to "impartially discharge and perform" all her or his duties. Acting as a political partisan is not "impartially discharging" one's duties.

Why the five justices broke the law:

Any human behavior is, of course, complex. Nevertheless, the most useful explanation of the five justices' behavior can be simply expressed. They, like all human beings, acted in the way they believed would maximize their pleasure and minimize their pain. Maximizing one's pleasure might involve, for some people, doing volunteer work in a hospital. For others, it might mean living in a fourteen-room house. The differences among people with regard to their notions regarding pleasure and pain certainly complicate the design of adequate reward and punishment systems. Nevertheless, it is abundantly clear that the rewards and the penalties associated with rendering (or not rendering) impartial justice by the justices of our supreme court—are both faulty and inadequate. In short, the rewards they anticipated for breaking the law exceeded the penalties.

What can be done to reform the judiciary?

The civil officers of all three branches of our federal government are out of control. That is, they are out of our control and are coming more-and-more under the control of special interest groups. Even more frightening, the increasing politicization of the judiciary fosters the union with the executive branch that was so feared by our founding fathers. Add to this mix the abdication of its war powers by the legislative branch and we have all the ingredients of a major political crisis.

In considering what can be done to deal with our crisis, we must first acknowledge that out federal government will not (and, in point of fact, cannot) reform itself. It will not because its 1,000 or so civil officers are quite content with the status quo. In fact, their power, glory and comfortable life styles all depend on maintaining the status quo. It cannot because our federal government does not have the power to reform itself. Genuine reform will require comprehensive constitutional amendments. Fortunately, our present Constitution gives the federal government virtually no legitimate role in amending the Constitution. Madison said that the uniqueness of our form of government lies, in large part, in the fact that our government cannot amend our Constitution. Only we can do that—acting through our state legislatures or conventions.[57] A constitutional convention is needed. This convention could devise a system of appointment and conditions of service on the judiciary that would make it more pleasant for judges and justices to render impartial justice that to serve partisan interests.

THE LAWLESS 106ᵀᴴ SENATE (1999)

. . . every breach of the fundamental laws, though it be dictated by necessity, impairs that sacred reverence, which ought to be maintained in the breast of rulers towards the Constitution.
—Alexander Hamilton in *Federalist 25*

---

[57] See Article V of the Constitution and *Federalist 53*.

Former President Clinton's alleged breach of our fundamental laws was not dictated by necessity. It was, instead, dictated by Clinton's personal desire to conceal his philandering. Polk was willing to violate our law in an attempt to gain territory for the US. Clinton apparently reverenced it so little that he was willing to violate it in an attempt to conceal his sexual behavior.

The record: [58]

On May 6, 1994, Ms. Paula Jones sued Clinton for sexual harassment. According to a BBC Special Report on Jan. 17, 1998, she alleged that, on May 19, 1991, an Arkansas State Trooper took her to Mr. Clinton's hotel room at the Excelsior in Little Rock, "where Mr. Clinton dropped his trousers and, alluding to his genitals, asked her to 'kiss it.'" Mr. Clinton gave sworn testimony in connection with the Paula Jones case later in 1998. In December of that year, the House charged him with perjury and the obstruction of justice in connection with his testimony. On Feb. 12, 1999, the Senate found him "Not Guilty" of perjury by a vote of 55 to 45 and was split by 50 to 50 with regard to the obstruction of justice charge. A number of senators went on record, saying that they believed him to be guilty but voted to acquit because they thought an acquittal would be "best for the country." The writers of our Constitution, of course, disagreed. They believed that the rendering of impartial justice would be best for the country.

The reaction of our civil society:

Some non-governmental organizations (NGO's) that we depend upon to defend the rule of law attempted to prevent

---

[58] For a lengthier and more detailed account of the Clinton impeachment and trial, see Richard A. Posner's *An Affair of State*, or Part II of my 2009 book, *After Patrick Henry*.

Clinton's impeachment. On Sept. 24, 1998 the leaders of fourteen major women's groups (organized by NOW President Patricia Ireland) issued a statement calling upon their members to urge their representatives in Congress to vote against impeachment. They took this position because "while President Clinton's record for women's rights has not been perfect, on balance we have had an ally in the White House."[59] NOW, which often acts on behalf of women alleging sexual harassment, chose in this case to ignore Paula Jones in order to curry favor with a miscreant president...

The ACLU believed that Judge Starr threatened Mr. Clinton's civil liberties by asking him questions that Mr. Clinton's desire for privacy prompted him to answer with lies.[60]

The ACLU failed to take into account the effect that Clinton's escape from conviction and removal would have on future presidents. Certainly George W. Bush, for example, would not have been so reckless in his attacks upon civil rights had he respected the impeachment provisions. The ACLU seemed determined to "shoot itself in the foot."

The media:

There were several major journalists that provided a faint voice of reason. However, more often heard were voices such as that of Time contributor and former reporter Nina Burleigh. She claimed to have said, when being interviewed by Howard Kurtz of the *Washington Post*, "I would be happy to give him (Clinton) a blow job just to thank him for keeping abortions legal. I think American women should be lining up on their presidential kneepads."[61]

---

[59] Press release issued Sept. 24, 1998, Contact, Loretta Kane, NOW.
[60] ACLU NEWS, "The ACLU of Southern California decries impeachment vote as dangerous to civil liberties and constitutional values," Dec. 14, 1998.
[61] *The New York Observer*, July 20, 1998.

The defense:

Mr. Clinton's main defense was a simple and very clever example of "doublethink." We were asked to believe that, while his charges read "perjury and obstruction," he was really on trial for sexual indiscretions. Perjury and obstruction, whatever the motive, are attacks upon our legal system and upon the rule of law. They are extremely serious offenses, especially when committed by a civil officer who is sworn to "protect and defend the Constitution." Sexual indiscretions are none of our or Congress's business. The more our "masters" train us in this sort of doublethink, the more gullible we become and the more vulnerable to absolute tyranny.

The trial in brief:

The 100 senators took a special oath to render impartial justice. The presiding officer, Chief Justice Rehnquist, took the same oath. Yet not one Democrat voted to convict on either charge. Only a few Republicans cast votes to acquit. Rehnquist, while he was sworn to render impartial justice, chose not to make any rulings. Senators from both parties said they believed Mr. Clinton to be guilty—yet voted to acquit. For example, Sen. Robert C. Byrd (D-WV) said he believed that George Washington would have "voted the defendant guilty." He explained his own vote to acquit as a reaction to the partisanship of the Senate Republicans. Sen. Snowe (R-ME) said that, if she had been a prosecutor in a criminal case, she would have indicted Clinton and that, if she had been a juror, she would have convicted him. She explained her vote to acquit by suggesting that his misconduct was not an "immediate threat to our government."

Flaws of the trial:

First, many senators took it upon themselves to decide whether or not it would be good for the country to convict a civil officer who committed perjury or obstruction. The framers and ratifies, however, had already settled that question more than two hundred years ago. The framers' decisions are binding until a constitutional amendment changes them. Second, it was a partisan trial. The framers assigned impeachment trials to the Senate (rather than to the judiciary) because they believed the Senate would be more capable of rendering impartial justice. Third, the senators disregarded Hamilton's caution (in *Federalist 65*) that rules such as those that "in common cases" protect the "personal security" of defendants (that is, the rules of due process) should never apply in a court of impeachment. Fourth, the Constitution gives the House the "sole power" to impeach. This limits the Senate's role to deciding whether or not the defendant committed the offense charged. Some senators wrongly voted to acquit Clinton because, in their opinion, the alleged offenses were not impeachable. The Constitution gives the House the final say on this matter. Finally, the framers would never have agreed to the Senate as our court of impeachment without being assured that the role of the Chief Justice as presiding officer would guarantee impartial justice. In the Clinton trial, the Chief Justice played a purely ceremonial role.

The price of lawlessness:

As Hamilton pointed out in *Federalist 61*, "There is a contagion in example . . .," the pernicious effects of Clinton's alleged perjury and obstruction were increased by his acquittal. They were further increased by the public admissions of some senators that they believed him to be guilty. This situation was made even worse by the success of the defense in convincing us that Clinton was being tried for sexual indiscretions rather than for perjury and obstruction. All this contributed to the cynicism with which we regard our government.

What can be done?

While little can be done to repair the effects of the Clinton acquittal, a great deal can be done to prevent future impeachment trials from becoming travesties of justice. A constitutional amendment putting "teeth" in our impeachment provisions is badly needed. This amendment, among other things, would transfer the power to try most impeachments from the Senate to the judiciary. The eroding effect of the Clinton proceedings (and government lawlessness in general) can be repaired only by genuine governmental reform.

THE EL-SHIFA MISSILE STRIKE (1993)

To hold simultaneously two opinions which cancel out, knowing them to be contradictory and believing in both of them.
—George Orwell, defining the term "doublethink" in *1984*

The authoritarian government in Orwell's classic book, *1984*, used self-contradictory pronouncements to develop in its people a capacity for "doublethink"—for believing whatever they were told, however absurd. Mr. Clinton's explanation for his 1993 missile attack upon Baghdad was (and is) an extreme example of doublethink.

Missiles and presidential powers:

Missile airstrikes and drones have become presidential

weapons of choice. It is no longer necessary for presidents to order generals to order colonels to order captains to order sergeants to order privates to "pull the trigger." They can pull the trigger themselves. Clinton was one of the first to understand the advantages of button-to-button combat. Congress neither expects nor wishes to be consulted every time a president thinks it would be well to launch a missile. This has opened the gates to the arbitrary use of military force for whatever reasons— political, personal or national security. The date June 26, 1993 is not, however, memorable primarily because of its association with the presidential use of air power. It is made memorable by Mr. Clinton's explanation for the Baghdad attack, and our acceptance of his explanation. It is memorable as a warning that we are losing our ability to think for ourselves.

The context of the 1993 Baghdad strike:[62]

Two Iraqi nationals were among sixteen suspects arrested on suspicion of planning an assassination attempt on former President Bush in Kuwait. The CIA thought that the Iraqi Intelligence Service was involved in planning the attempt, Mr. Clinton, therefore, decided it would be well to launch missiles aimed at the building in which the Intelligence Service was housed. Three of his twenty-three Tomahawk missiles went astray, killing eight civilians and wounding twelve others. The other twenty destroyed the facility. The attack was not only contrary to our own and international law. It was morally wrong.

Reasons given for the strike:

Mr. Clinton explained that the Baghdad strike was "essential

---

[62] The details of the attack are taken from *Presidential War Powers*, by Louis Fisher, historian and researcher at the Library of Congress (1st ed. p. 152).

in order to affirm the expectation of civilized behavior among nations." It is this "doublethink" explanation and the approval with which it was received by the public that makes this event memorable. We were asked to hold two contradictory ideas in our minds at the same time. First, most of us believe that it is wrong to kill innocent human beings. Mr. Clinton asked us to believe, at the same time, that his lawless taking of innocent human life "affirmed the expectation of civilized behavior among nations." And we did as we were asked. Public opinion approved the strike. This capacity for "doublethink" suggests that we are becoming a nation of sheep—unwilling or unable to think for ourselves.

The problem:

Technology has combined with the (illegal) concentration of the war powers in our president to enable him or her to order unmanned attacks upon other weaker countries. While Mr. Clinton may have been especially reckless in his use of missile attacks and air strikes, this lawless behavior is neither a partisan problem nor a problem that applies only to reckless presidents. So long as our presidents have the power to make pin-point attacks upon other countries, unchecked by Congress, they will do so when it seems to them to be expedient. This is a development that places the inhabitants of smaller and weaker nations at risk. It also places us at risk by aiding the recruitment efforts of terrorist groups.

This problem is worsened by our courts, which have found that neither our presidents nor our government are liable for the damage done by air attacks, however misguided and wrong these attacks may be. In August, 1998, for example, Mr. Clinton ordered an attack upon the El-Shifa Pharmaceutical Company in Sudan, calling it "a chemical weapons-related facility" which posed a threat to America's national security (*El-Shifa v. US*, 2001). The Pentagon later conceded that El-Shifa was harmless to us and, further, that it had, before being destroyed, produced a large share of the medicine used in Sudan.[63] Nevertheless, the US Court of Federal Claims decided against El-Shifa's request for compensation, saying that it "could not 'look behind' the President's discharge of his constitutional duties as Commander in Chief, including his declaration of what constitutes an enemy target and his determination to use military force to destroy that target." This decision ignored the fact that our president has no constitutional power to decide when to use military force. This power is reserved to Congress. Far from discharging his presidential duties, he was violating the Constitution.

Conclusions:

The story of Clinton's attack upon Baghdad contains two serious warnings. First, we must recognize that missile technology, taken with the presidency's usurpation of the war powers, gives our presidents the power, not only to declare war, but to use arbitrary military force to back up their own biases, opinions and goals.

Second, we should be alerted to the fact that it is becoming easier and easier for our government to control public opinion. By continually being exposed to ideas that contradict each other, we are losing our ability to (as Iredell put it), "watch over our rulers."

Third, this Clinton story is a warning. It is a warning that missile drones attacks and air strikes that are uncontrolled by Congress are becoming a threat to our national security. They fuel the hostile feeling that appears to be growing among radical groups in the Middle East.

---

[63] Louis Fisher, *Presidential War Powers*, p. 196-8.

Remedies:

We need to decide what war powers we wish our executive branch to possess, define these powers precisely and establish an effective mechanism for checking presidents who exceed them. We also need to develop means of protesting and rejecting governmental "doublethink." There should be a UN ban against the use of missile, drones and air strikes by individual countries that are not in a declared war.

FORD'S PARDON OF NIXON (1974)

If the president had the power of pardoning in such a case (the impeachment of a civil officer) this great check on high officers of state would lose much of its influence.
—James Iredell, in the North Carolina convention of 1788

The impeachment provisions, according to our fifth president, James Monroe, are the "pivot" upon which our government turns. If, he added, they are "preserved in full vigor, and exercised with perfect integrity, every branch will perform its duty."[64] As James Iredell pointed out, however, a presidential pardon in an impeachment case would rob the impeachment provisions of their power.[65] He and the other framers felt so strongly about this that they made one exception to the presidential power to pardon. Article II, Section 2 of our Constitution reads in part, "The President . . . shall have power to grant reprieves and pardons for offenses against the United States, except in cases of impeachment."

---

[64]James Monroe, *The People, the Sovereigns*, James River Press, 1987, p. 16.
[65]James Iredell, at the North Carolina Convention, July 28, 1788, in B. Bailyn, ed. *Debate on the Constitution*, Part II, p. 784.

Nixon and impeachment:

On June 17, 1972 five employees of the Committee to Re-elect President Nixon were caught in the Watergate offices of the Democratic National Committee. The investigations that followed revealed the involvement of Nixon and his top aides in the Watergate cover-up and other illegal activities. Nixon attempted to weather the storm until, on July 24, 1974, the Supreme Court ruled that he had to release a set of tapes he had made of meetings in his office. Six days later the House Judiciary Committee approved three articles of impeachment charging Nixon with "obstruction of justice," "abuse of power," and "contempt of congress." Several Republican senators, including Sen. Barry Goldwater (R-AZ) advised Nixon that, should the articles be approved by the House, the Senate would convict him. He resigned before he could be removed.

Ford and the pardon:

Upon the resignation of Spiro Agnew on October 10, 1973, Gerald Ford, a US representative from Michigan, was the first person to be appointed vice president under the terms of the 25th Amendment. He became president upon Nixon's resignation on Aug. 8, 1974. One month later he pardoned Nixon. In a 2004 interview, he told journalist Cokie Roberts there was no "deal" involved. He explained his reasons for the pardon, saying: "During the first month of my presidency I spent at least twenty-five percent of my time on Mr. Nixon's problems. . . the only way to 'clear the decks' was to pardon him." [66]   Ms. Roberts did not ask him about Article II, Section 2 of the Constitution.

---

[66] WHYY, Presidential Conversations on the Constitution (2004).

The Profiles of Courage award:

Mr. Ford was chosen to receive the John F. Kennedy Profiles in Courage award for 2001. The committee that selected him for the award included the late Sen. Edward M. Kennedy (D-MA), Sen. Olympia Snowe (R-ME), historian David McCullough and former president of CBS News Paul G. Kirk. The award's stated purpose is to honor public servants for "standing up for particular ideals or principles . . . even when it is not in their best interests to do so" Presumably, the committee was thinking of the negative public reaction to the pardon and of the possible effect of this reaction on Ford's bid for election to the presidency.

The consequences:

The Nixon resignation was a "mixed bag." Some observers from abroad gave us credit for forcing his resignation and overlooked the pardon as a necessary "deal." On balance, they seemed to admire our "idealism." The negative public reaction to the pardon in the US was encouraging. The incredible selection of Ford for the Profiles in Courage award on May 21, 2001, however, has no "up side." Whether or not Mr. Ford made a "deal," he never even claimed to anticipate a public reaction that would affect the presidential election.

To pardon a president who resigns because he is sure to be impeached (and convicted) is flying in the face of our Constitution. It is a direct violation of Art. II, Section 2. That Section exists for the specific intent of discouraging miscreant civil officers. Mr. Ford committed an action that ignored the Constitution he had sworn to "protect and defend." Just what "ideals and principles" did the Kennedy committee think Mr. Ford was "standing up for"?

The pardon was bad, but the award was worse. First, it was an insult to the Constitution-abiding Americans who protested the pardon. It expressed an elitist contempt for the opinions of the people. Second, and even more critical, the Kennedy award of 2001 encouraged (and continues to encourage) the civil officers of our government to disregard our laws and our Constitution. In *Federalist 25* Hamilton tells us ". . . every breach of the fundamental laws . . . impairs the sacred reverence which ought to be maintained in the breast of rulers toward the Constitution."

Louis de Montesquieu praised constitutional monarchies for the strength and honesty of their governments. He characterized the basic principle of monarchies as "honor." According to de Montesquieu, human nature has a strong desire to be honored and to receive the recognition and status that a prestigious honor provides. The English annual honors list is an example of this kind of monarchial motivation. However, a particular honor loses its power when it is bought and sold or when it is given to a civil officer who does not appear to the public as deserving.

Imagine, then, the consequences of giving an honor to a civil officer specifically for an unlawful, destructive and unthinking act. The negative consequences of such an honor are not limited to discounting the award itself. When, as is the case with the award given Mr. Ford, it is given for an unconstitutional act, it announces a general societal disrespect for the law and, in particular for the Constitution. Add to this the double irony that the constitutional provision against pardons in cases of impeachment was explicitly designed to help create an honest and lawful federal government, and that the purpose of the Kennedy Award is presumably to encourage lawful, courageous behavior among our civil officers.

What can be done?

The erosion of our national virtue (without which, as Montesquieu tells us, democracies fail) has gone too far to be controlled by statute. A second constitutional convention is needed.

THE GULF OF TONKIN RESOLUTION (1964)

Until the people have . . . annulled or changed the established form (the Constitution) it is binding upon themselves collectively, as well as individually, and no presumption, or even knowledge of their sentiments, can warrant their representatives in a departure from it prior to such an act (prior to its amendment)
—Alexander Hamilton in *Federalist 78*

The Tonkin Gulf Resolution of August 7, 1964 illegally amends the Constitution. It takes the power to declare war away from Congress and assigns it to the executive branch. In re-writing the Constitution, Congress did not even pretend to be responding to sentiments of the people. There had been no great surge of public opinion urging Congress to abdicate its war powers.

If there had been such a sentiment, it would not have justified Congress in doing so. If we wish to change the Constitution, we must exercise our constitutional powers. Admittedly, this is no easy task. The procedures of Article V do not (as Madison said they should in *Federalist 49*) "mark out and keep open . . . a road to the decision of the people." The road marked out in Article V is so muddy, full of ruts and overgrown that it has never been traveled. There has never been a 2nd constitutional convention and all twenty-seven of our amendments have been proposed by the federal government—not by the people.

Congress is responsible for passing laws "pursuant to" our Constitution. Hamilton also wrote, in *Federalist 78*, that "No legislative act . . . contrary to the Constitution can be valid." He also said that it is the duty of our courts " to declare all acts contrary to the manifest tenor of the Constitution void." Our courts, however, have failed to perform this duty by declaring the Tonkin Gulf Resolution (and other war resolutions) unconstitutional.

The Tonkin Resolution is also worth remembering because it is an ironic comment on the wisdom of the framers. Madison wrote, in Helvidius IV: "In no part of the Constitution is more wisdom to be found than in the clause which confides the question or war or peace to the legislature, and not to the executive department."

The War Powers Resolution of 1973:

The Tonkin Gulf Resolution established a lawless precedent. Nine years later, the War Powers Resolution of 1973 confirmed the abdication of the war powers by Congress and their usurpation by the presidency. In *Doe v. Bush* (2003), the plaintiffs asked the Court of Appeals to find the 1973 Resolution unconstitutional, but the Court declined.

A major reason for this abdication was that Congress had failed to make the "necessary and proper" law that would have provided it with the resources needed to make war and peace decisions. Instead, it made an unconstitutional law (the National Security Act of 1947) providing the presidency with these resources. With the Gulf of Tonkin Resolution, Congress formally "passed the buck" to the President. It is worth noting that Mr. Nixon vetoed the Resolution, but was overruled. Mr. Nixon felt that the Resolution did not go far enough. He claimed it violated the Constitution by imposing conditions on the executive's use of force.

The alleged incident in the Tonkin Gulf:[67]

LBJ claimed to have received reports of an August 4, 1964 North Vietnamese attack on a US destroyer. He asked Congress for a resolution. He told Congress that the United States "intends no rashness and seeks no wider war." He simply wanted to assure that all attacks by North Vietnam were met. The House passed the resolution unanimously and the Senate approved it by a vote of 88-2. Subsequent investigations revealed the August 4 attack "may never have happened." The Commander of the destroyer (the USS Maddox) said that the reports of torpedoes fired were doubtful and that "Freak weather effects and an over-eager sonar man may have accounted for many reports."

The Gulf of Tonkin Resolution:

Basing his request on these reports, LBJ asked Congress for a resolution "supporting freedom and protecting peace in Southeast Asia." Congress responded on August 7 stating that the US was "prepared, as the President determines, to take all necessary steps, including the use of armed forces" to help Southeast Asian nations defend their freedom. This Resolution went on to give LBJ the power to "take all necessary measures to prevent any further aggression" by North Vietnam. The Gulf of Tonkin Resolution was to expire "when the President determines." With these words, Congressed formally transferred the power to declare war from itself to the presidency. Only Senators Wayne Morse (D-OR) and Ernest Gruening (D-AK) voted "No."

---

[67]This account of the Tonkin Gulf "attack" by North Vietnam draws heavily on Chapter 6 of Louis Fisher's *Presidential War Power*, University Press of Kansas, (1995).

The dynamics of a losing war:

Presidential actions authorized by the Gulf of Tonkin Resolution increased the number of US troops from about 23,000 in 1964 to a peak of about 537,000 in 1968. According to VA statistics, by the time the US was driven from Vietnam in 1974, 58,202 US military personnel had died. About 75,000 had been severely disabled. Some of the disabled are still in VA hospitals. Countless Vietnamese, Cambodians and residents of Laos and Thailand lost their lives or suffered physical, economic and emotional wounds. Yet, according to a classified report released by the National Security Agency in 2002, " no attack happened that night." Hundreds of thousands of lives were lost to retaliate for an alleged act of aggression that did not happen.

Ten years of death and destruction in Vietnam might have been avoided had Congress not given the presidency control of our strategic intelligence services in 1947. Congress illegally transferred the war powers to LBJ in 1964 because it believed his claim that the North Vietnamese had attacked a US destroyer. Congress had little choice. It had no way of knowing whether his claim was true or false. The CIA, of course, did have ways of knowing. But it reported to LBJ. If it had reported to Congress, LBJ would probably not have even attempted his apparent deception.

Conclusions:

The House and the Senate authorized a war costing billions of dollars and many thousands of lives. They did this because of an "attack" on a US destroyer that its commander thinks was probably nothing more than an "over eager sonar man." Questions of war and peace should be decided by organizations that (1) are accountable to the people and (2) have access to accurate information regarding international events and circumstances. In the matter of the Tonkin Gulf Resolution, the entire House and Senate, with the exceptions of Senators Morse (D-OR) and Gruening (D-AK), authorized a long and bloody war on the basis of incorrect intelligence. The Constitution should be amended to transfer our strategic intelligence services from the executive branch to Congress's General Accountability Office.

CHAPTER 3

FIVE HISTORICAL EVENTS (1913-1960)

- The Greensboro Four tells the story of four North Carolina A & T students who re-energized the civil rights movement (1960).

- The National Security Act, in effect, illegally transferred a governmental power (1947).

- The Taft-Hartley Act began the decline of our trade union movement (1947).

- The Marshall Plan gave the US a world reputation for good citizenship (1947).

- The 17th Amendment snatched defeat from the arms of victory (1913).

THE GREENSBORO FOUR (1960)

*The only security of liberty in any country is the jealousy and circum-
spection of the people themselves. Let them be watchful over their
rulers. Should the government be found to want amendment, those
amendments can be made in a regular method, in a mode prescribed
by the Constitution itself.*
—James Iredell, speaking at the North Carolina convention
on July 28, 1788

Four students from North Carolina A&T College ignited
the "sit in" movement, and reenergized the civil rights movement itself. On February 1, 1960, Franklin McCain, Ezell Blair,
Joe McNeil and David Richmond took their seats at a
Greensboro, NC Woolworth's lunch counter. This courageous
act inspired the youth of America to produce a vast wave of sit-
ins throughout the upper south. The civil rights movement,
reenergized, produced the Civil Rights Act and the ratification
of the 24th Amendment, both in 1964. The "Greensboro Four"
had no organizational backing and received no salaries. They
made no speeches to thousands of cheering supporters. Instead,
they returned day after day to ask for service at a Woolworth
lunch counter, were spit upon, had spaghetti sauce poured on
their heads, and changed America for the better.

The road to the Civil Rights Act and the 24th Amendment:

Twenty or so more A & T students joined the "Greensboro
Four" at the Woolworth Lunch Counter the following day.
They were followed by hundreds more each day until the City
closed the store a week later. By then the sit-in "movement" had
spread through the upper south. It is estimated that more than
70,000 people "sat in" during the spring, summer and winter of

1960. In April, sit-in activists organized the Student Nonviolent Coordinating Committee. The sit-ins, according to Vol. II of *Who Built America*, "pumped new life into the civil rights movement." [68] In 1964 LBJ signed the Civil Rights Act. The 24th Amendment (which prohibited the denial or abridgement of the right to vote in a federal election because of a failure to pay any poll or other tax) became law during the same year. The Civil Rights Act and the 24th Amendment were made "in a regular method in a mode prescribed by the Constitution."

Elements of reform:

A successful reform movement requires icons. Spontaneous and incredible acts of courage on the parts of a few oppressed people are not enough. There is also a need for inspiring speeches cheered by thousands and tens of thousands. The character and courage displayed spontaneously by individuals and small groups of oppressed people are different from the character and courage displayed by icons. Both, however, are necessary and both must be displayed at a time when there is a widespread desire for change present in the people at large.

They must also be displayed in a country where the government does not react with violence, imprisonments and persecutions. In order to be successful, they must occur in countries that are structured to allow change. The United States, in the early 1960's, was just such a country. We had an elected legislature capable of producing the Civil Rights Act and state legislatures capable of ratifying the 24th Amendment. However, times have changed. The "war on terrorism" has produced immediate encroachments on our civil liberties. The Patriot Act is only one example. Even more serious than these specific encroachments,

---

[68] Stephan Brier (ed.) *Who Built America?* Vol. II (1992), p. 546. Much of the factual information in this essay comes from *Who Built America?*

however, our governmental powers are becoming more and more concentrated in the hands of the executive branch. If we are to continue as a nation that is capable of non-violent change, we must re-form our federal government. As Madison wrote in *Federalist 41*, "The accumulation of all powers, legislative, executive and judicial, in the same hands . . . whether hereditary, self-appointed, or elective, may justly be pronounced the very definition of tyranny."

The road to governmental reform:

New life could also be pumped into the lackluster, present-day governmental reform movement by a handful of college or university students. The road to the reform of our federal government, however, does not pass through the US Congress. It is unrealistic to imagine that our federal civil officers will ever enact (by statute) or propose (by amendment) any genuine reform. Neither would you or I if we were in their shoes. If we drew their salaries, enjoyed their benefits and basked in the glory of their celebrity lifestyles, it would be madness on our parts to give all that up by building a firewall between Congress and big-money campaign donations. The road to governmental reform must lead, not through Congress, but through our state legislatures. A national (truly representative) constitutional convention is needed to propose the many changes that need to be made in our Constitution. Our state legislatures have the power to both call a convention and to ratify (or fail to ratify) the amendments proposed by the convention.

Conclusion:

The Greensboro Four were not cheered by thousands. Instead, they had ketchup dumped on their heads. Now our country is threatened again, this time by an out-of-control federal government. Should a small group of university students ignite petitioning movements in 34 states? They would not be cheered either. Their rewards would come sometime in the future when they entered an airplane, took their seats in economy class, and found themselves sitting next to a Member of Congress.

THE NATIONAL SECURITY ACT (1947)

To make all laws which shall be necessary and proper for carrying into Execution the foregoing powers, and all other powers vested by this Constitution in the Government of the United States.
—Article I, Section 8 of the U.S. Constitution

On July 16, 1947, President Truman signed the National Security Act (NSA). This Act assigns the strategic intelligence services including the Central Intelligence Agency (CIA) to the executive branch. The NSA is unconstitutional. The Constitution vests the power to declare war in Congress. It also makes Congress responsible for providing the branches of government with the resources necessary to do their jobs. Article II, Sec.8 explicitly instructs Congress to make "all laws which shall be necessary and proper for carrying into execution the forgoing powers." Yet Congress, in the National Security Act, gave to the executive branch the resources necessary to carry out its own (Congress's) power to "declare war."

Moreover, Congress has been lax in other respects. For example, it has allowed questionable court decisions to be made without making rules preventing the same kind of decisions from being made in the future (See Part II, Chapter 10). Congress has never provided itself with the resources needed to make the war and peace decisions that the declaration of war involves. Instead, the National Security Act (NSA) gave these resources to the presidency. The reluctance of Congress to exercise its powers is also discussed in Chapter 10.

The National Security Act:

The NSA assigned the task of collecting strategic intelligence to the executive branch. Along with this task, it provided the presidency with the resources then being used to gather strategic intelligence. These resources included the agency now known as the Central Intelligence Agency.

The Constitutions and delegations:

The Constitution seeks to keep the powers separate. This does not mean, however, that the branches should have no influence over the exercise of powers assigned to other branches. Madison clarified the "separation of powers" principle in *Federalist 48*. He considered it "evident" that the branches should be connected "so as to give each a constitutional control over the others. However, he added that, "It is equally evident that none of them ought to possess, directly or indirectly, an overruling influence over the others" in the administration of their respective powers." The executive does possess, in effect, an overruling influence over Congress in regard to the congressional war powers. This, according to Madison, makes the war powers resolutions unconstitutional.

The Constitution and Strategic Intelligence:

By passing the NSA, Congress violated the will of the people—as expressed by the Constitution. Article I, Section 8 assigns to Congress the power "To declare war . . . To raise and support armies . . . To provide and maintain a navy . . . To make rules for the government and regulation of the land and naval forces," and "To provide for calling forth . . . organizing, arming and disciplining the militia."

Article II, Section 2 reads, in part, "The President shall be Commander-in-Chief of the Army and Navy of the United States, and of the militia of the several states, when called into the actual service of the United States." That is, the President is our commanding general/admiral. His or her job is to fight any war that Congress declares. According to Article II, that is the extent of the presidential war powers.

Why the NSA is unconstitutional:

The power to declare war involves the making of decisions to initiate, continue and cease hostilities. Strategic intelligence is the main resource needed to make these decisions. The NSA violated the Constitution when it assigned the strategic intelligence services to the executive branch. The Constitution gives the presidency no role at all in the making of such decisions. Madison said, in the Pacificus-Helvidius Debates of 1793-94, "Those who conduct a war cannot in the nature of things, be proper or safe judges, whether a war ought to be commenced, continued, or concluded." The framers intended to keep the hands of the president totally removed from the war powers. Further, the NSA violates the provision in Article II that requires Congress to provide the necessary resources to the responsible branch. The executive branch has no responsibility for making war and peace decisions. Yet the NSA gives it, instead of Congress, the strategic intelligence capability.

Why the violation occurred:

The CIA was formed during World War II, when the need

was for tactical intelligence. It was placed in the executive branch, since the president needed its services to carry out his duties as "supreme general." By 1947 it had become embedded in the executive branch and was gathering peacetime (strategic) intelligence. Congress, evidently without considering the implications of its action, transferred the power to make war to the presidency when it wrote the NSA.

What can de done to correct the mistake?

To move the strategic intelligence services from the executive to their constitutional home in Congress could theoretically be done by statute. This would be consistent with Article I, Sec. 8, of the Constitution. As a practical matter, while the war powers are extremely attractive to presidents, they are a political liability to Members of Congress. This means they must be moved by constitutional amendment. Fortunately, the federal government lacks the power to prevent constitutional amendments. As Madison said in *Federalist 49*, the people should be "recurred to," and when it is necessary to "new model" the powers of government. The "buck," therefore, stops with us.

THE TAFT-HARTLEY ACT (1947)

The possibility of particular mischiefs can never be viewed, by a well-informed mind, as a solid objection to a general principle that is calculated to avoid general mischiefs and to obtain general advantages.
—Alexander Hamilton in *Federalist 80*

One particular mischief that was viewed as a solid objection to trade unions in the late 1940's was the association of some union officers with communism. Another mischief was the increase in the number and duration of strikes following World War II. The "general principles" Taft-Hartley attacked (and still attacks) can be expressed as follows: "Strong labor unions are supportive of democracy, competitiveness, prosperity, and the dignity, safety, health and economic security of ordinary people."[69] They act as constraints to oppressive governments, excessive executive compensation, and the widening income gap between rich and ordinary Americans. While the "particular mischiefs" that led to Taft-Hartley are things of the past, the problems created by Taft-Hartley are still with us today. It continues to attack the general principles that "are calculated to avoid particular mischiefs and obtain general advantages."

The creation of Taft-Hartley:

During the years immediately following World War II, organized labor was becoming stronger and strikes were becoming more frequent. During 1946, more than five million workers went out on strike. Strikes were lasting an average of four times longer than those that occurred during the War.[70] While Taft-Hartley was being written, a strike threatened the coal industry. There was also concern that some labor leaders were members of the communist party or communist sympathizers. President Truman, to his great credit, vetoed the bill when it was submitted to him for his signature. He pointed out, in a June 20, 1947 radio address, that it was "deliberately designed to weaken labor unions." He went on to say, "Because of unions, the living standards of our working people have increased steadily until they are today the highest in the world." He alluded to the

---

[69] See Tables 1 and 2 in Chapter 7 for data consistent with these general principles.
[70] Bert Cochran, *Labor and Communism: the conflict that shaped American unions*, Princeton University Press, (1979).

Marshall Plan when he went on to say, "As our generous American spirit prompts us to aid the world to rebuild, we must, at the same time, construct a better America in which all can share equitably in the blessings of democracy."[71]

The provisions of Taft-Hartley:

Taft-Hartley made sympathy strikes and boycotts more difficult, allowed states to ban the union shop, and "gave the federal government a veto over union politics and strike strategy... To survive, the unions would have to function less as a social movement and more as interest groups protecting their own turf."[72]

Truman's veto:

Truman sent a strongly worded veto to Congress on the day of his radio address. He cited principles violated by the bill and made economic and constitutional objections. His prescience is quite remarkable. He told Congress that he had asked himself a fundamental question with regard to the provisions of the bill: "Would they strengthen or weaken democracy?" He concluded that its provisions would weaken democracy. They violated our principle of "fairness" by favoring management over labor. They would make us vulnerable to totalitarianism by attacking our unions which, he wrote, were our "bulwark" against it. By opening the door to "right to work" states, the Taft-Hartley Bill would violate another principle, the "uniform application of public policy." Truman provided Congress with an analysis showing the specific ways in which the Taft-Hartley provisions

---

[71]Harry S. Truman in a radio address given on June 20, 19487 titled "On the veto of the Taft-Hartley Bill."

[72]*Who Built America?* Stephen Brier (ed.), American Social History Project, (1992), p. 493.

violated our principles and weakened both the trade union movement and democracy.

His Taft-Hartley veto was Jeffersonian in its tone. Jefferson wrote that, in addition to a "benign religion" and various other benefits provided in America, people needed "a wise and frugal government, which shall restrain men from injuring one another, shall leave them otherwise free to regulate their own pursuit of industry and improvement, and shall not take from the mouth of labor the bread it has earned." [73]

The consequences:

Taft-Hartley violates many constitutional principles. The Preamble to our Constitution gives us the right to "life, liberty and the pursuit of happiness." Taft-Hartley, by weakening the labor movement, also weakens a check on our concentration of powers. This places our liberty in jeopardy. We can see now, even more clearly than Truman saw in 1947, how the Taft-Hartley provisions increase the role of government in our lives. He was concerned that government would be present at the bargaining table. As it has turned out, Taft-Hartley has minimized the role of the bargaining table. After Taft-Hartley, labor moved more and more away from collective bargaining as a means of improving wages and working conditions. More and more it has taken the political approach. It now relies on its ability to "get out the vote" as a way to gain influence in Washington. Then it uses this influence to secure the passage of laws that transfer its old functions to government agencies. For example, workers with safety or health problems can now get help from OSHA. Workers with discrimination problems have their own federal or state agency to ask for help. Whether this is good for workers is

---

[73] Thomas Jefferson in his first inaugural address on March 4, 1801 (Kindle 1629.

an open question. It certainly is not good for organized labor that many workers, when faced with problems at work, look to the governments for help—instead of to their unions. This transfer of union powers and functions to our government has strengthened our perception of government as all-powerful. This is consistent with our present tendency to protest against our government instead of taking action to improve it.

Since Taft-Hartley, the percentage of workers who belong to unions has decreased from thirty-seven to 11.9 per cent. In the private sector, only 6.9 percent of workers belong to unions.[74] In 1947, Truman—as a matter of course—alluded to the fact that the US had the highest standard of living in the world. The first Legatum prosperity index (2007) tended to agree with him.[75] It had the US tied for 1st place with Norway and Sweden. In 2008, we were ranked 6th, in 2009, 9th, and in 2010, 10th. In 2010, the four most heavily unionized countries (Sweden, Denmark, Finland and Norway) were ranked 6th, 2nd, 3rd and 1st in the world by Legatum.[76] According to the "Gini" index, our income gap is now the widest of all developed countries.[77] Of course, the decline of organized labor is not the sole cause of these disparities. Neither is Taft-Hartley the sole cause of the decline of organized labor. However, the countries ahead of us on the Legatum rankings do tend to have strong labor movements. At the least, this suggests that strong labor movements are not necessarily detrimental to competitiveness, prosperity, income equality and life satisfaction.

---

[74] These figures are from a Bureau of Labor Statistics news release dated January 21, 2011.

[75] However, a prosperous country with a large gap between its rich and its ordinary citizens cannot be said to have a high standard of living for the strong and the weak alike...

[76] The Legatum Institute For Global Development issued prosperity indices in 2007, 2008, 2009 and 2010.

[77] The Gini index measures the income gap between the top ten percent of a country and the bottom ten percent. CBS News, Washington, Sep. 28, 2010 reported that the "Income gap between rich, poor the widest ever."

Conclusion:

The main lesson to be drawn from our Taft-Hartley experience is that we should be very cautious about abandoning principle in favor of expediency. It is perhaps true that, in the short run, a few wealthy people benefited from Taft-Hartley. In the long run, however, it appears to have affected most of us negatively.

THE MARSHALL PLAN (1947)

The history of human conduct does not warrant that exalted opinion of human virtue which would make it wise in a nation to commit interests of so delicate and momentous a kind, as those which concern its intercourse with the rest of the world, to the sole disposal of a magistrate created and circumstanced as would be a President of the United States.
—Alexander Hamilton in *Federalist 75*

Our intercourse with our global neighbors should be peaceful. Our treaties, our military policies and actions and our participation in global projects should all be aimed at establishing and maintaining peaceful relationships. The text of our Constitution supports this view. It gives Congress the sole power to declare war. The intent of the framers was to keep the presidency as far removed as possible from any decisions having to do with the commencement, continuation or cessation of hostilities.[78] Madison, the father of our Constitution called this its wisest feature. The presidency was to do the "nuts and bolts" negotiation of treaties, but under the substantive supervision of the Senate. After all, treaties can lead to either peace or war. Questions of peace and war belong with Congress: the "people's branch."

---

[78]Fisher. *Presidential War Power*, 1st ed. pg. 9

Yet our presidency has now gained virtually absolute control over both our war and treaty powers. As recently as the late 1940's this was not the case. In those days the executive could propose but only Congress could approve. One result was a diplomatic triumph—the Marshall Plan. We extended the hand of friendship to our recent enemies and, for a time, earned the esteem and trust of many throughout the world.

About the Marshall Plan:

Nine months after "Little Boy" was dropped on Hiroshima, Congress authorized the Marshall Plan. During these nine months the US had already begun giving assistance to some of the countries devastated by World War II. In those early post-war days, our wartime ally, the USSR, played a part in providing this assistance. For example, it shipped quantities of wheat to France. It now appears that, in 1947, we had an opportunity to establish a cooperative relationship with the USSR based on our joint participation in the Marshall Plan. However, we set conditions to Soviet participation that guaranteed its refusal. In this way, we lost an opportunity to foster international cooperation.

During the four years of the Plan's existence, we donated $13 billion in economic aid.[79] We also established "counterpart funds" that loaned capital to private enterprises. Much of the money provided under the Plan was spent to purchase US goods, thus helping create our own post-war boom. The Marshall Plan was a textbook case of "enlightened self interest." While the Marshall Plan would prove to be beneficial to the United States in terms of both our economy and world opinion, the fact remains that, at that time, our Congress was willing to commit substantial funds to peaceful purposes. Our present-day

[79] Michael Cox and Caroline Kennedy-Pipe, "The Tragedy of American Diplomacy?" MUSE, *The Marshall Plan and the Origins of the Cold War*.

Congress passed a military budget for FY 2010 of $680 billion. This was $16 billion more than President Obama had requested.

About our Middle Eastern war:

A 2010 Congressional Research Service report analyzing the FY 2010 Appropriations Act, estimated that about $748 billion would go for Operation "Iraq Freedom," and about $304 billion for Operation "Enduring Freedom."[80] As of April 29, 2011, US fatal casualties totaled 4,452 in Iraq and 1,566 in Afghanistan.[81] Iraqi civilian casualties from 2004 to 2009 are estimated at 92,000.[82] For every casualty, about three people have been seriously wounded.

Toward a global Marshall Plan:

In 1992, then Senator Al Gore proposed what he termed a "Global Marshall Plan." His plan would allocate money to help impoverished nations achieve patterns of sustainable economic progress. The US alone, by redirecting the funds now spent supporting armies of invasion and occupation, could contribute $100 billion dollars a year for ten years to such a plan. A UN fund of $200 billion per year (used in this way) could make a substantial impact on the world economy, thus benefiting the people of the developed, as well as of the impoverished nations. Used in this way, the money could improve the quality of our children's lives instead of placing their lives in jeopardy.[83]

It would help matters somewhat if the power to declare war

---

[80] CRS Report for Congress 7-5700, Amy Belasco. "The cost of Iraq, Afghanistan, and other global war on terror operations since 9/11." (July 16, 2010).

[81] These figures were accessed from antiwar.com on May 7, 2011.

[82] These figures are from Wiki Leaks classified Iraq war logs, accessed May 6, 2011.

was returned to Congress. Congress, however, has itself become aggressive. While the framers believed that assigning the power to declare war to Congress would make us a peaceful country, things have not turned out quite that way. Congress does not act as a check on US military aggression for several reasons. First, it has abdicated its war powers to the presidency. This has not only placed the power to make war and peace decisions in the hands of a branch the framers considered prone to war. It has also placed Congress in a position where it votes to authorize (rather than to order) war. It can do this without being held accountable by the electorate. If things go wrong, as they usually do, we rally behind our embattled president instead of blaming our representatives in Congress. Second, our electoral system (further damaged by *Citizens United v. FEC*) tends to place Congress under obligation to corporations.

The ball is in our court:

We cannot rely on our political or corporate leaders to support a Global Marshall Plan. Their self-interest, at present, lies with the production of military goods and the amassing of power and wealth. Our self-interest, on the other hand, lies with promoting general peace and prosperity. It follows that we must restructure our government in such a way that our leaders come to see their self-interests as being congruent with ours. The

---

[83] It is true that a great deal of our present foreign aid tends to enrich the politicians of the countries being aided—instead of helping the ordinary people. However, this is not inevitable. A world Marshall Plan could by-pass local politicians and focus on training and making loans to private entrepreneurs. NPR's "State of the Nation" recently interviewed an aid worker who told of how local entrepreneurs took over the "well maintenance" function in an African village from aid workers and turned it into a profit-making enterprise. It is possible to use aid resources to foster local initiatives. Much of the original Marshall Plan consisted of loans to business enterprise and entrepreneurs.

means of doing so are at hand. While Congress controls the making of statutes, it has no power over the making of constitutional amendments. This power is reserved to us, the people, acting through our state legislatures.

THE 17th AMENDMENT (1913)

The law of unintended consequences is what happens when a simple system tries to regulate a complex system.
—Unknown

The process that produced the 17th Amendment was simple in that its framers dealt with a single issue and focused on information directly bearing on that issue. The political system it sought to improve, on the other hand, was complex and involved information indirectly bearing on the Amendment. Surely enough, the passage of the 17th Amendment produced unintended consequences. It is true that the election-year behavior of senators was found by researchers to be slightly more responsive to the views of their constituents after the Amendment was passed. The major consequence of the Amendment, however, was both unintended and undesired by its framers.

Why a 17th Amendment? [84]

The US Constitution originally provided for the election of senators by state legislators. The direct election of senators by the people was first proposed in 1826.[85] Congress proposed the 17th Amendment on May 13, 1912 in response to a general

---

[84] This paragraph draws heavily from "Direct election of senators," US Senate Historical Office, accessed on Feb. 23, 20010.
[85] Senate historical office, "Direct election of senators," Accessed Feb. 23, 2010.

belief that it would avoid stand-offs in state legislatures that resulted in vacant Senate seats, reduce corruption in the Senate and give us more control over our federal government. In the mid-1890's, the Populist Party included the direct election of senators in its party platform. In the early 1900's, Oregon and Nebraska experimented with measures that consulted the people's preferences. By 1912, twenty-nine states had adopted similar measures. Thus the consequences intended by the various supporters of the 1913 Amendment had to do with vacant Senate seats, corruption and populism

The 17th Amendment and the impeachment provisions:

The impeachment provisions also have to do with corruption and populism. They were intended to make the civil officers of all three branches lawful, responsive and dedicated to the needs of the people. However, the framers of the impeachment provisions violated the general "separation of powers" principle by assigning the Senate a crucial judicial power (the power to try impeachments). They committed this violation on the grounds that the early Supreme Courts would be too weak and small to render impartial justice, especially in cases involving high government officials.

Federalist 65 and *66* make it clear that the framers would never have considered the Senate as an appropriate body for the trying of impeachments had they suspected that its member might someday be elected by the people directly.[86] Above all

[86] This is, perhaps, unfair. There is ample evidence in the *Federalist Papers* that the framers knew that the impeachment provisions (and many other provisions of the Constitution) would require revision by future generations. They were counting on us when, for the sake of expediency, they assigned the power to try impeachments to a legislative body. Where they made their mistake was in assuming that future generations would frequently revise the Constitution.

they wanted the nation's court of impeachment to render impartial justice. They fully understood that an elective body would become politicized and could not, therefore, render this impartial justice. The original assignment of the power to try impeachments to the Senate led to the failure of impeachment courts to render impartial justice and this, in turn, led to lawlessness on the parts of our civil officers. In 1797,[87] the Senate began the erosion process by exempting itself from the impeachment provisions, thus demonstrating the value of another general principle (this one set forth by Hamilton in *Federalist 80*) that "no man ought . . . to be a judge in his own cause." This exemption by the Senate encouraged lawlessness in both houses of Congress. It was followed by the partial politicization of the Senate and the exemption of subordinate officers of the executive branch. By 1913, the *de facto* elective nature of the Senate had rendered the impeachment provisions worthless. The framers of the 17th Amendment could have rejuvenated them by including a provision transferring the power to try executive and legislative impeachments to the judiciary. Yet they let this golden opportunity slip by. When they made the Senate officially elective, they should have taken the opportunity to transfer the power to try most impeachments to the judiciary. Instead, they thrust a sword into the already feeble heart of the impeachment provisions.

It would have been well if the framers of the 17th Amendment had recognized and taken their opportunity to remedy the damage done by Hamilton and his fellow framers. A provision transferring the power to try most impeachments to the judiciary could have re-established the original intent of the framers in a number of respects. For example, it could have explicitly re-extended the reach of the impeachment provisions to Members of Congress and to subordinate civil officers of the executive branch.

---

[87] Raoul Berger, *Impeachment, the Constitutional Problems*, Harvard University Press, 1973, p.224.

Were these consequences unintended?

The framers of the 17th Amendment failed to notice the likelihood that it would administer the *coup de grace* to the impeachment provisions. This was not due to any lack of intelligence or political acumen on the part of the Amendment's framers. Their failure to notice the connection between their efforts and the impeachment provisions was due to the nature of the amendment process. This process tends to consider one issue as separate from the other elements of our overall system of government. The unspoken assumption is that the particular issue or issues of the proposed amendment, if resolved, will fit in with our general system of governance. This is not necessarily the case. The ease with which the unfortunate consequences of the 17th Amendment could have been avoided went unnoticed. These consequences, were certainly unintended.

What can we learn from the 17th Amendment?

Our experience with the 17th Amendment is a strong argument for the periodic constitutional conventions proposed by Jefferson.[88] The structure, process and nature of a convention not only brings out conflicting views that need to be resolved, but identifies the "unintended and undesirable" consequences in time to avoid them. Periodic conventions would supplement, individual amendments, not replace them.

We can also learn that Congress cannot be trusted to propose constitutional amendments. Congress is conditioned to respond to pressure according to its intensity and its political importance. It is not conditioned to look for unintended consequences. Congress is also disproportionately influenced by special interest money. This hampers its ability to produce amendments that are for the general good.

---

[88] In a letter to James Madison dated Sept. 6, 1789.

What actions can we take to mend matters?

We need an "unlimited"[89] national convention of at least four months duration to consider constitutional problems that have developed or become apparent since 1787. Such a convention should be charged with developing and proposing a comprehensive set of provisions dealing with these problems.

---

[89] An unlimited convention makes a comprehensive review of all Articles and provisions. A limited convention would consider only one amendment.

CHAPTER 4

SIX HISTORICAL EVENTS (1787-1876)

- Belknap's acquittal (1876) in effect, exempted subordinate officers of the executive branch from the impeachment provisions.

- In *Ex Parte* Milligan (1866), Justice David Davis stated an admirable principle that, however, has been ignored by subsequent US governments.

- In 1846, Polk precipitated a war with Mexico. de Tocqueville arrived in America in 1831 to research his classic analysis, *Democracy in America*.

- The charges against Senator Blount were dismissed by his fellow senators in 1799.

- **The Federalist Papers were first published on Oct. 27, 1787. The framers had agreed to the proposed constitution in September and the ratification process was beginning.**

THE BELKNAP ACQUITTAL (1876)

*There is a contagion in example which few men have
the strength to resist.*
—Alexander Hamilton in *Federalist 61*

On August 1, 1876, Secretary of War Belknap was acquitted of "basely prostituting his high office to his lust for private gain." Belknap had set a poor example for the civil officers of our federal government—past, present and future. The Senate that acquitted him, however, did the real damage.

When he made the above statement about the power of example, Hamilton was arguing for the election of all members of the House at one time. He felt that this would allow each Congress to start fresh. Every two years a new and idealistic group of members, uninfected by the example of a previous Congress, would be free to concern itself with the well being of its constituents. Each group of new members would be uninfected by any self-interested values and behaviors that it might otherwise "catch" from holdover members. Hamilton's words would no doubt have been just as valid if applied to the Senate. It is extremely difficult to change an organization's culture once its values, or lack of values become established. It is likely that Belknap's acquittal was one factor in the establishment of a lawless culture in the Senate.

The Belknap Impeachment and resignation:

The Senate *Historical Minutes* for May, 1876 read, in part, "On May 2, just minutes before the House was scheduled to vote on (his) articles of impeachment, Belknap raced to the White House (and) handed Grant his resignation." Nevertheless, the

House unanimously approved five impeachment charges. It accused Belknap of receiving substantial quarterly payments from a certain Caleb Marsh over a period of some six years. Belknap was charged with receiving these payments in return for his appointment of John Evans (an associate of Marsh's) to operate the lucrative Fort Sill military trading post.[90] On August 1 the Senate failed to muster the required two-thirds majority and thus acquitted Belknap on all five counts. The August 2, 1876, the *New York Times* reported that all but one of the "not guilty" votes were based on the senators' belief that, since Belknap had resigned, Congress had no jurisdiction over the case. It is also noteworthy that only one Democrat voted "not guilty."

The Belknap "virus" is still with us:

The way an organization deals with its first experience of a given kind is especially important. However destructive and illegal it may be, it sets a precedent that is difficult to overturn. The Belknap acquittal did incalculable damage to our federal governments, past and present.

First, the Belknap affair was contagious in that it assured all subordinate officers of the executive branch, present and future, that they had (and have) nothing to fear from the impeachment provisions. If worst comes to worst, they can simply resign and thereby avoid conviction, removal and (the greatest deterrent of all) disqualification. Yet the framers relied on the impeachment provisions as our main "check" to corrupt behavior on the part of our civil officers. As James Monroe wrote, the impeachment provisions are the very "pivot" on which our government turns.[91] He added that, only if the impeachment provisions were maintained in their "full vigor" would our government be suc-

---

[90] The *New York Times* of March 31, 1876.
[91] James Monroe, *The People, The Sovereigns*, James River Press, 19087, p. 16.

cessful. The *New York Times* of August 2 editorialized: "it is here-after a part of the law . . . that a civil officer may be corrupt in his office, and escape the penalty fixed by the Constitution by hastening to resign as soon as his deeds are disclosed." In fact, the contagion from the Belknap affair has extended even further into the enforcement of our Constitution than the *New York Times* anticipated. Since Belknap, no House has impeached a subordinate civil officer of the executive branch. Evidently our representatives have felt that it would be "love's labor lost" since an impeached miscreant could escape by resigning his or her post. The precedent set by the Belknap Senate exempted, in effect, the subordinate civil officers of the executive branch from the impeachment provisions. This has been its most serious consequence.

Second, the Belknap verdict strengthened the feeling among senators that they are justified in disregarding their special impeachment oath (or affirmation) to render impartial justice. This pernicious precedent had already been established by the admittedly political nature of the 1868 trial of President Andrew Johnson for exceeding his lawful powers. More recently, members of the Clinton court of impeachment voted to acquit, yet freely admitted their belief in Clinton's guilt. Some said they voted to acquit him because, in their opinion, acquittal would be for the "good of the country." Yet they had taken oaths to consider only the evidence and the law. Their votes were blatant violations of both their oaths and the rule of law. The rule of law is designed to prevent just such arbitrary verdicts.

Third, the acquittal contributed to the general feeling among Grant appointees that corruption was the name of the political game. As Hamilton pointed out, it takes a person of very strong character to behave honestly when honest behavior is a joke to his or her colleagues. To cite a contemporary example, imagine a member of our present Congress admonishing his or her colleagues for flying first-class or business-class. Rubbing shoulders with the wealthy and with corporate officers—rather than with the ordinary citizens they are paid to represent—is, while legal, certainly dishonest. Yet what Member of Congress, however careful about his or her own conduct, would dare say so?

Who is accountable?

The damage was done, not by Belknap, but by the senators who acquitted him. The people, however, are ultimately responsible for the behavior of their civil officers, whether miscreant senators or miscreant executive appointees. Just as the people of the 1870's were responsible for both Belknap's misdeeds and for his acquittal, we are responsible for any corrupt behavior on the part of our civil officers. The buck stops with us.[92] Acting through our state legislatures, we have both the power to call a constitutional convention and the power to propose and ratify amendments that would prevent governmental corruption. Since we have not done so, we have no grounds for complaint. If we are unhappy with our government, we should take action rather than complain. We should set strict rules governing the behavior of our civil officers and provide for the vigorous enforcement of these rules.

---

[92] Madison made it clear that "the buck stops with us" in *Federalist 53* (and in other *Federalist Papers*. In *Federalist 53*, he pointed out that our government is "established by the people and unalterable by the government."

EX PARTE [93] MERRYMAN (1861) AND EX PARTE MILLIGAN (1866)

No doctrine involving more pernicious consequences was ever invented by the wit of man than that any of its (the Constitution's) provisions can be suspended during any of the great exigencies of government.
—Justice David Davis (1866)

Lincoln illegally suspended *Habeas Corpus* in 1861. During that same year, in *Ex Parte* Merryman, Chief Justice Taney found the suspension unconstitutional. The Constitution gives the power to suspend the writ of *Habeas Corpus* to Congress, not to the president. Accordingly, Taney ordered John Merryman, a Maryland secessionist, freed from a union prison under the writ of *Habeas Corpus*. Lincoln ignored the Taney order. Taney had no means of enforcing it and the suspension continued in effect. This set the stage for Justice David Davis's famed 1866 words in *Ex Parte* Milligan.

Ex Parte Milligan (1866):

Justice David Davis earned a place of honor in our history when he took the matter of *Habeas Corpus* up again in writing the US Supreme Court's decision in *Ex Parte* Milligan. The Union Army had arrested Milligan (and four other civilians) in Indiana in 1864. A military court sentenced them to death for plotting to steal weapons and arm Confederate soldiers held in prisoner-of-war camps.

The Supreme Court found that the military court's sentence

---

[93] "Ex Parte" refers to "motions, hearings or orders granted on the request of and for the benefit of one party only." Definition provided by Legal explanations.com, accessed on March 24, 2011.

violated Article II, Section 9 of the Constitution which reads, in part, ". . . the writ of *Habeas Corpus* shall not be suspended except when in case of rebellion or invasion the public safety may require it." The writ of *Habeas Corpus*, among other things, protects civilians from military trials. It can only be suspended by an act of Congress. The Milligan decision was made after the war. Milligan and his compatriots were freed. *Ex Parte* Milligan is remembered especially for Justice Davis's condemnation of the suspension of constitutional provisions in times of national crises.

What all this means today:

Former Justice David Davis and the Milligan decision provide us with a clear and eloquent statement of principle. This statement should inspire our present-day Congress, Judiciary and President to abide by the Constitution, even where circumstances seem to make unlawful actions expedient. Civil disobedience is one thing; lawlessness on the parts of civil officers is quite another. Civil officers have taken oaths to support the Constitution and should be impeached, removed and disqualified when they fail to do so. As Hamilton wrote in *Federalist 80*, "The possibility of particular mischief's can never be viewed . . . as a solid objection to a general principle which is calculated to avoid general mischiefs." We should ask ourselves what we can do to assure that our federal government adheres to the "David Davis principle."

A broader question:

The story of John Merryman, Chief Justice Taney and President Lincoln raises another question: What can be done when a president, backed by the armed forces, defies a court order? It seems reasonable to suppose that many US Supreme Court justices have reflected, since 1861, on the precedent set by Lincoln in the *Ex Parte* Merryman case. Let us suppose that a court is faced with a constitutional case asking that a president be enjoined from some action he is taking or contemplates taking. Would it not be natural for the court to reflect upon Lincoln's defiance of the Taney order in *Ex Parte* Merryman? After all, US presidents control the world's greatest military force. The court controls only its pen and paper.

Schlesinger v. Holtzman (1973) comes to mind. In this case, Congresswoman Elizabeth Holtzman obtained an injunction from a district court to stop the bombing of Cambodia. The Second Circuit ordered a stay of the injunction on the grounds that the matter was a "political question" to be settled between Congress and the President. The Supreme Court affirmed this decision.[94] The illegal killing of innocent Cambodians continued. This piece of legal history is difficult to understand except in the light of a possible fear on the part of the judiciary that Nixon would disregard the Holtsman injunction. If this had occurred, it would have created a national crisis.

Conclusions:

The issues raised by *Ex Parte* Merryman and *Ex Parte* Milligan are difficult questions to resolve. However much we humans revere the David Davis principle, we toss it aside if and when we assume the mantle of power. Power corrupts and power seduces. These concomitants to power, combined with the pressures of office, make the adherence to principle in times of crisis seem absurd to the civil officers involved. Hamilton spoke eloquently about the need for adhering to principle, and

[94] Congressional Research Service Report for Congress, August 18, 1999, p. 16.

then he masterminded a disastrous violation of the separation of powers principle (the assignment of the power to try impeachments to the Senate). Lincoln, while a Congressman, criticized Polk for exceeding his constitutional powers (Polk provoked a war with Mexico). Later, President, Lincoln himself illegally suspended *Habeas Corpus* and defied Chief Justice Taney's court order to release Mr. Merryman.

As for the difficulty that would arise should a president disregard a court order, the impeachment provisions, would be our only recourse. The crux of this problem is that the president controls our military both in times of peace and in times of war. Without changing this arrangement, it would be difficult indeed to enforce a court order on the executive. However, it might be possible to create a constitutional transfer of control to Congress under specified circumstances.

POLK'S WAR WITH MEXICO (1846)

This (a presidential war), our convention understood to be the most oppressive of all kingly oppressions, and they resolved to so frame the Constitution that no one man should hold the power of bringing the oppression upon us.
—Abraham Lincoln from *the Collected Works of Abraham Lincoln*, 451-52 (Roy Basler, ed. 1953)

In the above quote, then Congressman Lincoln was referring to what was known in 1846 as "Mr. Polk's War" (with Mexico). After he became president, Lincoln viewed the exceeding of presidential powers in a different light. In April of 1861 he issued proclamations (illegally) calling forth the state militia and (illegally) suspending the writ of *habeas corpus*. Then he defied a court order that found his suspension of *habeas corpus* unconstitutional. When Chief Justice Taney instructed him to release one John

Merryman, who was being illegally detained, he ignored the court order. Neither Polk nor Lincoln, however, can be held accountable for taking the law into their own hands. It is our Constitution that is at fault for not giving efficacy (Hamilton's word) to its own provisions. For example, it requires our presidents to swear that they will "protect and defend the Constitution of the United States." Yet it neglects to provide us, or our representatives, with any effective means of assuring that they do so. Our Constitution , unlike our federal statutes, belongs to the people. Its amendment is our responsibility.

Mr. Polk's War:

Andrew Jackson, our seventh president, took the constitutional war powers of Congress so seriously that he refused to recognize the independence of Texas because this act might have led to war with Mexico. Mr. Polk, our eleventh president, did not hesitate to usurp Congress's powers. He provoked a hostile reaction from Mexico in 1846 by sending General Zachary Taylor and his troops into disputed territory along the Texas-Mexico border. When a military clash resulted, Polk sent a message to Congress stating that "Mexico has invaded our territory and shed American blood . . . and war exists." [95] Congress declared war two days later. Even congressmen who disagreed with the war voted for it, on the grounds that it was a *fait accompli*.

Polk's Censure:

The House of Representatives of that time had second thoughts. The same body that had voted overwhelmingly for war in 1846 declared in 1848 that the war had been "unnecessarily and unconstitutionally begun by the President of the United

---

[95] As quoted in Louis Fisher's *Presidential War Power*, 1st ed., p. 32.

States." The Polk censure, however, was not enough to deter President Pierce from shelling, in 1854, a coastal town of Nicaragua. That Country's offense was that it declined to apologize for arresting an American citizen and attempting to charge him with murder.[96] We have failed to include in our Constitution any effective means for preventing constitutional violations on the parts of our federal civil officers.

The Migration of the War Powers:

When Polk, Pierce and Lincoln violated our Constitution, it was generally conceded that their actions were unlawful. While Polk was not impeached, removed and disqualified, he was at least censured. Lincoln's actions could be defended on the grounds that the Civil War made them necessary. Modern presidents, on the other hand, blatantly disregard the Constitution and go essentially unchallenged by us, the people. Clinton said in 1993, ". . . clearly, the Constitution leaves the President, for good and sufficient reasons, the ultimate decision-making authority" (for making decisions that might lead to war).[97] George W. Bush cited his authority as President, rather than the Iraq Resolution, to justify his invasion of that country. When, on Dec. 2, 2009, Mr. Obama announced his escalation of the war in the Middle East, he never even mentioned Congress.

What we can learn from Mr. Polk's War:

The best of human beings, when given the powers we allow our presidents, will come to look on foreign policy as a game of chess, with no rules other than "win or lose." Polk moved his black Knight into disputed territory in order to provoke an inju-

---

[96] *The Arkansas News*, July13, 1854,
[97] Fisher, p. 158.

dicious response from the Mexican government. The Mexican government obliged and Mr. Polk gave the world a lesson in the "chain rattling" that was held in such contempt by Patrick Henry. The framers knew that presidents could not be trusted with the power to make war. Madison said that the wisest provision of the Constitution was the one that confided "the question of war and peace to the legislature, and not to the executive department . . . in war, the honours (sic) and emoluments of office are to be multiplied and it is the executive patronage under which they are to be enjoyed." The power to declare war should be returned to Congress. This is the body that represents the people who must pay for wars—both with their money and the lives of their children and grandchildren.

We can learn from Mr. Polk's War, and from many more recent wars, that what Madison considered the "wisest" provision of the Constitution has failed to do its job. Mr. Polk's usurpation of congressional powers, and the "slap on his wrist" that resulted, was well- known to Mr. Pierce in 1854 when he ordered the shelling of Greytown, Nicaragua. Pierce's attack on the inhabitants of Greytown was later used by Woodrow Wilson as a precedent for his occupation of Veracruz, Mexico in 1914. We can learn from Polk, and others that something must be done to bring our presidents (and the rest of our federal government) more nearly under our control.

The Remedy:

Our presidents, justices and federal legislators did not create this chaos, nor have they the power to remedy it. A constitutional solution is required. Constitutional solutions are the province of the people.

DE TOUQUEVILLE'S ARRIVAL IN AMERICA (1831)

If men are to remain civilized, or to become so, the art of associating together must grow and improve.
—Alexis de Tocqueville. In *Democracy in America*, Book II, Part Two, 28.

de Tocqueville, visiting America in 1831-2, admired the way we created "associations to give entertainment, to found seminaries, to build inns, to construct churches, to diffuse books, to send missionaries to the antipodes" (and to build) "hospitals, prisons, or schools." He admired our associations for standing "in lieu of those powerful private individuals" (in Europe) "whom the equality of conditions" (in America) "has swept away." The giving of entertainment and the building of inns are now, for the most part, accomplished by corporations, at a profit. Our non-profits, whose revenues increased from $802 billion in 1995 to $1.6 trillion in 2005, provide health care and education, do health research, perform charitable works, advocate causes and act as restraints on our government's bias in favor of corporations. They are staffed, in large part, by paid workers and form a "shadow government" performing many useful tasks that might otherwise be neglected. Despite these positive aspects of our present "shadow government," our "art of associating together" needs improvement in order to keep up with changing times.

The down side to our large NGO's:

There is no down side to such small associations as volunteer fire departments, service organizations and theater groups. They retain the many virtues noted by de Tocqueville. In addition to performing important functions, they educate their members to political action and, as de Tocqueville noted, incline them to be considerate of their neighbors. Our larger NGO's, however, are beset by the same general problem that plagues our government. They, like it, have spun out of our control. While the civil officers of our government have transferred their allegiance, in large part, from us to corporations and other special interest groups, the staffs of some large non-profits are accountable to no one. This lack of accountability is the over-riding issue, not only with our domestic non-profits, but among the large non-profits of the world.

This mini-essay, however, deals only with one particular kind of US non-profit: the NGO that solicits individual members of the public for all (or for a portion) of its revenue. We contribute to the budgets of these non-profits. However, we have no say in their governance and operations. We should be able to assure ourselves that (1) our contributions are being used frugally and effectively and (2) that we are in agreement with both the administrative and program policies governing their use. However, the advents of paid staff, substantial budgets and non-member funding have given rise to the same accountability problems among NGO's that, for a variety of different reasons, plague our elective government.

Paid staff:

There is no doubt that changes in scale have made it necessary for most NGO's to employ paid staff. However, our "art of associating" has not been improved to deal with the consequences of this development. The staffs of many NGO's are paid from our individual contributions. Yet we, the contributing public, have no way to hold them accountable. We receive professionally prepared fliers in the mail telling us of an NGO's good works. We then write our checks and hope for the best. We neither participate in writing codes of ethics for NGO staffs, nor do we have any significant role in developing or monitoring NGO policies or programs. We simply provide a portion of the organization's budget. The staff members do with our money pretty much what they please. Members of Boards of Trustees appear to be selected for their "name recognition" value and, in my experience, have little to do with developing or monitoring codes of ethics or programs.

Substantial budgets:

Madison, in discussing the civil officers of government, alluded to the fact that human beings are not "angels." NGO staff members, since they are human, are no more "angels" than are the civil officers of government. They do what brings them pleasure and avoid doing what brings them pain. Fortunately, non-profit work attracts many people who derive pleasure and satisfaction from doing worthwhile work. Nevertheless, they are human: The easier their access to money provided for charitable purposes (and the less strictly they are supervised) the more pleasant they find it to yield to temptation. Whether this leads to illegal behavior or simply to a profligate culture (for example, one that condones business class and 1st class air travel for NGO managers), the result is the same: the misuse of contributed funds and the abuse of trust.

It should be noted here that "transparency" is not an adequate remedy. For example, the fact that National Public Radio (NPR) receives one-third of its funds from government, another third from corporations and a final third from individual contributions is posted on its internet site—along with its strict code of ethics. Despite its posting of both its corporate funding and its strict code of ethics (which requires its news staff to report both sides of an issue) you will rarely hear a discussion on NPR that involves guests holding opposing points of view. In the matter of crop-based ethanol, for example, *Talk of the Nation* sympathetically interviewed a proponent of crop-based ethanol on Aug. 15, 2008, but failed to include in the discussion a member of the "Princeton Study." This study, published in *Science* magazine on Feb. 8, 2008, concludes that, if we continue to subsidize crop-based ethanol, "greenhouse emissions will increase by 50-100 percent in thirty years." [98]

"No strings attached" funding:

Typically, individual contributors to these NGO's have no say in either their governance or operations. They are introduced to the non-profit by pamphlets in the mail describing the urgent need for the NGO's efforts and telling of its accomplishments. They note that the need is great, that the accomplishments sound good, and that they agree with the stated goals of the organization. They write their checks and have no further involvement until another solicitation arrives in the mail. They have no means of influencing either the governance or the operations of the non-profit—other than, perhaps, the casting of a meaningless vote for a "name" being proposed for its board of trustees.

The nature of the non-profit accountability problem:

There are three aspects of accountability to be taken into account with non-profits. First, they are accountable to the government for abiding by the law. Second, they should be accountable to the people they serve for providing them with the goods

---

[98] Searchinger, Timothy et al. "Use of US croplands for bio fuels increases greenhouse gases through emissions from land use changes," *Science* magazine, Feb. 8, 2008.

and services they need and want. Third, they should be accountable to their sources of revenue for operating effectively, effi-
ciently and in accordance with the wishes of these sources of revenue. Clearly, defining the nature of any given NGO's accountability is a complex and difficult matter. For example, some
NGO's receive funds from corporations, from government and
from the individuals they purport to serve. Often, the interests
of their funding sources are in conflict. Even where there is no
obvious conflict of interest (for example, an NGO formed to
fight governmental corruption might receive all of its contributions from among the same people it has been formed to serve),
in practice NGO's rarely make themselves accountable to either
their contributors or to their beneficiaries. Their boards are "for
show" and their staffs are often accountable only to themselves.
Individual contributors and beneficiaries have no way to exercise
the authority they possess by virtue of their ownership, other
than by withholding their contributions when an NGO's performance is poor. This option is of little use, however, since the
only way contributors have of evaluating an NGO's performance
is by reading the fund-raising material generated by either its
staff or by a public relations firm in its employ.

A non-governmental solution:

We can improve our "art of associating"—(as de Tocqueville
hoped we would) by taking advantage of internet technology.
We can simply decline to support any NGO that does not adopt
and enforce a computer-based "Members Bill of Rights." Under
such a bill of rights, all contributors would become members of
the NGO and entitled to a say in its governance and operation.
Members would, upon payment of their annual dues, be
assigned code ID's and passwords which would give them, for
the membership period, access to a management information

page and a voting page. Each member would be entitled to cast an equal, and binding vote on all matters of both governance policy and operational policy. The management information page would provide, as a minimum, a breakdown of the annual budget and specific figures on the total compensation package of the CEO and on the average compensation packages for each level of management and professional personnel. Another crucial set of data would give the total number of business trips made by the staff at each level (including the trustee and CEO levels) broken down at each level by 1st class, business class and economy class. These two indicators would give contributors an excellent non-gloss-able insight into the overall frugality (or profligacy) of the non-profit's staff and trustees. Members could use the voting site to cast their votes on such matters as: travel policies, staff salaries, the process for selecting trustees, the duties of trustees, the duties of the CEO, the allocation of resources to an NGO's various activities, etc. Since operations would be funded by membership dues rather than contributions, there would be no need for frequent telephone and mail solicitations or for the services of fund-raising firms. An annual membership drive should suffice.

THE BLOUNT DISMISSAL (1799)

No man ought certainly to be a judge in his own cause, or in any cause in respect to which he has the least interest or bias.
—Alexander Hamilton in *Federalist 80*

In January of 1799, when the US Senate dismissed the impeachment charges against Senator William, Blount, the senators were acting as judges in their own cause. They were, in effect, exempting themselves (and, as it turned out, the House of Representatives) from the impeachment provisions. Blount was the first and last Member of Congress to be impeached. The impeachment provisions were intended by the framers to check lawless behavior by the civil officers of government. The senators chose that congressional lawlessness should go unchecked.

The Blount case:[99]

Blount was charged with conspiring to assist Great Britain in wresting Florida and Louisiana from Spain. The Senate immediately expelled him. In his answer to the impeachment, Blount claimed that only "civil officers" were subject to impeachment and senators were not civil officers. He also claimed that he was not "charged with misconduct in office." The Senate dismissed the charges on the grounds that "it ought not to hold jurisdiction."

Are senators civil officers?

In dismissing the Blount charges, the Senate did not specify the reason it did not have jurisdiction. However, since the Blount dismissal no Member of Congress has been impeached. Yet there can be little doubt but what both the framers and the ratifiers of the Constitution understood the impeachment provisions to cover Members of Congress. The evidence that they intended to cover senators and representatives is overwhelming. Some framers resisted giving the Senate the power to try impeachments on the ground that it would be trying its own members. It is clear from this that the framers assumed the impeachment provisions would apply to the Senate. They were concerned, however, that the senators would be made "judges in their own cases." But the Senate out-witted them. It decided in 1799 that there would be no cases to judge.

[99] These comments on the Blount case draw heavily on Chapter 5 of Raoul Berger's Impeachment: *The Constitutional Problems*.

There is little, if any, support in the debates or in the *Federalist Papers* for exempting Congress from the impeachment provisions. The framers assumed that the impeachment provisions would be a necessary check against corruption and lawlessness in Congress, as well as in the judicial and the executive branches. For example, Edward Rutledge of South Carolina said, during the 1788 debates, "... if the president or the senators abused their trust, they were liable to impeachment."[100] John Stevens, Jr. wrote in the *New York Daily Advertiser* of January. 21, 1788 that the Constitution should ". . . provide a tribunal instead of the Senate for the impeachment of senators..."[101]

Judges in their own causes:

The framers and ratifiers were concerned about the Senate trying its own members because this would present a conflict of interest. After all, "No man should be a judge in his own cause." However, the Senate, within a decade of its creation, judged its own cause once and for all, by seeming to accept Blount's plea that senators were not civil officers. The 1797 senators, not wishing to judge their own members (and, perhaps, not wishing themselves to be defendants in impeachment trials) simply exempted themselves from the impeachment provisions. This was the fault of the framers and ratifiers. They set the fox to guard the hen-house and, of course, the fox helped himself.

Isn't the criminal code a sufficient check on the Senate?

The criminal code has had little deterrent effect on the behavior of Members of Congress. First, they know that Grand Juries are reluctant to indict them. For example, Vernon L.

---

[100] Bernard Bailyn, ed., *The Debate on the Constitution*, Vol. II, p. 28.
[101] Ibid, p. 61.

Jackson of Kentucky was convicted of paying $400,000 to former Representative William E. Jefferson (D-LA). Yet Jefferson was not indicted until he had been re-elected and finished out another term in Congress.

Further, the criminal courts are designed to protect the personal security of defendants. Defendants are assumed to be innocent until proved guilty and our legal system is prepared to acquit many guilty defendants in order to avoid convicting one defendant who is innocent. The rules of due process are a critical feature of our free society. They protect all of us ordinary people from oppression by our government . . . They do not, however, apply to the impeachment provisions. Defendants in impeachment cases do not appear as ordinary people. They appear in their official capacities as representatives of the government. The very purpose of the impeachment provisions is to protect us ordinary people from being oppressed by the civil officers of government. The framers were explicit on this point. Hamilton wrote, in *Federalist 65*, that impeachment trials " . . . can never be tied down by such strict rules . . . as in common cases serve to limit the discretion of courts in favor of personal security." The "strict rules" Hamilton alluded to are now termed "due process." To rely on the criminal courts as a check to governmental lawlessness is ineffective.

The price of expediency:

It is ironic that Hamilton (almost single handedly) persuaded the framers to violate the "separation of powers" by assigning a critical judiciary power to the Senate. It is ironic because, first, he advised against making a man the judge in his own case, Second, he wrote, in *Federalist 80*, "The possibility of particular mischiefs can never be viewed . . . as a solid objection to a general principle which is calculated to avoid general mischief's."

Because of a particular mischief (the small size and poor reputation of the Supreme Court) Hamilton nevertheless persuaded his fellow framers to abandon their assumption that the Court should try impeachments. His powers of persuasion created a "general mischief" that is at the root of many present-day governmental problems. The Senate soon became politicized and, therefore, incapable of rendering impartial justice.

Congress today:

It is difficult to accurately estimate the extent to which Members of Congress violate the law today. This is so because Members of Congress ignore, and seem to condone offenses. Grand juries are slow to indict. It would seem, however, from individual cases such as that of William J. Jefferson and that of Walter Nixon, that congressional culture tolerates a considerable amount of unlawful behavior.

Conclusions:

The Members of Congress should be checked by strict impeachment provisions and by an effective investigatory and judicial process giving teeth to these provisions. The first step in creating these provisions and this process would be to transfer the power to try congressional and executive impeachments to the judiciary. This would require a constitutional amendment of a kind that can only be produced by a constitutional convention.

PUBLICATION OF THE *FEDERALIST PAPERS*

The book known by the title of "The Federalist" (is). . rarely declined or denied by any as evidence of the general opinion of those who framed and those who accepted the Constitution . . . on questions as to its genuine meaning.
—Thomas Jefferson (Rector), James Madison and three other members of the Board of Visitors of the University of Virginia, 1825

Jefferson, Madison and their fellow "Visitors of the University of Virginia" resolved that "The Federalist," along with the Declaration of Independence, Washington's Valedictory Address and the Virginia Resolutions on the Alien and Sedition laws "should . . . be used as the text and documents of the school." They accepted the *Federalist Papers* as evidence of the general opinion of the framers and the delegates to the state conventions. These 85 papers by Madison, Hamilton and Jay were written to explain the meaning of the proposed constitution in clear and specific language. They were first published on October 27, 1787 and widely printed in the newspapers of the time. They were also widely discussed by the voters who were to choose the delegates to the state ratifying conventions. Since the voters who ratified the proposed Constitution drew their understanding of its meaning from the *Federalist Papers*, those papers are a uniquely valid indicator of constitutional intent.

What the "genuine meaning" consists of:

The "genuine meaning" of the Constitution is the meaning the framers and delegates to the state conventions thought they were agreeing to or disagreeing with when they cast their votes for or against the proposed constitution. There was a great deal of disagreement as to the desirability of certain constitutional provisions. There was, however, very little disagreement as to their genuine meaning. For this we can thank Madison, Hamilton and Jay, the authors of the *Federalist Papers*.

Genuine meaning and substantive intent:

The genuine meaning of a constitutional provision is found in its substantive intent. That is, its genuine meaning is not necessarily consistent with its literal meaning. For example, the literal meaning of the impeachment provisions is that the Senate has the power to try impeachments. A core substantive intent of these provisions is that impeachment courts render impartial justice. Yet, due to various historical events, the Senate is now incapable of doing so. If we are to carry out the genuine meaning of the provisions, we should now transfer the power to try executive and judicial impeachments to the judiciary.

Why we should care about the Constitution's genuine meaning:

We are constitutionally bound to abide by the intent of the Constitution until we have altered its intent in accordance with Article V. Where its substantive intent differs from its literal intent, our courts should be guided by the former. Where our courts are guided by its literal intent, they threaten our freedom. For example, the executive's usurpation of the congressional war powers threatens our freedom by involving us in costly and unnecessary wars. If we had promptly transferred the power to try executive impeachments to the judiciary when it first became apparent that the Senate could not render impartial justice, it is probable that the impeachment provisions would have been enforced with sufficient vigor to motivate lawful presidential behavior. A government that disregards its constitution is a threat to its own people.

Insofar as it is enforced, our Constitution protects us from the possibility of a tyrannical federal government. It protects us, for example, by separating the powers of government into three separate branches—thus preventing any one branch from becoming dictatorial. Every time our federal government alters the genuine meaning of our Constitution, it illegally overrules our wishes and substitutes its own arbitrary views in their place.

We should care about the genuine meaning of our Constitution because, without an immutable law to appeal to, we are at the mercy of our federal government. It is true that our statutes are mutable. Our federal government has the power to change them at its pleasure, subject only to the judiciary's power to find them unconstitutional. However, we (the people), acting through our state legislatures, have the sole power to make our supreme law (to which all statutes must conform). To the extent we exercise this power we are a free country. To the extent our federal government overrules us by departing from the Constitution's genuine meaning; it nudges us down the slippery slope to tyranny. To quote Madison in *Federalist 53*, our Constitution should be "established by the people and unalterable by the government."

The genuine meaning and a 2nd constitutional convention:

The only way we can bring our Constitution back to life is to hold a national convention and alter it so that it expresses the needs and desires of our present population. The best way to keep it alive in the future is to alter Article V so that it calls for periodic conventions to be held no less often than once each twenty years. This was Jefferson's proposal and it was a good one.[102] Especially in their literal and specific provisions, the

---

[102] In Jefferson's letter to Madison of Sept. 6, 1789, he wrote, ". . . every constitution expires at the end of nineteen years" and "The earth belongs to the living generation."

framers could not anticipate the rapid changes in our population, in our culture and in our technology. Despite these changes, however, our Constitution has principles that are immutable—such as the "rule of law" and "impartial justice."

How we can act to preserve our freedom:

In the name of a "living" Constitution, our judiciary disregards the genuine meaning of the Constitution as explained by the *Federalist Papers*. In *Citizens United v. FEC*, it decided that our Constitution intends us to be a government controlled by money instead of a nation self-governed by its people. In the name of a "living" Constitution, our Congress abdicates its powers and our presidents usurp them. The result has been more than a half-century of illegal, costly and inhumane wars. We should insist that the courts decide constitutional cases on the basis of the "genuine meaning" of the Constitution—not on the basis of mutable case law. As Hamilton tells us in *Federalist 81*, Congress has the power to establish rules for the guidance of the courts.[103] Since Congress has not done this, we should do it ourselves.

---

[103] Hamilton wrote, "A legislature, without exceeding its province, cannot reverse a determination once made in a particular case, though it may prescribe a new rule for future cases."

CHAPTER 5

FIVE HISTORICAL EVENTS (1776-1787)

- The core virtue of our Constitution is vaguely expressed in Article V, which was intended to make us (the people) its "establishers" and controllers (1787).

- The Framers laid the groundwork for our mutable Constitution (1787).

- Shays' rebellion illustrates the dissatisfaction that is created when people have no legitimate means of improving their government (1786-7).

- The Declaration of Independence reminds us of the sacrifices our forefathers made so that they (and we) could be free. It suggests that we might pay our debt by taking steps now to exercise the right it gives us to reform our government (1776).

- The Virginia Bill of Rights illustrates the weakness of general statements of rights that are not given "efficacy" by the provision of specific procedures for exercising these rights (1776).

OUR CONSTITUTION—ITS CORE VIRTUE (1787)

(The U.S. Constitution is). . the most remarkable work . . . (in)
modern times to have been produced by the human intellect, in its
application to political affairs.
—William Gladstone, British Statesman in a letter
of July 20, 1887

It is a great irony that the core virtue of what Gladstone
called "the most remarkable" (political) "work in modern times"
may also be its most serious flaw. I am thinking of Article V.
Hamilton and Madison claimed (in the *Federalist Papers*) that the
people of the US would be more powerful than their government. [104] Madison suggested Article V as the probable basis for
that claim when he wrote, in *Federalist 53*, that our Constitution
would be, "established by the people and unalterable by the government."

The Philadelphia convention:

In early 1787, Congress called a convention in Philadelphia.
On May 14 the delegations from Virginia and New York arrived.
By May 25 a quorum of states was represented. Four months
later, the convention approved the "work" so praised by
Gladstone and later said by British philosopher Lord Acton to
have "transformed the world."[105] This was America's first and
last constitutional convention. In 1791, ratification was completed and the proposed constitution became our supreme law.
Philadelphia hosted our first and only constitutional convention.

---

[104] Certainly the four principles discussed by Hamilton in *Federalist 9* are both
powerful and necessary to a well-functioning democracy. However,
Hamilton's description of us as America's "only legitimate fountain of power"
is difficult to support when, in practice, we have been unable to make our
supreme law.
[105] In *The History of Freedom and Other Essays* (1907) Ch. 2.

More about the Constitution's core virtue:

I believe Madison was alluding to our Constitution's core virtue when he wrote that it was "established by the people and unalterable by the government." Our democracy and our freedom depend on this core virtue. It consists of our having the final say with regard to proposed changes in the Constitution. Neither Congress nor the president nor the courts are given any decisive constitutional role in "establishing" our Constitution. The congressional role is limited to calling national conventions, proposing amendments and "proposing" whether they are to be ratified by state legislatures or by state conventions. Neither the president nor the courts have any legitimate role at all.

The core virtue in practice:

In practice, it has not delivered what the framers promised. It is so vague that our government has been able to usurp our power to "establish" the Constitution. It is true that Congress has no actual power as regards amending the Constitution. In theory, state legislators could make our supreme law and thus control both the arrangement of governmental powers and the rules governing the conduct of our civil officers. In theory, we could control our state legislatures. In theory, therefore, Madison was right. We have the power to "establish" our Constitution. In theory, it is "unalterable" by the government. However, despite our having the final say and Congress having only a procedural role according to Article V, Congress has gained and maintained the actual power. It has proposed all twenty-seven of our constitutional amendments. It has "proposed" state legislatures (instead of state conventions) as having the final say in all instances but one.[106] Since having the final say

---

[106] Congress specified state conventions to repeal prohibition with the 21st Amendment in 1933.

over establishing the Constitution is the most critical power in our government, the failure of Article V to make our means of exercising this power explicit has resulted in our abdicating this power to our federal government. This failure of Article V is, I believe, the Constitution's most serious flaw.

The specifics of Article V:

Article V gives two-thirds of our state legislatures the power, in effect, to call a national constitutional convention. That is, if two-thirds of the state legislatures ask for a convention, Congress has no choice. It must call one.[107] Article V also gives three-fourths of the state legislatures (or state conventions should Congress so "propose" and should the state legislatures accept the proposal) the power to ratify proposed amendments, even in the face of opposition from all three branches of the federal government. The 1st Amendment gives us the right to petition our state legislatures (for a constitutional convention or for other purposes). The 9th and 10th Amendments, taken together, give our petitions force.[108] In short, if an appropriate number of the people in thirty-four states petitioned their state legislatures to call for a national convention, it would be a crucial first step toward genuine governmental reform. The lawlessness of our federal government is not the fault of our federal civil officers. They are well pleased with their present arrangements and have neither the power nor the duty to change them. The buck stops with us.

---

[107] Madison also believed that, if two-thirds of the states asked Congress to propose a specific amendment to all the states (without the need for a convention) Congress would be obliged to do so. See Farrand, pp. 629-630.

[108] This appears to the case from a reading of the Constitution and the *Federalist Papers*, but I can find no instance of its having been tested in court.

We are at fault:

Genuine reform requires that a "fire wall" be built between Congress and money from corporations and other special interest groups. Without such a "fire wall," our principle "each person is entitled to one vote" falls to the ground. It is replaced by a principle to the effect that "money talks." Statutes could construct a fire wall, but they are the sole province of Congress. The Members of Congress are not (as Madison suggested in *Federalist 51*) angels. They are rational human beings. Why should we expect them to voluntarily cut off their supply of campaign donations? Of course they will continue to make palliative "reform" statutes instead. Genuine governmental reform can be achieved only by constitutional amendments proposed and ratified by us, the people. We are the ones who have the power and we are the ones who would benefit (in both the short- and the long-term) from reform.

The constitutional problem:

Proposing a constitutional amendment is a relatively easy matter for our federal government. After both houses agree that it should be proposed, it goes to the states for ratification. On the other hand, it is not so easy for us (the people) to propose one. It is, in fact, so difficult that it has never been done. This is the great anomaly of the US government. Our Declaration of Independence gives us the power to alter our government. The framers wrote over and over again in the *Federalist Papers* that the people would be the "fountain of power" in the US. Hamilton wrote in *Federalist 78* that "the power of the people is superior to" the powers of the judiciary and the legislature. Yet, in practice, the basis for these statements does not exist. It is true that the framers provided us with a "road to a people's decision" just as Madison promised. This road, however, is so poorly "marked" it has never been used. Nevertheless, we should consider how much our forefathers did for us and how little we have done for ourselves and for future generations. It does not seem unreasonable that we should take the trouble to find our own way over the unmarked road they provided. We should make the constitutional decisions needed to protect our freedom, and the freedom of our children and grandchildren. We have a rare opportunity—the opportunity to rejuvenate the competitiveness, prosperity, income equality and international reputation of our country.

The practical problem:

Two of the key groups in any reform effort are our youth and our non-governmental organizations (NGO's). Potentially, our students are the "tinder" in the sense that four North Carolina A&T students: Franklin McCain, Ezell Blair, Joe McNeil and David Richmond, were the tinder that ignited the sit-in movement in 1960. One problem is that our NGO'S are not tinder. They are accustomed to working for reform by trying to persuade the government to reform itself. Another problem is that our young activists are dividing their efforts among many different causes—most of which are symptoms of our underlying problem: an unresponsive and lawless government. These approaches to activism produce only palliative statutes.

A Rallying Point for Reform:

The recent *Citizens United v. FEC* decision has inspired Public Citizen, one of our finest and most powerful NGO's, to take action. It is responding with a campaign aimed at persuading Congress to propose a constitutional amendment. This amendment, instead of prohibiting the use of private funds in federal elections, would provide those congressional candidates who decline donations of more than $100 with public campaign funds. If and when it emerges from Congress, it will almost certainly have been further diluted. Public Citizen is relying on the fox to guard the chicken coop.

The road to a solution:

Our federal government has become increasingly lawless over the past half-century. This lawlessness both causes and is exacerbated by the illegal migration of some critical powers from Congress to the presidency. This centralizing of power in the executive branch threatens our freedom and requires a solution. Lobbying Congress to reform itself, however, is futile. It also makes a mockery of Madison's characterization of our Constitution as "unalterable by our government." The difficulty with this solution is that we have become too dependent upon our federal government. If we have a problem, we think we have done our duty when we have lobbied Congress to provide a solution. We must learn that, when the problem to be remedied is a lawless federal government, more is required of us. We must find our way through the Article V thicket to a national constitutional convention.

THE FRAMERS LAID THE GROUNDWORK FOR OUR MUTABLE CONSTITUTION

" . . mutable legislation is not more an evil in itself than it is odious to the people." . . .
—James Madison in *Federalist 37*

On September 17, 1787, thirty-nine of our founding fathers signed a proposed constitution and sent it off to be ratified by the states. It saved the Confederation from anarchy and has kept us relatively free for over two centuries. However, we have failed to either correct its original flaws or keep it current. Because of our failure to alter our Constitution legally, our federal government has altered it illegally—thus making of it nothing more or less than "mutable legislation." This has opened the door to anarchy and to the loss of our freedom. We have made this mutability seem less "evil" and "odious" by calling the result our "living" constitution.

A "living" Constitution v. "originalism":

President Obama believes that our Constitution is a "living" document. He wrote in his second autobiography[109] that, with regard to the "truly big arguments," our courts must interpret it in the light of "context, history and the practical consequences of a decision." With these words, Mr. Obama supports arbitrary judicial decisions. Justice Scalia defended his own "originalist" views at Princeton's Conference on James Madison in 2001. He said he interprets the Constitution according to the "common sense" meaning and definition of its words at the time they were written.

---

[109] *The Audacity of Hope*, 2006.

Obama and Scalia make the same assumption:

President Obama and Justice Scalia both assume that the people whose views, values and policies we should hold sacred are the people who framed and ratified our Constitution and its amendments. Mr. Obama would hold their views sacred except "on the truly big arguments." Justice Scalia would make no exceptions.

Their assumption is unfounded:

We should certainly hold sacred the essential views of our forefathers. That is, for example, we should revere the ideal that our government should reflect the needs, values, and wishes of its people. It follows, however, that our Constitution should change as these needs, values and wishes change. In short, the road should be clear for us to amend our Constitution as we see the need. Jefferson wrote Madison on Sept. 6, 1789 that, if a constitution is to serve the "living" generations, it must "naturally expire at the end of nineteen years."

We should not hold our Constitution sacred because of any misguided notion that the words of our forefathers continue to express our needs, values and wishes. Rather we should hold it sacred because it introduced to the world a practical form of self-government guided by the rule of law. Article V was intended to provide the key to this form of self-government. The framers expected that, whenever the Constitution conflicted with the needs, values or wishes of a "living" generation, the people of that generation would amend it—acting through their state legislatures or conventions.

There is a need for constancy:

This is not to deny the need for an immutable Constitution.

Hamilton underscored this point in *Federalist* 77. He wrote, "Until the people have changed the" (Constitution) . . . no presumption, or even knowledge of their sentiments, can warrant their representatives in a departure from it . . ." In order to respect and have confidence in our federal government, we must conclude from our own experience that our government respects our Constitution. This means that neither our courts, nor our president, nor our Congress should alter or otherwise tinker with our Constitution. Madison believed that the Constitution prohibits any such tinkering. In *Federalist 53*, he alluded to our Constitution as "established by the people and unalterable by the government." While Madison believed that this was "well understood in America," in his day, this is certainly not the case today.

There is also a need for flexibility:

The people and their views, values and policies change from generation to generation. A constitution that does not change accordingly flies in the face of self-government. It also puts pressure on the civil officers of the federal government to alter arbitrarily the very fabric of our lives by illegally violating and/or rewriting the Constitution. Our Congress abdicates its constitutional powers to our presidents. Our presidents gladly usurp them. Our mutable case law has evolved in such a way as to transfer (or sanction the transfer) of the power to declare war from Congress to the president. In this way statutes and court decisions have illegally taken precedence over the Constitution. That is, government has taken precedence over the people. We need flexibility but we should not tolerate the alteration of our Constitution by our federal government.

Both needs can be met legally:

Hamilton's words "Until the people have changed the

Constitution" suggest the solution. Legal changes in the Constitution, made by the people in accordance with Article V, do not make it mutable in any negative sense. The framers agreed. Madison said in *Federalist 49* that a "road to the decision of the people ought to be marked out and kept open for certain great and extraordinary occasions." Any occasion (like the present), in which our Constitution is being violated and illegally altered by civil officers of the federal government, is great and extraordinary. It is true that the road now provided by Article V is poorly marked. This, however, does not excuse our negligence. The 1st, 9th and 10th Amendments, taken with Article V and with our Declaration of Independence, give us the power to call a constitutional convention. We are duty-bound to exercise this power.

Conclusion:

We should amend Article V in at least four ways in order to make our Constitution more supportive of the rule of law and of self-government. First, it should require (in accordance with Jefferson's advice) that a national constitutional convention made up of non-governmental delegates (elected especially for the purpose) be held at least once every 20 years. Second, it should require either the calling of a national convention (or the proposal by Congress of a specific amendment) upon applications by two thirds of the state legislatures. State legislatures should be required to apply to Congress upon receipt of petitions from eight per cent of their constituent voters. Third, Article V should require the ratification of proposed amendments either by referendum or by state conventions. Fourth, it should prohibit the use of private money in the election of delegates to state or national conventions. Part III of this book suggests several approaches to amending Article V.

SHAYS' REBELLION (1786-87)

I hold that a little rebellion now and then is a good thing, and as necessary in the political world as storms in the physical. Unsuccessful rebellions, indeed, generally establish the encroachments of the rights of the people which have produced them. (They are) a medicine necessary for the sound health of government.
—Thomas Jefferson in a letter to James Madison dated January 30, 1787

A privately funded Massachusetts militia defeated Shays' Rebellion about four months prior to the Philadelphia convention. These words of Jefferson's are certainly supportive of Shays. They should be read, however, side-by-side with his letter of Sept. 6, 1789 also to James Madison. In this later epistle he wrote ". . . every constitution . . . naturally expires at the end of 19 years, if it be enforced longer, it is an act of force and not of right." He evidently believed that non-violent revolutions brought about by changes in a country's constitution might not only call "encroachments to the rights of the people" to the country's attention. They might also bring about remedies to these "encroachments." Generational constitutional conventions might, therefore, achieve results even more beneficial than those brought about by unsuccessful armed rebellions. They might also avoid the loss of lives that accompanies armed rebellions.

The Rebellion:[110]

In August of 1786, groups of farmers and rural artisans began stopping the courts in their western Massachusetts counties

---

[110] I am indebted to "Shays' Rebellion" in *West's Encyclopedia of American Law* for much of the factual material in these pages. Except where otherwise indicated, the opinions expressed are mine.

from granting judgments in civil cases. Many were losing their farms and other property through foreclosures and debt collections. On January 25, 1787, Captain Shays, a veteran of the Revolutionary War, led an "army" of more than a thousand of these disgruntled "Bay Staters" in an attempt to seize the weapons in the Springfield armory. Much to the surprise of Captain Shays and his men, they were greeted by cannon fire. They hadn't thought their former comrades-in-arms would fire on them. In fact, the militia general had only ordered a warning shot. Nevertheless, four "Shaysites" were killed by cannon fire. Twenty more were wounded and two were subsequently hanged.

The armed resistance in Massachusetts ceased the following month. This sad end to Shays' Rebellion happened about four months before George Washington arrived in Philadelphia in mid-May, 1787. Shays and his followers believed they were acting in a manner consistent with the principles of the American Revolution. They were protesting, among other things, heavy taxation by a Massachusetts government they felt ignored their plight while favoring commercial interests.

Its Beneficial Results:

There is no doubt, however, that Shays "unsuccessful" Rebellion did achieve beneficial results. Not only did Massachusetts enact laws easing the financial plight of its farmers and artisans. At least one historian (L. Richards in *Shays' Rebellion*, 2002) believes that Shays' Rebellion caused George Washington to emerge from retirement and attend the Constitutional Convention in Philadelphia.[111] Without his attendance and without the fear of anarchy that was exacerbated by Shays and his followers, many historians doubt that the

[111] Leonard L. Richards. *In Shays' Rebellion: The American Revolution's Final Battle*, University of Pennsylvania Press, pp. 1-4, 129-30, (2002).

Philadelphia Convention would have produced a constitution capable of bringing order to the chaos of the Confederation.

The Issue Raised by Shays:

However, Shays and his rebellion raise a long-term issue: Are violence and rebellion the best ways to deal with oppression and injustice? While Jefferson and others endorsed the method adopted by the Shaysites in 1786, would it not be better to avoid oppression and injustice in the first place? Would it not be better to re-structure government so that it responds to the needs of its citizens before they become desperate and resort to violence?

Our Present Situation:

In the 21st century, we must deal with a different set of dynamics. While our government, like that of Massachusetts in 1786, favors commercial interests over the interests of ordinary citizens, our "safety nets" and our powerful standing army protect us from armed rebellion. Instead, we are faced with a deep cynicism and distrust of our federal government. We attempt to "take arms against a sea of troubles" once every two years by voting the old rascals out and voting some new rascals in. We seek to solve the problem presented by our unresponsive and corrupt government by what we believe to be the only means at our disposal: our federal elections. However, the outcomes of these elections have come to be greatly influenced by campaigns funded by corporations and other special interest groups. It is true that many of our non-governmental organizations are member-funded and tend to represent the concerns of ordinary citizens. They are, however, only able to negotiate marginal improvements (see de Toqueville's arrival in America in Chapter 4). It is also difficult for them to compete with the NGO's funded by corporations.

A Logical Solution:

A change in parties does not make our government any more responsive to us or any less responsive to money and special interests. We need a means of achieving genuine reform. It cannot be achieved by statute since Congress makes our statutes and corporations have an undue influence on Capitol Hill. However, we—and not Congress—have the power to rewrite the Constitution. We need to take Jefferson's suggestion seriously and require a constitutional convention at least once each twenty years. At these periodic conventions, which would be attended only by non-governmental delegates elected by us for this sole purpose, we could establish meaningful reforms such as term limits, a balanced budget and election campaigns funded solely by public money.

Our road to a "people's decision" is not "well-marked," despite Madison's belief that this should be the case,[112] but it is nevertheless possible for us to find our way. Any group of 34 state legislatures has the power to call a 2nd constitutional convention. We have the right, under the first amendment, to petition our state legislatures to this end.[113]

---

[112] Madison wrote, in *Federalist 49*, ". . . a constitutional road to the decision of the people ought to be marked out and kept open for great and extraordinary occasions." Now is just such an occasion.
[113] Alternatively, constitutional scholars such as Akhil Amar of Yale believe we could by-pass our state legislatures and petition Congress directly for a constitutional convention.

THE DECLARATION OF INDEPENDENCE (1776)

*. . . there are more instances of the abridgement of the freedom
of the people, by the gradual and silent encroachments of those in
power, than by violent and sudden usurpations.*
—James Madison, in the Virginia convention of 1788

One of the ironies of 21st century American life is the 4th of July parade. We sing and cheer to celebrate the courage our ancestors showed in fighting for their (and our) freedom. Yet we seem unwilling to devote a few hours of our leisure time to a peaceful revolution aimed at protecting the freedom they gained for us from the "gradual and silent encroachments" of our federal government.

Our Plight in 1776:

Virginian Thomas Jefferson drafted the Declaration of Independence in June of 1776. While it was mainly devoted to justifying our revolution against England, Jefferson also set forth some principles of government. One of these principles is revolutionary. "Whenever our government threatens "life, liberty and the pursuit of happiness," Jefferson wrote, we have the right and duty to "alter or abolish it." It should be noted, however, that he was not necessarily advocating violent revolution. Governments can be altered or abolished by changing their constitutions peacefully. This is especially true of a government like ours. Article V of our Constitution provides for (in a tangled, ineffective and implicit way) its amendment by the people.

The Declaration of Independence charged King George III with twenty-six offenses. These offenses ranged from maintaining a standing army to "transporting us beyond seas to be tried for pretended offenses." The colonists repeatedly petitioned their King regarding these offenses. When their petitions were ignored, they declared themselves "free and independent." Shays and his fellow citizens in western Massachusetts did not rebel until the government had ignored their petitions for relief from foreclosures and seizures. Many of Shays followers were veterans of the revolution who were accustomed to live by bartering their crops for the necessities of life. They had been paid little or nothing for their military service and had no cash with which to meet the tax demands imposed by the Massachusetts legislature.

Our plight today:

There is no need for us to "abolish" our federal government. It and our Constitution are monuments to man's search for a form of government strong enough to protect and serve us, yet responsive enough to remain within our control. Our need is to "alter" and improve our government. Fortunately, Article V of our Constitution makes this possible by means of a peaceful revolution. Madison and Hamilton wrote in the *Federalist Papers* that the Constitution of 1787 was imperfect and that it would be the duty of later generations to correct its flaws. Jefferson also wrote that it would be our duty to alter or abolish" our government when it threatened, "life, liberty and the pursuit of happiness." Viewed in this light, it is not only our privilege to carry out the kind of peaceful revolution provided for by our Constitution. It is our duty. Our list of charges against our governments of the past sixty years might read something like this:

- Congress has abdicated its war powers in full and its legislative powers in part.

- The presidency has usurped the war powers and, with its use of signing statements and executive orders, has partially usurped the legislative powers.

- The judiciary has condoned the congressional abdications and the presidential usurpations.

- Congress has made, the presidency has signed and the judiciary has upheld laws and resolutions that invade our privacy, deprive us of our rights, and respond disproportionately to the interests of corporations and wealthy Americans.

- Over the past sixty years, our presidents have illegally initiated and continued wars that have cost hundreds of thousands of lives and trillions of dollars.

Any one of these charges justifies us in carrying out a peaceful revolution. Congress, the presidency and the courts have threatened our lives by combining to involve us in illegal wars. They have threatened our liberty by making and upholding laws that invade our privacy and deprive us of our civil rights. Even more serious, they have threatened our liberty by illegally transferring more and more of our governmental powers to the executive branch. As Madison warns us, the concentration of all governmental powers in one branch is "the very definition of tyranny." [114] Our federal government threatens our pursuit of happiness by spending tax money and sacrificing lives on illegal wars. This money could better be spent on improving our domestic infrastructure, funding research in clean energy and improving our foreign relations by proposing to the UN a World Marshall Plan. [115]

---

[114] He wrote, in *Federalist 47*, that "The accumulation of all powers . . . in the same hands, whether . . . hereditary, self-appointed or elective, may justly be pronounced the very definition of tyranny."
[115] Such a plan was proposed by former Vice-President Gore. See Chapter 3.

Our Duty Today:

Our forefathers anticipated our government's potential for lawlessness and understood that it would be incapable of reforming itself. Madison wrote, in *Federalist 49*, "whenever it may be necessary to enlarge, diminish or remodel the powers of government," the people, who are the "only legitimate fountain of power," should decide the matter. Hamilton conceded the flaws in the Constitution when he argued, in *Federalist 85*, that the convention should approve it and leave the correction of its many flaws to later generations.

Amendments are the province of the people. Madison wrote that our Constitution is made by the people and "unalterable by government." The executive and judiciary branches have no constitutional role in its amendment. Congress itself has no power. It can only "propose" amendments and "propose" whether they are to be ratified by state legislators or by state conventions. Only we the people, acting through our state legislatures or conventions, can amend the Constitution.

Summary:

Just as it was our forefather's duty in 1776 to abolish the English government in America, it is our duty to alter our present government. We should petition our state legislatures to either require Congress to call a constitutional convention or to forward a specific proposed amendment to Congress for proposal by Congress to all the states. This amendment should, among other things, require the calling of a national convention. This convention would consider amendments aimed at reforming our lawless federal government and restoring to us (the people) our role as America's "only legitimate fountain of power."

THE VIRGINIA DECLARATION OF RIGHTS (1776)

. . . made by the good people of Virginia, assembled in full and free convention, which rights do pertain to them, and their posterity, as the basis and foundation of government.
—Preamble to the Virginia Bill of Rights

George Mason wrote the first draft of the Virginia Declaration of Rights. It was approved on June 12, 1776, just twenty-four days before the signing of the Declaration of Independence. Mason later declined to sign the federal Constitution, in part because it lacked a bill of rights. The Virginia Declaration is a strong statement of the supreme power of the people. It has since been incorporated into the Virginia Constitution as Article I.

Virginia's Bill of Rights is important nationally :

Much can be learned from Virginia (and from the other states) that is relevant to the alteration of our US Constitution. Virginia is especially appropriate because it adopted the first state bill of rights and set a high standard for other states as well as for our federal framers and for other countries. Section 2 of the Virginia Constitution vests "all power . . . in the people." It continues, ". . . magistrates are their (the people's) . . . servants and at all times amenable to them." Section 3 reads, in part, ". . . a majority of the community hath a . . . right to reform, alter or abolish" a government they believe does not meet their needs. Much can be learned from Virginia's actual performance as well as from its words. We should consider the gap between stated rights and actual experience in Virginia, Illinois and other states as we prepare for a 2nd national convention. This experience suggests that specific methods for use in exercising stated rights must be set forth either in constitutions or in the statutes made pursuant to them. If this is not done, our constitutional rights are meaningless. Another crucial lesson to be learned from Virginia is that elected legislators cannot be relied upon to voluntarily make laws giving effect to their constituent's constitutional rights.

Parts of the Virginia Bill of Rights are meaningless:

Hamilton wrote, in Federalist 80, "There ought always to be a constitutional method of giving efficacy to constitutional provisions." A provision can be given efficacy by statute, or by the Constitution itself if the enabling constitutional provision is sufficiently specific. Sections 2 and 3 of Virginia's Bill of Rights have not been found by the courts to be sufficiently specific.

Further, Virginia's statutes are far from enabling its constitutional provisions. Paragraph 24.2-684 of the Virginia State Code prohibits referenda "unless specifically authorized by statute or by charter." In effect, this makes it almost impossible for the people of Virginia to initiate a referendum. Since they do not have the right to initiate a statute, they cannot successfully request a referendum. Since Section 3 requires a majority of the community and since a referendum is usually needed as evidence of a majority, the Virginia Code opposes, rather than enables, the Virginia Constitution.

The empty promises of Article I affect Virginians' daily lives: [116]

In *Feagan v. Hudgins* (2008), for example, the plaintiffs complained against the Board of Supervisors of Mecklenburg

---

[116] The writer was one of the plaintiffs in Feagan v. Hudgins.

County, Virginia for not "being amenable" to the will of a "majority of the community." The Board had approved a zoning request for the construction of a crop-based ethanol plant. At a public hearing, thirty people had spoken in opposition to the rezoning and only eleven had spoken in favor. For every "lawn sign" in nearby Chase City favoring the ethanol plant, there were three in opposition. However, these indicators did not, of course, hold up in court. A referendum of County voters was needed.

On Feb. 8, 2008, the Princeton study of bio-fuels had concluded that, if the US continued its policy of making ethanol from materials grown on crop lands, greenhouse emissions would increase by fifty to one hundred percent in thirty years. It urged that ethanol be produced using waste materials rather than from materials grown on crop lands.[117] The plaintiffs were not successful in their efforts to secure legal help from Earth Justice, Public Citizen and other concerned non-governmental organizations (NGO's),

Article I did not stand up in court:

The plaintiffs asked the court to declare Paragraph 24.2-684 of the state code void on the grounds that it is unconstitutional. A referendum could then be held. This would have settled the question of whether a majority of the "community" opposed the Board's zoning decision. The case never went to trial. It was stricken from the docket on technical grounds. The plaintiffs had neither the legal skills nor the financial resources to support an appeal.

Yet Article I, Sections 2 and 3 of the Virginia Constitution

---

[117]Searchinger, Timothy et al, "Use of croplands for bio fuels increases greenhouse gases through emissions from land use change," *Science* magazine, Feb. 7, 2008.

clearly state that, where a majority of a Virginia community (in this case, the voters of Mecklenburg County) opposes an action of their government, they have the right to "reform" it. In *Feagan v. Hudgins*, the plaintiffs did not wish to "reform" their Board of Supervisors. They merely desired the Board to be "amenable" to the wishes of a majority of the "community" as required by Article I of the Virginia Constitution. Article I also says that "all power" resides "in the people' and requires Virginia magistrates to be "amenable" to them. These constitutional provisions, however, are all promise and no practice.

Summary:

Our experience with state constitutions combines with our experience with Article V of the US Constitution. This combined experience strongly suggests that we make it a guiding principle to provide, by constitutional provisions themselves or by statutes, methods and procedures giving "efficacy" to the provisions of our state and national constitutions. Both the US Constitution and the Virginia Constitution promises their people powers and rights that Congress and some state legislatures do not deliver. Further, there is no clear way for us to claim these powers and rights. Some state constitutions, along with the US Constitution, fail to provide any specific methods for use in proposing constitutional conventions, constitutional amendments, or enabling statutes. Our inability to alter our constitutions affects both our national well-being and our individual daily lives. We must find our own methods and procedures for altering our constitutions.

SIX HISTORICAL FIGURES (1689-1758)

Our forefathers were not only statesmen and men of action. They were also political philosophers.

- James Monroe (born in 1758) was our fifth president. He was the last president to have fought in the Revolution. He recognized and wrote about the pivotal nature of the impeachment provisions.

- James Madison (born in 1751) was a framer and our fourth president. In later years, he was called the Father of the Constitution.

- Thomas Jefferson (1743) was our third president and the principal author of the Declaration of Independence.

- Patrick Henry (1736) was a strong advocate of the Revolution.

- George Washington (1732) commanded the revolutionary forces and was our first president.

- Charles-Louis de Montesquieu (1689) was a French political philosopher whose theories were influential in the framing of our Constitution

JAMES MONROE (1758)

Let us . . . promote intelligence among the people as the best means of preserving our liberties.
—James Monroe, in his first inaugural address

James Monroe, born in Virginia on April 28, 1758, placed a high value on education as a means of "promoting intelligence among the people"—thus enabling us to "preserve" our own liberties. He was the last of our presidents to have fought in the Revolution, dropping out of The College of William and Mary at age eighteen to join the Continental Army. He was wounded at Trenton and fought at Brandywine, Germantown and Monmouth, attaining the rank of Lieutenant Colonel. He became our 5th President in 1817.

Monroe's expectations:

Monroe believed that the US Constitution was ushering in the most important "epoch" in the history of mankind.[118] He wrote, "If we fail, the fault will be in ourselves, and we shall thereby give the most discouraging example to mankind that the world ever witnessed."[119] He added, "If they" (the people) "make judicious selections for office, reward those who have merit, and punish those who commit offenses, the whole movement" (toward representative democracy) "cannot fail to be . . . successful." [120]

---

[118] James Monroe, *The People, The Sovereign*, James River Press, 1987, p. 1.
[119] Ibid, p. 2.
[120] Ibid, p. 69.

The extent to which Monroe's expectations have been met:

In *Federalist 9*, Hamilton predicted that we would become "the broad and solid foundation of other edifices, not less magnificent . . ." A century ago, Lord Acton could still write about our forefathers' ideas "bursting forth" from America and transforming the world.[121] Today, however, our national conduct is far from exemplary. Our judiciary opens the floodgates to special interest campaign funding. Our legislature trades its constitutional powers for donations and favors. Our presidents usurp congressional powers, illegally invade other nations and "turn a blind eye" to torture. According to *The Nation*, our mercenaries "are at the center of a secret program" (in Pakistan) "in which they plan targeted assassinations" and "snatch and grab."[122] The US is the only one of 191 signatories that has failed to ratify Kyoto.[123]

America's "fall from grace" is not the fault of our presidents, judges or representatives. They are simply acting rationally. They weigh the consequences of honest, lawful behavior (frustration and reduced campaign donations) against the consequences of corrupt, lawless behavior (gifts, favors and increased campaign donations)—and choose the latter. The fault is not theirs; it is ours. Monroe tells us that, when acts of the federal government are constitutional but objectionable, "the people might correct the evil by an amendment of the Constitution."[124] We have not done so.

---

[121]Lord Dalberg-Acton, *The History of Freedom and Other Essays* (1907), Chap. 2.
[122] Jeremy Scahill, *The Nation*, Dec. 21-28, 2009, p. 11.
[123] "The Kyoto Protocol is a legally binding agreement under which industrialized countries will reduce their collective emissions of greenhouse gases by 5.2% compared to the year 1990" UN Environmental Program, Official Website.
[124] Monroe, p. 17.

Monroe's philosophy of government:

Monroe took a realistic view of human nature. He said, "The principles and passions of men are always the same. Self-interest is the ruling passion." [125] The provisions of our Constitution determine whether it is in the self-interest of our civil officers to be lawful, or lawless. Madison tells us that these provisions are established by us and "unalterable by the government." [126]

Learning from Monroe:

Monroe's views on impeachment are particularly relevant to our situation today. Here we will consider the broad and specific intents of the impeachment provisions, the principles involved, the means the framers chose to carry out these intents, the efficacy of these means, and the steps that might be taken to make them more effective. We will consider what Monroe had to say about impeachment and discuss various aspects of the impeachment problem.

What Monroe wrote about impeachment:

Monroe considered impeachment to be the most important check on lawless and self-seeking behavior by civil officers of government. He wrote:

The right of impeachment and of trial by the legislature is the mainspring of the great machine of government. It is the pivot on which it turns. If preserved in full vigor, and exercised with perfect integrity, every branch will perform its duty, and the people will be left to the performance of theirs, in the most simple form, and with complete effect, as the sovereign power of the state. [127]

---

[125] Ibid, p. 69.
[126] James Madison, the *Federalist 53*.
[127] James Monroe. *The People, the Sovereigns*, James River Press, 1987, p. 16.

The legislature (the Senate) did not live up to Monroe's expectations. Far from preserving the impeachment provisions in full vigor, it twisted and turned them until they became useless. However, Monroe was prescient. He foresaw the consequences of "partial justice," but mistakenly assumed that the Senate would be capable of acting as an impartial court.

Intents of the impeachment provisions:

The goal of the impeachment provisions, as Monroe suggested, is to help motivate our civil officers to behave lawfully and in the interests of most people. The election provisions, of course, share this goal.

Principles and Objective of the impeachment provisions:

The two general principles that apply to the impeachment provisions are the rule of law and the idea that we should do what is best for most people. The objectives that dominated the writing of the impeachment provisions were the speed of acquittal or conviction, the certainty of convicting guilty defendants and impartial justice. It was clear to Monroe that, if these principles were not realized and these objectives not achieved, the provisions would fail.

Means and their efficacy:

The principal means of realizing speed (provided by the framers) was to bar the application of rules providing for the personal security of defendants.[128] This prohibition also made it more certain that guilty defendants would be convicted. The means adopted by the framers to achieve impartial justice were:

---

[128] See Hamilton in *Federalist 65*.

(1) assigning the power to try impeachments to the most prestigious non-elective body in government (the Senate), (2) requiring a two-thirds vote to convict, (3) requiring the Chief Justice of the Supreme Court to preside over presidential trials, and (4) requiring the senators to be under oath or affirmation when they serve as members of an impeachment court.

The bar against the use of personal security rules in impeachment cases has been routinely ignored. The Senate became politicized in the mid-1830's and, therefore, incapable of rendering impartial justice. The two-thirds vote to convict was effective in preventing partisan removals. However, in order to guide a court towards rendering impartial justice, the presiding officer must make rulings. The Chief Justices in the Johnson trial (1868) and the Clinton trial (1999) failed to do so. Further, many senators have violated their oaths to render impartial justice, especially in the two presidential trials. For example, some senators serving as court members in the Clinton trial said they believed him to be guilty but, nevertheless, voted to acquit.

Conclusions:

Monroe's emphasis on the importance of "vigorous" enforcement of impeachment was justified. We would almost certainly have a more lawful government today had the impeachment provisions been vigorously enforced. Based on this analysis, it would be well to transfer the power to try non-judicial impeachments to the judiciary, retain the two-thirds vote to convict, and declare Senate Impeachment Rule 7 void (it gives the Senate the power to overrule the rulings of the presiding officer [129]).

There are key requirements we could establish for our civil officers that would make lawfulness in their self-interest. Term limits and a prohibition against the use of private funds in feder-

---

[129] Senate Rules for Impeachments.

al elections come to mind. But perhaps the most important requirement would be for the swift and certain removal and disqualification of miscreant civil officers. Removal by itself is nothing more than a "bump in the road" when it not accompanied by disqualification. Monroe tells us, ". . . impeachment . . . is the main spring of the machine of government. . . If (it is) preserved in full vigor . . . every branch of government will perform its duty." [130] We should now reestablish impeachment in its full vigor by, among other things, transferring the power to try congressional and executive impeachments to the judiciary.

JAMES MADISON (1751)

The important distinction so well understood in America between a Constitution established by the people and unalterable by the government, and a law established by the government and alterable by the government, seems to have been little understood and less observed in any other country.
—James Madison (March 16, 1751—June 28, 1836) in *Federalist 53*

James Madison, "Father of the Constitution," and our fourth president, was born in Port Conway, Virginia, 259 years ago. He is remembered for the major role he played in making us a country "of, by and for the people."

Madison the peacemaker:

One of his contributions was made in vain. He argued for our establishment as a non-aggressive nation. He wrote in 1791, "In no part of the Constitution is more wisdom to be found than in the clause which confides the question of war and peace to the

---

[130] Monroe, p. 16.

legislature, and not to the executive department" (*Helvidius, No. 1*). He explained, in part, the executive's tendency to violence when he added, "In war, the public treasures are to be unlocked and it is the executive hand that is to dispense them." Despite Madison and the crystal-clear language of the Constitution, our government has slid out of our control. Congress, with the assistance of the judiciary, has abdicated its war powers and the executive branch now (illegally) exercises them.

Madison the political philosopher:

Madison also made important statements of principle that helped guide the framers in their work. We have already noted a prime example. In *Federalist Paper 49* he wrote that, ". . . a constitutional road to the decision of the people ought to be marked out and kept open, for certain great and extraordinary occasions." Madison and his fellow-framers attempted to give these statements "efficacy" (to use Hamilton's term) when they crafted Article V of the Constitution. Their efforts, however, fell short. Instead of explicitly giving the people the power to initiate constitutional amendments, they gave this power to Congress and to state legislatures. Instead of giving the people the power to approve amendments, they gave this power to either state legislatures or state conventions (depending, in practice if not in law, on the whim of Congress).

Nevertheless, the intent of the Constitution is clear from the writings of those who framed it. They intended us to have the power to amend our Constitution. Hamilton says, in *Federalist 33*, that—should the government "overpass the just bounds of its authority," the people, "whose creature it" (the Constitution) "is, should take such measures . . . as the exigency may suggest." The circumstances of our present crisis suggest the writing of reform legislation bringing the federal government back under our control. While the writing of statutes is reserved to Congress, the Constitution is our "creature." We should take advantage of this by proposing and ratifying "responsive government" amendments.

The road to our decision is not "marked out":

The difficulty, of course, is that the "constitutional road to the decision of the people" is far from being "marked out" and "kept open" as Madison said it should be. In fact, it is so obscure and hidden that it has never been used. Our federal government has abstained, of course, from "marking out" and "keeping open" a constitutional road for us to use in initiating constitutional amendments. It would be expecting too much of human nature to expect our civil officers to encourage genuine reform. Why should they interfere with their own enjoyment of the favors provided by corporations and other special interest groups?

This makes the "road to our decision" bumpy and overgrown from disuse. It does not, however, excuse us from exerting ourselves to make a path through the thicket. For example, the 1st Amendment gives us the right to petition our state legislatures. Again, why not petition them to propose an amendment (1) prohibiting the use of private funds in delegate elections and (2) requiring that Congress call a constitutional convention. Should Congress receive applications from 34 state legislatures, it would be required to propose the amendment to call a constitutional convention.

One of Madison's gifts to us:

A lesson taught us by history and by James Madison is that we should not complain because our government has slid out of our control. We have no one to blame but ourselves. We possess the motivation, the power and the means for restoring our government to lawfulness. Our forefathers did most of the work for us. They expected us to find our own way along the road "to our decision."[131] We should live up to their expectations.

THOMAS JEFFERSON (1743)

Men . . . are naturally divided into two parties: 1. Those who fear and distrust the people . . . . and 2. Those who identify themselves with the people, have confidence in them, and consider them as the most honest and safe, although not the most wise, depositary of the public interests.
—Thomas Jefferson in a letter to Henry Lee of
August 10, 1824

Thomas Jefferson, born on April 13, 1743, was in France at the time of the 1787 convention. Nevertheless he exerted an influence among the delegates, partly through his correspondence with James Madison. Jefferson belonged to the "party" that identifies itself with the people and considers them to be the "most honest and safe . . . depositary of the public interest."

Jefferson and the people:

Jefferson believed that the "people" should control their government—rather than the other way around. Government, especially the federal government, was a necessary evil. It is true that the voting "people," during the early 1800's, consisted of male, white property owners. The property restriction on voting

---

[131] Hamilton wrote, in *Federalist 84*, that it appeared to him "to be susceptible of absolute demonstration" that it would be far easier to amend the Constitution after it was ratified than to make it perfect during the debating and compromising of the Philadelphia convention.

was not removed until the Jackson era. It is also true that Jefferson relied heavily upon the people's elected representatives and upon state governments to put into place laws and policies benefiting the populace.

Jefferson and strict constitutionalism:

Jefferson agreed with Madison and Hamilton that the Constitution should be strictly interpreted and enforced. It should be closely adhered to regardless of public opinion. Nothing could excuse or justify its provisions being ignored, loosely interpreted or tampered with by the federal government. Each provision should be revered as our supreme law until such time as the people amend it in accordance with Article V.

Jefferson and his "living" Constitution:

Jefferson believed that the Constitution should always reflect the desires, needs and wishes of the current generation. It should be amended whenever the current generation (not the federal government) feels that changes are necessary. In a Sept. 6, 1789 letter to James Madison, Jefferson wrote, "every constitution expires at the end of nineteen years." He believed that the Constitution should be reviewed by the rising generation every twenty years and made consistent with the current generation's desires, needs and wishes. For the twenty years that a constitution is in effect, however, it should be held sacred. It should be strictly interpreted and enforced. It should not be a living constitution in the sense that it can be twisted and adapted by the federal government. Jefferson wrote in his Sept. 6, 1789 letter to Madison, "The earth belongs to the living generation." He saw and feared the danger of illegal alterations by the three branches of the federal government.

Jefferson and corruption:

Like Madison, Jefferson was well aware that men are not "angels." Since corrupt actions have become more profitable, pleasant and convenient than honest actions, some of our "non-angelic" federal civil officers yield to temptation as a matter of course. Corporations compete for the favors of these civil officers. Jefferson predicted, in an 1816 letter to George Logan, they would "challenge our government in a trial of strength." As it happens, they have found it more convenient to co-opt our government than to challenge it. Jefferson and the framers would, I think, urge us to restructure our government so that corporate and other special interest money is banned from federal elections. This would help make honest behavior in the personal interests of our civil officers.

The Jeffersonian remedies:

Jefferson believed that citizens should resist corruption, federal powers should be constrained, the Bill of Rights should be strictly enforced, church and state should be separate and state's rights should be protected. He also believed that our freedom of speech is crucial, that we have a right to be educated, that wealth should be more evenly distributed through a graduated income tax, and that (as mentioned before) we should bring the Constitution up to date at least once every 20 years. In short, if Jefferson were alive today, he would no doubt remind us that it is our duty to petition our state legislatures for the calling of a national constitutional convention. Should we do this, we could consider his and other possible remedies, and amend our Constitution accordingly. In this way we could free ourselves from the ills caused by our federal government's attacks upon our inspired but disregarded present Constitution.

PATRICK HENRY (1736)

Is life so dear, or peace so sweet, as to be purchased at the price of
chains and slavery? Forbid it, Almighty God! I know not what
course others may take; but as for me,
give me liberty, or give me death!
—Patrick Henry

Patrick Henry, born in Virginia on May 21, 1736, joined Thomas Paine in urging us toward revolution. In 1775, he addressed the House of Burgesses in Richmond asking that it mobilize forces against the English army of occupation. Our forefathers had to choose between living peaceful lives under a government they could not control and fighting a bloody war for the right to live under a government they could control. We are now faced with a similar choice. Our choice is between living peaceful lives under a government we cannot control and taking time out from our busy schedules to conduct a peaceful revolution. Is our leisure time so dear or our leisure pursuits so sweet, as to be purchased at the price of life under an elective monarchy?

English philosopher Lord Acton was still able to say, in 1907, "It was from America that the plain ideas . . . burst forth . . . upon the world . . . under the title 'the rights of man' . . . and the principle gained ground that a nation can never abandon its fate to an authority it cannot control." These words describe our heritage—our past. Our present era is one of out-of-control presidents, passive legislatures and an "activist" judiciary. Our presidents fight illegal wars against our will and sometimes against the will of "the people's branch" (Congress). Our Congress abdicates its war powers and allows the presidency to encroach upon its law-making powers by adding "signing statements" to its bills. Our judiciary declares corporate donations to Congress constitutional.

How did we come to our present sad state of affairs? The "Father of our Constitution," James Madison, said in *Federalist 47*, "The accumulation of all powers . . . in the same hands . . . may justly be pronounced the very definition of tyranny." He and his fellow-framers attempted to balance the powers of government among the three branches. They provided "checks" for each branch to use in defending its powers from raids by the other branches. We have arrived at our present predicament because this system of checks and balances has broken down. Many powers of Congress and some powers of the courts have migrated to the presidency.

Patrick Henry, however, was prescient. He refused to attend the 1787 convention in Philadelphia. Speaking at the Virginia ratifying convention, he opposed ratification saying, "What can avail your specious, imaginary balances, your rope-dancing, chain-rattling, your ridiculous ideal checks and contrivances."[132] This was harsh, since the framers' "rope-dancing" gave us almost two centuries of reasonably balanced government. Technological, economic and demographic changes, however, have combined (with flaws in the Constitution itself) to destroy our balance of powers and set us on the slick slope leading to tyranny.

What can be done to preserve our representative democracy? Expecting our federal government to balance its own powers is as fruitless as expecting the fox to guard the chickens. However, the framers anticipated a situation in which our powers would need to be re-balanced (or new-modeled, as Madison put it in *Federalist 48*). No doubt realizing that the federal government would be unlikely to "new-model" itself, they gave us Article V. This Article is pivotal for two reasons. First, it makes our Constitution "unalterable" (to use Madison's words again)

---

[132] Ralph Ketcham (Ed.). *The Anti-Federalist Papers and the Constitutional Convention Debates*, A Mentor Book, (1986), p. 208.

by the federal government. Second, it allows us, the people, to alter it, acting through our state legislatures or conventions.

So you and I face a choice analogous to the one faced by Patrick Henry 235 years ago when he made his speech (on liberty v. death) to the Virginia House of Burgesses. Which future shall we choose? We have a less difficult choice, however. Our choice is between taking the trouble to bring about a constitutional convention and running the risk of eventually losing our liberty.

GEORGE WASHINGTON (1732)

The basis of our political systems is the right of the people to make and to alter their constitutions of government. But the Constitution which at any time exists, until changed by an explicit and authentic act of the whole people, is sacredly obligatory upon all.
—George Washington, in his Farewell Address, Sept. 8, 1791

It seems likely that Washington would be saddened if he were aware of the later twisting and rewriting of our Constitution by our federal government. He concluded his farewell address by hoping that his words might "now and then recur to moderate the fury of party spirit, to warn against the mischiefs of foreign intrigue, and to guard against the impostures of pretended patriotism." He had personally experienced the aggravations of excessive party spirit, foreign intrigue and pretended patriotism during his two terms as President and felt it might conceivably be of use to warn us against them. As James Iredell said, while speaking to the North Carolina Convention in 1788, "The only security of liberty in any country is the jealousy and circumspection of the people." Washington was justified in advising us to be moderate. However, we must take care not to neglect our duty under the banner of "moderation."

Iredell also said, "Should the government, on trial, be found to want amendments, those amendments can be made in a regular method, in a mode prescribed by the Constitution."[133] Washington placed the responsibility for changing the Constitution "by an explicit and authentic act" upon our shoulders. Should we undertake this "explicit and authentic act," it would positively affect the lives of people all over the world for generations to come. Yet, while it would be an act of great importance, it would also be an action taken in the interests of moderation. This leads us to a Washingtonian interpretation of Article V and to some comments on how his view of the Constitution relates to other aspects of his political philosophy—as expressed in his Farewell Address.

Washington and Article V:

Article V does not explicitly give the people of the United States the power to change the Constitution. Washington seems to have assumed that it did. Hamilton, in *Federalist* 78, says that the power of the people is "declared in the Constitution" and is superior to the power of both the judiciary and the legislature. He says the Constitution must stand until the people, "by some solemn and authoritative act" annul or change it. However, while the ratifiers no doubt assumed that these statements in the *Federalist Papers* were accurate, the framers failed to follow through on their implied promises. Article V says that, on the application of two-thirds of the state legislatures, Congress shall call a constitutional convention. This has never happened. Article V also says that ratification of proposed amendments shall be by either three-quarters of the state legislatures or by conventions in three-quarters of the states "as the one or the other mode of ratification shall be 'proposed' by Congress." The closest it comes

---

[133] James Iredell. He made this statement in his speech to the North Carolina Convention in 1788. In Bailyn, (Ed.) Vol. II, p. 887.

to mentioning "the people" is where it alludes to state conventions as possible ratifiers of amendments. Even this allusion is weak. It is left to Congress to, in effect, decide between the two possibilities. Nevertheless, it is the clear intent of the framers that the people have the power to amend the Constitution. While the road to our exercise of this power is not paved, it does exist. The Declaration of Independence grants us this right explicitly. The 1st Amendment gives us the right to petition our state legislatures the 9th and 10th Amendments give us the right to compel compliance with our petitions. Our petitions should explicitly require that civil officers of the federal government be ineligible for election as delegates to the convention.

Washington's Political Philosophy and the Constitution:

Perhaps our most serious error of omission over the past two centuries has been our failure to observe the following rule laid down by Hamilton in *Federalist 80*: "There ought to always be a constitutional method of giving efficacy to constitutional provisions." For example, no constitutional method has been put into effect giving efficacy to the "oath or affirmation" required of senators acting as members of a court of impeachment. The two presidential trials have been blatantly political. The following principles alluded to in Washington's farewell address have suffered from the same neglect.

In a free country, it is important that those entrusted with power do not encroach or exceed their constitutional spheres. Note: Our Constitution clearly assigns the power to declare war (and all the associated powers) to Congress. Yet neither the Constitution nor any statute made pursuant to it, has given efficacy to the war provisions of the Constitution.

If in the opinion of the people the Constitution needs amendment, let it be amended—but observed until it is amended. Note: As Jefferson maintained, the genuine intent of the Constitution is to be found in the writings of the framers. These writings reserve the power to amend the Constitution to the people. Yet all three branches of our federal government amend our Constitution routinely.

Do not extend our commercial relationships abroad to the political sphere. Note: Nowhere in the Constitution is there a provision authorizing presidents to impose our system of government on the people of other nations. Yet they have engaged (and are engaging) in "nation building by force" as a matter of foreign policy.

A free, enlightened and great nation should give to mankind an example of justice and benevolence. Note: Hamilton had given voice to a kindred thought in *Federalist 9*, "I trust that America will be the broad and solid foundation of other edifices, not less magnificent." Needless to say, we have made no constitutional provisions or statutes to prevent our military adventures and "nation building" in the Middle East. Our military adventures involve the killing of civilians and the use of torture.

How can we return to Washingtonian principles?

Genuine reform will require a constitutional convention. Article V gives us the "road to travel" (albeit a muddy road) to bring about a convention for reforming our federal government. All that is required is that we find our way along this difficult road.

CHARLES-LOUIS de MONTESQUIEU (1689)

*In a popular state (a democracy) more (than law) is necessary,
namely, virtue. . . As virtue is necessary in a republic, and in a
monarchy honor, so fear is necessary in a despotic government.*
—Charles-Louis de Montesquieu in
The Spirit of the Laws, Book III (1698)

The writings of Baron de Montesquieu are evidence that, in some instances at any rate, the pen is mightier than the sword. de Montesquieu was very nearly a contemporary of Shakespeare. Yet his writings continue to influence the framers of constitutions throughout the world. James Madison, often called "The father of the US Constitution," was influenced by his political philosophy. de Montesquieu is cited and/or summarized in many of the *Federalist Papers*. In *Federalist 47*, for example, Madison calls him the ". . . oracle who is always consulted . . . on this subject." (the separation of powers).

The separation of powers and democracy:

As Madison pointed out in *Federalist 41*, "The accumulation of all powers . . . in the same hands . . . may justly be pronounced the very definition of tyranny." The question then becomes: How are the powers of a government, once they have been properly assigned by its constitution, to be kept in their proper places? How are the civil officers of government to be prevented from abdicating inconvenient powers and usurping desirable ones? It is with respect to this question that de Montesquieu and his principles are of particular interest to those of us who live in a democracy. The framers of our Constitution did, in general, an excellent job of separating the powers of government. However, they had no way of anticipating the great changes that have taken place in the cultural and political contexts of our government. They could not, therefore, devise adequate ways of keeping the powers separate over time. Neither could they rely on our civil officers to perform this task. Therefore, they placed the responsibility and the power with us, the people. As mentioned before, In *Federalist 49* Madison calls us "the only legitimate fountain of power" and alludes to the necessity of "recurring" to us "when it may be necessary to enlarge, diminish, or new-model the powers of government." Our Constitution, he adds in *Federalist 53*, is "established by the people and unalterable by the government."

How the framers attempted to deal with the problem as they saw it in 1787:

de Montesquieu identified virtue as the principle upon which democratic governments depend. He saw this dependence, however, as a weakness of the republican form of government. The love of honor required by monarchies is so naturally strong in human beings that it motivates civil officers to serve honestly and well. The fear of punishment required by despotic governments is so strong in human beings that it motivates civil officers to do the bidding of their despot. The love of virtue for virtue's sake, upon which democracies depend, is less powerful.

The framers acknowledged this special weakness of democracy. They knew that they must take special care to instill in both their civil officers and in the American people a love of virtue. They disliked the honor principle because it separates those who are knighted or otherwise honored from their fellow citizens. The framers considered the honor principle to be inconsistent with the republican system of government. Article I, Section 9 of our Constitution reads in part: "No title of nobility shall be granted by the United States."

This left the framers with the task of forming a constitutional system that would motivate its civil officers to act "virtuously." That is, they needed to devise a system that would make it more pleasant and convenient for civil officers to respect and obey the law and apply themselves to the good of the country, than to disrespect the law and pursue their own personal self-interests. One result was the impeachment provisions of our Constitution. Our 5th president, James Monroe, called these provisions, in *The People, The Sovereigns* (p. 16), "the mainspring of the great machine of government . . . the pivot on which it turns . . . if preserved in full vigor . . . every branch will perform its duty."

The impeachment provisions aimed at instilling a love of virtue without either the British "honors system" or the despotic punishment system. The impeachment provisions aimed at dishonoring miscreant civil officers without punishing them by depriving them of their lives, liberty or property. They attempted to assure the swift and certain "dishonoring" of miscreants by denying them the right to the rules of personal security (due process) and, in the case of presidential trials, appointing the Chief Justice of the US Supreme Court as presiding officer. Since, in impeachment proceedings, the welfare of the population would be opposed to the welfare of a single defendant, the framers evidently believed it would be better to convict a hundred innocent defendants than to free one who was guilty. The object was of great importance: to deter governmental corruption and lawlessness. The framers apparently also believed that, by making the people responsible for making our supreme law (the Constitution) they were assuring that the impeachment provisions would be changed so as to operate with "full vigor" despite political or cultural changes. The dishonoring of miscreant civil officers must be swift and certain in order to deter corruption and lawlessness, however the political and cultural conditions might change.

What has actually happened?

The impeachment provisions, instead of being preserved in their full vigor, have eroded over time and are now worthless. Because it seemed expedient at the convention of 1787, the framers violated the separation of powers by assigning the power of trying impeachments (a crucial judicial power) to a legislative body, the Senate. The Senate, a decade later, exempted itself (and, in effect, the House) from the impeachment provisions. The duty of impeachment courts to render impartial justice eroded. In 1868, the trial of Andrew Johnson was blatantly political. In 1999, the provisions lost all their deterrent power when former President Clinton was acquitted of perjury and obstruction. As noted above, he was acquitted despite the fact that a number of the senators who voted to acquit, admitted publicly that they believed him to be guilty.

The consequences:

The impotence of the impeachment provisions has encouraged our presidents to invade other countries and to usurp the legislative powers with "signing statements."[134] Members of Congress have been encouraged to write laws permitting the flow of money to them from special interest groups. The judiciary has found this flow of money constitutional. Further, the lawlessness of our civil officers is, as Hamilton put it in *Federalist 63*, a "contagion by example." de Montesquieu tells us, "It is exceedingly difficult for the leading men of a nation to be knaves and the (people) to be honest; for the former to be cheats and the latter to rest satisfied with being only dupes."

---

[134] Signing statements are statements appended to a bill by a president when he signs it into law. These statements sometimes decline to enforce those provisions of the bill with which the president does not agree. This encroaches upon Congress's authority under Article I to possess "all legislative powers herein granted."

Summary:

Our forefathers have given us the responsibility for altering the Constitution at times when such altering becomes necessary. Now is just such a time. It is true that the ambiguity of Article V (when taken with the *Federalist Papers*) makes our recourse to The Declaration of Independence 1st, 9th and 10th Amendments necessary in order to secure the needed constitutional amendments. However, we must either secure such amendments or allow our country to abandon the democratic principle of virtue and adopt the despotic principle of fear.

PART II

RE-FORMING OUR
FEDERAL GOVERNMENT

No man ought certainly to be a judge in his own cause, or in any cause in respect to which he has the least interest or bias.
—Alexander Hamilton in *Federalist 80*

Here Hamilton gives us a critical principle of reform. No member of the group of people being reformed should have any substantial role in the reform process. In the present case, the group needing reform is made up of 1,000 or so federal civil officers. They are highly organized and have immense resources at their command. If they were allowed to have any role at all in a reform process, it is probable that they would be able to convert a minor role into a decisive one. This would render the reform meaningless. How could it be otherwise? When it comes to looking after our own interests, we humans are quite rational. It would not be rational for our civil officers to change a system that provides them with power, status, wealth and an elitist life style. We will do well to keep the principle laid down by Hamilton in mind as we consider some of the various approaches to governmental reform.

The road to governmental reform does not pass through Congress. Our framers wisely gave our state legislatures the power to require constitutional conventions and the power to ratify (or arrange for the ratification of) the resultant proposals. It would be a serious mistake on our part to ask Congress to pass reform laws, write and propose reform amendments or attend reform conventions. Such laws, amendments or conventions would produce nothing of value to us and would take the energy out of any movement for genuine reform. This book is concerned with a peaceful, legal and constitutional approach to genuine structural reform. The following paragraphs put this in context by comparing several other approaches to reform with the structural approach. In chapters 7-10 we will discuss some issues and aspects involved in the structural reform of the US government.

VIOLENT REBELLION

Occasionally, violent rebellions have improved government. As Americans, our best example of this is our own Revolution. A post-revolutionary example is Daniel Shays' Rebellion of 1786-87. While the Massachusetts militia put down Shays' Rebellion with little bloodshed, the incident impressed the delegates to the 1787 Philadelphia Convention with the necessity for taking strong action. More than one of the delegates cited Shays' Rebellion and remarked that their choice was between a strong constitution on the one hand and anarchy on the other. They arrived in Philadelphia in May of that year charged by the Continental Congress with revising the Articles of Confederation. They left in September having designed a new and unique system of government. This system has given us more than two centuries of relative freedom and prosperity. It is also worth noting that, were it not for Shays' Rebellion,

Washington may not have attended the convention. As it happened, he was one of the first (and in one sense the most important) of the delegates to arrive in Philadelphia.

However, violent revolutions, in general, have a poor track record. Only two come to mind that replaced an oppressive government with a more responsive democratic one: our own and the Nicaraguan revolution of 1979-1990. Neither ended in a blood bath nor replaced one repressive regime with another. However, neither was fought against an oppressive domestic government. They were both fought against foreign colonizers and, therefore, left behind than no reigns of terror. By the time the US ceased funding its Contras in Nicaragua, however, that country's economy was devastated and has not yet recovered.

In any event, violence is not a credible option in the US. We are neither hungry enough nor dissatisfied enough to risk our lives in a violent revolution. We have a safety net, however tattered and torn, that keeps our revolutionary spirit in check. Further, our president has at his disposal the strongest military force in the world. A violent revolution would be given short shrift. In the unlikely event that one should occur, it would tear our country apart rather than unifying it.

PALLIATIVE /INCREMENTAL REFORMS

The term "palliative/incremental reform" describes our present situation. Non-governmental organizations (NGO's) lead reform movements. These movements lobby for statutes or constitutional amendments less favorable to corporations and more favorable to ordinary people. Often, however, the resultant reform laws are counter-productive. They simply dissipate any public pressure that may exist for genuine reform in the area concerned. Most campaign finance and ethics laws fit this description. Sometimes, however, new laws do move us a step in the right direction. These laws are often produced by tragedies. For example, the Farmington, West Virginia mining disaster gave impetus to federal mine safety legislation. This law, however, was aimed at reforming mining corporations rather than the federal government. It is unrealistic to expect even incremental reform legislation from a Congress that is, "acting as judge in its own case."

SPIRITUAL RENEWAL

This is an approach often endorsed by our political philosophers.[135] It places the responsibility for societal change on the shoulders of individuals and their churches and consists of civil disobedience and personal growth. According to this view, we are responsible for engaging in civil disobedience when we find our government's actions inconsistent with our beliefs. We are also responsible for living our daily lives in a non-profligate, loving, considerate manner. When enough of us have become spiritually healthy, our government will respond by becoming spiritually healthy itself. This is an attractive, long-range, evolutionary approach. It takes a more optimistic view of human nature than did the framers of our Constitution.

STRUCTURAL REFORM

Structural reform of our federal civil officers would act through changing the institutional arrangements that produce lawless, unresponsive and corrupt behavior on the parts of our federal government. Structural reform is most effective when it provides increased rewards as a consequence of lawful, responsive, honest, "public servant" behavior and increased pain as an inevitable consequence of lawless, unresponsive and corrupt behavior.

---

[135] For example, see Walter Brueggemann in *Journey to the Common Good*, WJK Press, 2010.

Structural reform must be carefully approached. It requires legislation. Yet Congress controls the making of all laws except the Constitution. We cannot trust Congress to make laws genuinely reforming itself. As Madison remarked in *Federalist 53*, however, the Constitution is the province of the people and "unalterable" by government. Since constitutional amendments can be both initiated and ratified by the people,[136] they are the logical vehicles for governmental reform. In point of fact, they are our only means of bringing about genuine reform.

SUMMARY

In summary, violent revolution rarely produces an honest, responsive replacement government and always produces death and destruction. Palliative/incremental change, while it is our *status quo*, is not working. Our quality of life is declining and our national moral code is in tatters. Our governmental powers are migrating to the executive branch. We will be doing our grandchildren an injustice if we stick to our *status quo*. The "spiritual renewal" approach has much to recommend it. It is clear that any efforts we make to be true to ourselves and humane to others will produce satisfying and virtuous results. Whether such efforts will make our government more honest and responsive in the immediate future is another question.

However, spiritual growth and structural change are not mutually exclusive. They might even be mutually supportive. I would suggest a joining of efforts by those who recommend the one, and those who propose the other. Ralph Nader tells us, "If you organize one percent of the people in this country along pro-

---

[136] It is true that Article V gives the power to call constitutional conventions to state legislatures and the power to ratify proposed amendments to state legislatures or conventions (as Congress decides). However, as is detailed in other parts of this book, the 1st, 9th and 10th Amendments implicitly give the power to call conventions and propose and ratify amendments to the people.

gressive lines, you can turn the country around." He bases his belief on our commonalities of interests. Certainly, we are all (but a very few) personally interested in honest, responsive government.[137] It seems likely that even those who advocate "spiritual renewal" approaches to reform (for example, social critic Dwight MacDonald) would support such a joining of efforts. MacDonald argued "any movement that did not pay fealty to the non-historical values of truth, justice, and love inevitably collapsed."[138]

The remainder of Part II of this book is devoted to discussions of reform issues and examples of reform amendments to the Constitution. Chapter 7 discusses alternative approaches to governmental reform and points out the related need for a revitalized labor movement. Our McCarthy-era fear of communism and the corruption that existed in some unions of that period led us to "throw out the baby with the bathwater." It is time we repaired the damage. A new labor relations act could take adequate measures to forestall corruption and—at the same time— take advantage of the positive aspects of a strong labor movement. Chapter 8 discusses two of the critical flaws in our Constitution that have led us to our present national crises. Chapter 9 identifies some congressional, judicial and executive issues that should be considered in pursuing structural reform. Chapter 10 suggests some language for use in altering and improving our Constitution.

---

[137] Ralph Nader is quoted in Chris Hedges, *Death of the Liberal Class*, Nation Books, Kindle 3338.
[138] Quoted in Hedges, Kindle location 2038.

CHAPTER 7

GOVERNMENTAL REFORM
AND US INSTITUTIONS

We the people of the United States, in order to form a more perfect union, establish justice, insure domestic tranquility, provide for the common defense, promote the general welfare, and secure the blessings of liberty to ourselves and to our posterity, do ordain and establish this Constitution for the United States of America.
—Prologue to the Constitution of the United States

These powerful words declare the United States to be a self-governed nation devoted to justice. It is paradoxical that these two principles, taken together, imply the innate goodness of humankind. Yet our constitutional checks and balances resolve this paradox. They acknowledge the tendency of power to corrupt human beings and the consequent necessity that, in order to create a self-governed nation devoted to justice, the power of our civil officers must be checked. The difficulties of giving "efficacy"[139] to this resolution of our magnificent paradox made flaws in our original Constitution inevitable. The framers acknowledged these flaws and relied upon future generations (not future governments) to correct them. For over two centuries "future" generations have neglected this duty. Now, at least partially as a

---

[139] Hamilton wrote, in *Federalist 80*," . . . there ought always to be a constitutional method of giving efficacy to constitutional provisions."

result of this neglect, we are faced with political, economic, ecological and moral crises. We must either reform our federal government or lose both our liberty and our standing in the world community. This book identifies some of our major constitutional flaws and suggests an approach to "new-modeling" our Constitution so as to remedy them. This Chapter first discusses the centrality of federal reform to dealing with our societal crises. Then it discusses the special[140] role of organized labor in federal reform. Organized labor was once (and could be again) the main non-governmental institution of our society capable of coming close to expressing a unified view of America's ordinary people. As our manufacturing sector becomes smaller and our white collar occupations increase, this potential also increases. Organized labor, while now on the decline, could play a major role in making our government more democratic. For this reason, the chapter emphasizes both the role it could (even now) play in bringing about government reform and the need for new labor-management relations legislation under a rejuvenated government. Finally, it comments on the relevance of five other institutions in instituting, effecting and maintaining a genuine reform of our federal government. These five institutions are our state legislatures, our political parties, organized religion, education, and our non-governmental organizations (NGO's).

REFORM AND THE FEDERAL GOVERNMENT ITSELF

Madison warned us that tyranny does not announce itself.[141] It comes quietly and gradually. One tyrannical act builds upon another. We are outraged, but we are never outraged enough to take action. In America today, there is no lack of early warning signs. Government has slipped out of our control. It's powers are

---

[140] Organized labor's role is special in that it is the largest of the special interest groups that represent us ordinary "90%" Americans.

[141] See Madison's speech to the Virginia Ratifying Convention, June 16, 1788.

out-of-balance. It has become dominated by our military-corporate complex. It is failing to exercise some of its constitutional powers and taking upon itself new powers that are unconstitutional. International indicators reflect a decline in our democratic structures, our governmental honesty, our competitiveness and our prosperity. Significantly, these measures now rank the US 15th among the 28 OECD nations in "democracy" and 17th in governmental honesty. A bit over a half century ago we earned the respect of the world by extending the hand of friendship to our former enemies. Now we invade other nations, torture our fellow human beings and refuse to join the rest of the world in confronting disastrous climate change.[142] Our bi-partisan dissatisfaction with our government is evidenced by the emergence of the Tea Party on the right and the Occupy Movement on the left. The Tea Party and Occupy are potentially two of the major actors in a genuine reform movement.

- **Our government powers are out-of-balance.**

Our most serious political problem is the extent to which US governmental powers are becoming concentrated in the presidency. This creates short-range problems (for example, unnecessary and expensive wars) and one long-range, mega problem. The long range problem is our slide toward tyranny. The reader may recall that Madison defined tyranny as the concentration of all governmental powers in one branch of government.[143] The power to declare war, placed by the framers in the sole care of Congress, is now in the sole care of the presidency. The presidency, with its signing statements, has the "final say" over legislation. Even Hamilton, who favored a strong executive, warned his fellow framers that the treaty powers must not be the sole

---

[142] Former President Clinton declined to send the Kyoto Protocol to the Senate for ratification and subsequent presidents have followed suit.
[143] See *Federalist 47*.

province of the presidency. Nevertheless, these powers are now, in effect, under the president's control.[144] The notion that we are in a state of war with "terrorism" has made our civil rights vulnerable to the arbitrary decisions of the president. His dual role as both president and leader of a major political party enables him, in effect; to "appoint" justices of the US Supreme Court on the basis of political ideology. Our first priority must be to balance the powers of our government.

- **Our government is dominated by our military-corporate complex.**

Our next most serious problem is the extent to which the making of our laws, administrative standards, policies and even legal decisions is dominated by corporations. These laws, safety standards and enforcement policies combine to create long-term damage to the environment in return for short-term corporate profits (for example, the Gulf Oil Spill). Our failure to alter the constitutional process for making judicial appointments contributed to the decisions in *Bush v. Gore* (2000) and *Citizens United v. FEC* (2010). Our energy legislation, until recently, provided for grants to support the production of croplands-based ethanol.[145] Our foreign policy is being driven by military and corporate influences. The less fortunate vast majority of our population must not only fight our wars. It must also pay for them. The money that pays for military supplies and equipment goes out of the pockets of the less fortunate ninety percent and onto the income statements of corporations. It is not that these

---

[144] See *After Patrick Henry*, Black Rose Books, pp. 53-54.
[145] The prestigious "Princeton Study" on bio fuels concluded that, if the US continued to subsidize the production of ethanol made from materials grown on croplands, greenhouse emissions would increase by 50-100 per cent in thirty years (Timothy Searchinger, "The use of US croplands for bio fuels," *Science Magazine*, Feb. 7, 2008). The ethanol subsidies were continued until 2011, when they were ended due to budgetary pressures.

military and corporate influences are illegal. Our problems are exacerbated by the fact that they are perfectly legal. The laws making them legal were made, of course, subject to military and corporate influence. Unless and until we view this as a problem requiring a constitutional remedy, we are caught in a classic "Catch 22" dilemma: we can't pass statutes to solve the problem until the problem is solved.

- **Our government is spending more than it is taking in.**

It is clear that we can check our government's spending only by means of a "balanced budget" amendment. Our military-corporate complex urges Congress to spend money to bolster our military supremacy. We urge our representatives in Congress to guard our "entitlements." These pressures drive us further and further into debt. Someone must "give ground." That someone will not be either Congress or the military-corporate complex. Their members have too much to lose personally from making the difficult decisions that are necessary to balance our budget. A rational and carefully thought out balanced budget amendment is only likely to be conceived and written by delegates to a 2nd constitutional convention who represent the "ninety percent" of ordinary Americans. Modeling their deliberations after those of our original framers, free from corporate pressures and advised by our leading conservative and liberal economists, these delegates could produce a reasonable solution to our financial dilemmas.

- **Our government is failing to exercise some of its powers.**

Congress is responsible for prescribing strict rules, "which define and point out" (the courts') "duty in every particular case that comes before them."[146] To my knowledge, Congress has

---

[146] In *Federalist 78*, Hamilton emphasizes the necessity for strict rules. In *Federalist 81*, he alludes to such rules as being the province of the "legislature."

never prescribed one such rule governing decisions in constitutional cases. Judges and justices apply their own ideological and procedural biases to each such case that comes before them. As a result, the same case might draw different decisions in different jurisdictions and at different points in time. This is inconsistent with both the concept of justice and with the "equal justice" clause of the 14th Amendment This failure of Congress to provide strict rules for the judiciary has contributed to the tendency of the judiciary to encroach upon the exclusive Article V power of state legislatures (and/or state conventions) to amend the Constitution.

The courts are responsible for "preserving" the integrity of the Constitution. This integrity depends in large part on preserving our separation of powers. Hamilton tells us, in *Federalist 78*, "Limitations of this kind" (for example, the constitutional prohibition against *ex post facto* laws) "can be preserved in practice no other way than through the medium of the courts of justice, whose duty it must be to declare all acts contrary to the manifest tenor of the Constitution void." The courts have found ways to avoid this duty. In the matter of the war powers they have (by their avoidance) sanctioned costly and unnecessary wars.

- **International measures** [147] **show the US in crisis.**

The principal measures of national performance show our country in decline. The World Competitiveness Index ranked America number one as recently as 2008. In 2009 it slipped to second. In 2010, it was ranked fourth and, in 2012, sixth. In 2007, the Legatum Prosperity Index ranked us number three in the world. We slipped down to number six in 2008, number nine in 2009, and number ten in 2010. The Gini Index measures the gap

---

[147] See Appendix A for brief comments on the criteria used by these six measures.

between the rich (the top ten percent) and the poor (the bottom ten percent). That is, it measures the extent to which ordinary people share in a country's wealth. The country with the smallest "gap" in 2007 was Denmark, with a ratio (UN) of 24.7 our Gini increased by 23 percent from 1967—2007. In 2007, we ranked 73 rd in the world in income equality. Turkmenistan was 72nd and Senegal was 74th.[148] The life satisfaction rankings were launched by OECD in 2011. They rank the US 13th among 32 OECD member nations. Seventy percent of American respondents expressed satisfaction with their lives. The Netherlands and Denmark are ranked 1st and 2nd with 93 percent and 90 percent respectively. In 2011 the US, the "cradle of democracy," ranked 16th among the OECD countries on the Economist Intelligence Unit's Democracy Index. Most critical, the US, was ranked 18th (among 32 OECD countries) on Transparency International's Corruption Perception Index in 2011. This Index, however, would more accurately be called the "honesty" Index since it ranks the nation perceived as the least corrupt (New Zealand) number one on its list. In 2006 (the first year of the Corruption Perceptions Index) we were given 7.8 points for governmental honesty (on a scale of ten). That figure had dropped to 7.1 by 2011. Our score on the Democracy Index was 8.22 (of a possible ten) in 2008 and 8.11 in 2011. The rankings presented in Tables 1 and 2 are intended to persuade the reader (1) that our country is in crisis and (2) that alterations in our public policies might be an effective approach to dealing with this crisis.

The associations shown in Tables 1 and 2 indicate that there are changes we can make in national political and economic policies that could improve our political and economic conditions. The structures of democracy and government honesty are both directly influenced by public policy. For example, prohibit-

---

[148]The increase from 1967-2007 was derived from Gini Coefficient data published annually by the US Department of Labor.

ing the use of private money in federal elections would improve the effectiveness of our election system. Altering the impeachment provisions so as to make them both strict and enforceable would reduce illegal and unconstitutional actions on the parts of our federal civil officers. These structures are also positively associated with competitiveness and prosperity. The relationship in these matters is indirect. That is, altered public policies could increase democracy and governmental honesty. These factors, in turn, are positively associated with competitiveness and prosperity. While it is true that associations do not prove causal relationships, they certainly point out possibilities for further investigation and consideration. The persistence of these associations when the 32 OECD countries are grouped by their levels of democracy, honest government etc., while it does not prove causality, makes it highly improbable that the groupings are a result of random selection.

Table 1 shows some associations between democracy and five other aspects of national life in 32 member nations of the OECD Ranking. Table 2 does the same for life satisfaction. While these associations do not establish causality, they do point out fruitful areas for further study. It is worth noting that the eight OECD nations with the highest democracy rankings have, on the average, significantly higher rankings in all the other aspects of national life. In turn, the second tier of eight nations has significantly higher rankings than the third tier and so on. It is possible that there is no causal relationship between democracy and the quality of life. It is possible that there is some unrelated characteristic shared by highly democratic countries that is responsible for their high quality of life. This question of causality is of the greatest importance and deserves intensive study, perhaps by the United Nations.

TABLE 1: DEMOCRACY

(1) Countries ranked and grouped by levels of democracy	(2) Union density ranks	(3) Govt. honesty ranks	(4) Competitiveness ranks	(5) Prosperity ranks	(6) Life satisfaction ranks and %'s	(7) Avg. ranks for columns 2-6
1. Norway	5	5	11	1	5 (84%)	5.4
2. Iceland	1	10	19	12	15.3 (66)	11.5
3. Denmark	3	2.5	9	2	2 (90)	3.7
4. Sweden	4	4	3	5	3 (87)	3.8
5. New Zealand	14	1	17	4	7.5 (77)	8.7
6. Australia	18.5	7.5	15	3	10 (75)	10.8
7. Switzerland	20	7.5	1	8	7.5 (77)	8.8
8. Canada	9	9	10	6	6 (78)	8.0
Group 1 Averages	9.3	5.8	10.6	5.1	7 (79.1%)	7.6
9. Finland	2	2.5	2	7	4 (86)	3.5
10. Netherlands	16.5	6	4	9	1 (93)	7.3
11. Ireland	8	15.5	18	11	11.5 (73)	12.8
12. Austria	10	13.5	12	14	11.5 (73)	12.2
13.Germany	16.5	11.5	5	15	18.5 (56)	13.3
14. Czech Republic	21	27	23	23	18.5 (56)	22.5
15. UK	11	13.5	7	13	14 (68)	11.7
16. USA	28	18	6	10	13 (70)	15
Group 2 Averages	14.1	13.4	9.6	12.8	11.6 (78%)	12.3
17. Japan	18.5	11.5	8	18	24 (40)	16.1
18. South Korea	29	25	14	21	26.5 (36)	23.1
19. Belgium	6	15.5	13	16	9 (76)	11.9
20. Spain	24	21	22	20	22 (49)	21.8
21. Portugal	15	22	27	22	26.5 (36)	22.4
22. France	31	19	16	17	21 (51)	22.8
23. Slovenia	12	23	29	19	25 (39)	21.6
24. Italy	7	30	25	25	20 (54)	21.4
Group 3 Averages	17.8	20.9	19.3	19.8	21.8	19.9
25. Greece	13	31	32	30	23 (43)	25.8
26. Estonia	30	20	21	28	31 (24)	26
27. Chile	25	17	20	26	15.5 (66)	20.7
28. Slovak Rep.	22	29	31	27	30 (27)	27.8
29. Poland	26	24	24	24	28 (35)	27.2
30. Hungary	23	26	30	29	32 (23)	28
31. Mexico	27	32	28	31	15.5 (66)	28.7
32. Turkey	32	28	26	32	29 (30)	31.4
Group 4 Averages	27	25.9	26.5	28.4	25.5	26.7

Table 2 shows the associations of the life satisfaction measure with five other aspects of national life. These associations are of special interest since life satisfaction can be regarded as the common goal of unionization, democracy, honest government, competitiveness and prosperity. The tables show that the "top tier" life satisfaction countries have an average quality of life ranking of 6.4, The comparable figure for the "top tier" democracy countries is 7.6 and for the "top tier" union density countries 10.5. All three average rankings are impressive since a random selection of eight countries from the 32 included in this study would produce an average ranking of 16.5. Rankings of one to 16.4 reflect positive associations. Rankings of 16.6 to 32 reflect negative associations. Positive rankings in any one factor are positively associated with rankings in all the other factors. This suggests that public policies aimed at improving a country's rankings in any one of the aspects of national life would be consistent with improvement in the other aspects.

- **It is irrational to expect our federal government to reform itself.**

Genuine governmental reform can be accomplished only by means of our constitutional amendment process. This is so partly because some reforms require the shifting of constitutional powers and cannot, therefore, be accomplished by statute. More important, statutory reform is controlled by the civil officers of the federal government—in whose interest it is to maintain the *status quo*. Historically, their strategy has been pre-emptive. When energy gathers for genuine reform, Congress typically dissipates this energy by passing expedient but ineffectual "reform" statutes. Fortunately, the federal government has no power to approve or disapprove constitutional amendments. This power belongs to the people. One method we have to exercise this power is to act through our state legislatures or state conventions.

TABLE 2: LIFE SATISFACTION

(1) Countries ranked and grouped by life satisfaction	(2) Union density ranks	(3) Democracy ranks	(4) Govt. honesty ranks	(5) Competitiveness ranks	(6) Prosperity ranks	(7) Avg. ranks for columns 2-6
1. Netherlands (93)	16.5	10	6	4	9	9.1
2. Denmark (90)	3	3	2.5	9	2	3.9
3. Sweden (87)	4	4	4	3	5	4
4. Finland (86)	2	9	2.5	2	7	4.5
5. Norway (84)	5	1	5	11	1	4.6
6. Canada (78)	9	8	9	10	6	8.4
7.5. New Zealand (77)	14	5	1	17	4	8.2
7.5. Switzerland (77)	20	7	7.5	1	8	8.7
Group 1 Averages	9.2	5.9	4.6	7.1	5.3	6.4
9. Belgium (76)	6	19	15.5	13	16	13.9
10. Australia (75)	18.5	6	7.5	15	3	10
11,5. Austria (73)	10	12	13.5	12	14	12.3
11.5. Ireland (73)	8	11	15.5	18	11	12.7
13. US (70)	28	16	18	6	10	15.6
14. UK (68)	11	15	13.5	7	13	11.9
15.3. Chile (66)	25	27	17	20	26	23
15.3. Iceland (66)	1	2	10	19	12	8.8
Group 2 Averages	13.9	13.5	13.8	13.8	13.1	13.6
15.3. Mexico (66)	27	31	32	28	31	29.8
18.5. Germany (56)	16.5	13	11.5	5	15	12.2
18.5 Czech Rep.(56)	21	14	27	23	23	21.6
20. Italy (54)	7	24	30	25	25	22.2
21. France (51)	31	22	19	16	17	21
22. Spain (49)	24	20	21	22	20	21.4
23. Greece (43)	13	25	31	12	30	22.2
24. Japan (40)	18.5	17	11.5	8	18	14.6
Group 3 Averages	19.8	20.8	22.9	17.4	22.4	20.7
25. Slovenia (39)	12	23	29	29	19	22.4
26.5. Portugal (36)	15	21	22	27	22	21.4
26.5. South Korea (36)	29	18	25	25	21	23.6
28. Poland (35)	26	29	24	24	24	25.4
29. Turkey (30)	32	32	28	26	32	30
30. Slovak Republic (27)	22	28	29	27	27	26.6
31. Estonia (24)	30	30	20	21	28	29
32. Hungary (23)	23	30	26	30	29	27.6
Group 4 Averages	24	26.4	25.4	26.1	25.3	25.5

REFORM AND ORGANIZED LABOR

Unions are crucial to governmental reform for two reasons. First, weak though they now are, they could provide an organized group of people in each state to carry and collect petitions. These petitions would be needed to bring about a constitutional convention. Second, should the reform movement be successful, a rejuvenated labor movement would be necessary to act as a continuing check to the military-corporate complex.

• **Present-day unions and the reform movement.**

Present-day unions are a "far cry" from our unions of the 1940's and 1950's. In those years, their membership included as much as 37 per cent of the workforce. In 2010, according to the Current Population Survey, "the percent of wage and salary workers who were members of unions was 11.9 percent, down from 12.5 percent a year earlier." However, 11.9 percent comes to 14.7 million workers. Over the past forty years or so, despite their lessening membership, unions have become quite proficient at getting out the vote for their candidates. This proficiency could be the deciding factor in a campaign to deliver petitions to all state legislatures calling upon them to "apply" for Congress to call a "money-free" convention or propose a specific amendment to Article V to the same effect. Should our unions make common cause with our churches, environmental groups and other non-governmental organizations (NGO's), the result would almost certainly be a 2nd constitutional convention.

• **Rejuvenated unions would be needed to perpetuate the reform**

A rejuvenated labor movement would be crucial to act as a

continuing check upon the military-corporate complex after the reform movement has produced a responsive government. Without continuing checks on the natural tendency of government to expand its powers, we might slip back into our present patterns. The factors that tempt civil officers to expand their powers would not all be removed—even by a "more perfect" constitution. However, the tendency of power to corrupt can be minimized by a vigilant population armed with a carefully altered constitution and strong independent institutions. An altered Constitution could pave the way for the repeal of Taft Harley and the passage of a more rational labor relations statute. This could lead to a rejuvenated labor movement capable of checking governmental and corporate excesses.

In short, a strong labor movement would be good for all working people. Strong unions are associated with national competitiveness, national prosperity, life satisfaction and income equality (See page 208 Table 3). Strong unions used to be our first line of defense against the excessive influence corporations can exert upon our federal government.

Strong unions are needed to keep corporations from totally co-opting government. In the past, strong private sector unions also checked the excessive compensation of corporate executive officers (CEO's). Unions are currently co-operating with stockholders in attempts to limit management's self-aggrandizement. A strong labor movement would tend to increase the incomes of employees in both the private and public sectors, thus attacking one of America's most serious social and economic problems: our ever-widening income gap. Organized labor, when faced with declining membership during the last century, did not focus on changing its organizing and collective bargaining strategies. Instead, during the past forty years or so, it has relied on its ability to "deliver the vote." This has produced incremental gains in the form of worker-friendly legislation, but has had little effect on the income gap. It has also tended to transfer many of labor's protective functions from the private sector to the government. Unions, like many other NGO'S, have concluded that they can best serve their constituencies by relying on government to do their work for them and on their ability to "get out the vote" to secure the election and appointment of civil officers who are friendly to their cause.

- **International comparisons suggest the value of unions**

Table 3 (see page 208) groups the OECD nations with high union densities, the countries with moderately high union densities, the countries with moderately low densities and the countries with low densities. There are eight countries in each group.[149] It also shows the rankings of each country based on the democracy rankings of the Economist, the competitiveness rankings of the World Economic Forum, Legatum's prosperity rankings and Gini's income equality rankings—and on the life satisfaction responses in a recent OECD survey.[150] The data shows that countries with high percentages of union workers tend to have high rankings on the democracy, governmental honesty, competitiveness, prosperity, income equality and life satisfaction indices. Second, it shows that countries with low percentages of unionized workers tend to have low ratings. This data does not establish causal relationships. The associations mentioned above are no doubt affected by political and cultural factors as well as by union density. The

[149] Israel and Luxembourg are not included because of their incomplete data. While the data is the most recent available, it is—unfortunately—not current. [150] The available democracy, governmental honesty, competitiveness and prosperity indices produce global rankings. This necessitated adjusting the global rankings to conform to the OECD rankings. For example, while the USA ranked 24th on Transparency International's "honesty" index, it ranks 13th among the 32 OECD countries. That is, the differences between very positive and very negative rankings are masked when the global rankings are adjusted to conform to the number of OECD countries.

Scandinavian social democracies, for example, are extremely high performers on all four outcome measures. While they all encourage unionization, they no doubt have other characteristics that are associated with desirable outcomes. An analysis that takes into account the forms of governments, the characteristics (as well as the densities) of unions, the degrees of governmental lawlessness and corruption (and, no doubt other factors) is needed in order to draw conclusions on the extent to which union density (and union characteristics) contributes to performance. At the least, however, we can conclude from this data that it is possible for high union density and high political, economic and social performance to co-exist. It is particularly noteworthy that, while 77.9 % of the people in the eight OECD countries with an average union density of 53.9% (the eight most unionized countries) say they are satisfied with their lives, only 62.1% of the people in the ten next most unionized OECD countries (with an average union density of only 20.5% report life satisfaction. In the eight countries with the lowest union density (11.9%), a mere 47.1% say they are satisfied. Union density is also consistent with democracy and governmental honesty. Since democracy and governmental honesty are especially sensitive to structural reform, it would make sense to include provisions encouraging unionization in a reform program.

It should be noted that the Global Competitiveness index focuses on the capacity for producing wealth, while the Legatum Prosperity Index, sometimes termed the "happiness index," looks more at the extent to which a country invests its wealth in programs that benefit the ordinary citizen (for example, health, education, parks etc.). See Appendix A for descriptions of the criteria used by the various measures. The OECD life satisfaction index, like the Legatum Prosperity Index, tends to reflect the ways governments invest their wealth. It is somewhat

TABLE 3: UNION DENSITY

(1) Countries ranked and grouped by levels of union density	(2) Democracy ranks	(3) Govt. honesty ranks	(4) Competitiveness ranks	(5) Prosperity ranks	(6) Life satisfaction ranks and %'s	(7) Avg. ranks for columns 2-6
1. Iceland (79.4 %)	2	10	19	12	15.5(66)	11.7
2. Finland (69.2)	9	2.5	2	7	4 (86)	4.9
3. Denmark (68.8)	3	2.5	9	2	2 (90)	3.7
4. Sweden (68.4)	4	4	3	5	3 (87)	3.8
5. Norway (53.8)	1	5	11	1	5 (84)	4.6
6. Belgium (52.0)	19	15.5	13	16	9 (76)	14.5
7. Italy (33.4)	24	30	25	25	20 (54)	24.8
8. Ireland (32.2)	11	15.5	18	12	11.5(73)	11.8
Group 1 Averages	10.4	10.6	12.5	10	8.8(77)	10.5
9. Canada (29.2)	8	9	10	6	6 (78)	7.8
10. Austria (29.1)	12	13.5	12	14	11.5(73)	12.6
11. UK (27.2)	15	13.5	7	13	14 (68)	12.5
12. Slovenia (25.6)	23	29	29	19	25 (39)	25
13. Greece (24.0)	25	31	32	30	23 (43)	28.2
14. New Zealand (20.6)	5	1	17	4	7.5 (77)	8.9
15. Portugal (20.5)	21	22	27	22	26.5(36)	19.6
16.5. Germany (18.8)	13	11.5	5	15	18.5(56)	12.6
Group 2 Averages	15.1	16.3	17.4	13	14.1(58.8)	15.2
16.5.Netherlands(18.8)	10	6	4	9	1 (93)	6.0
18.5 Japan (18.2)	17	11.5	8	18	24 (40)	15.7
18,5 Australia (18.2)	6	7.5	15	3	10 (75)	8.3
20. Switzerland (17.8)	6	7.5	1	8	7.5 (77)	6.0
21. Czech Rep. (17.3)	14	27	23	23	18.5(56)	23
22. Slovak Rep. (17.2)	28	29	31	27	30 (27)	29
23. Hungary (16.8)	30	26	30	29	32 (23)	29.4
24. Spain (15.9)	20	21	22	20	22 (49)	21
Group 3 Averages	16.4	16.9	16.8	17.1	18.1(55)	17.1
25. Chile (15.8)	27	17	20	26	15.3(66)	21.1
26. Poland (15.6)	29	24	24	24	28 (35)	25.8
27. Mexico (14.3)	31	32	28	31	15.3(66)	27.5
28. US (11.8)	16	18	6	10	13 (70)	12.6
29. Korea (10.3)	18	25	14	21	26.5(36)	24.9
30. Estonia (7.7)	26	20	21	28	31 (24)	25.2
31. France (7.6)	22	19	16	17	21 (51)	19
32. Turkey (5.9)	32	28	26	32	29 (30)	29.4
Group 4 Averages	25.1	22.9	19.3	23.6	22.4(47.3)	22.7

surprising that union density is more closely associated with the life satisfaction and "prosperity" measures than with the two more objective economic rankings. It is interesting (and worth further study) that the deterioration of the prosperity and life satisfaction rankings (in the lower density groups of nations) is so much greater than the deterioration of the economic indicators.[151]

- **Unions aid job protection.**

A recent article in *Mother Jones* described the success corporations are having in their efforts to get more work done by fewer employees (at less cost per employee).[152] The top two reasons it gave for this success are, "the turning over of elections to wealthy interests" and "making it harder for unions to organize." These two reasons are, in a sense, only one. Turning election financing over to corporations prevents the passage of laws that would enable unions to organize. The *Mother Jones* article also points out that, while corporate profits are up twenty-two percent since 2007 and the compensation of corporate executives has skyrocketed, the salaries and wages of working Americans (who now work 378 hours a year more than, for example, German workers) has "stagnated." All this suggests that it is not only our duty and the duty of all working Americans to reform our government and assist in the rejuvenation of organized labor. It is also necessary for our economic survival.

Labor can best rejuvenate itself by participating in a government reform movement, lobbying for the repeal of Taft Hartley and, even more important, by decentralizing its collective bargaining process. Our fear of communism was the major factor used to justify the anti-union Taft Hartley Act in 1947. This Act

---

[151] The average percentage of people saying they were satisfied with their lives decreases from 76.9% in the high union density group to 62.6 in the middle density group and 45.1% in the low density group.

[152] Monica Bauerlein and Clara Jeffery, "The Speed Up," *Mother Jones*, July-August, 2011.

was passed over a Truman veto and has been one cause of organized labor's decline in the U.S. The justifications for Taft Hartley were questionable in 1947 and irrelevant now. It has certainly damaged our national quality of life and may have negatively affected our national competitiveness, prosperity, income equality and ability to control our government. Its repeal and replacement by a rational labor reform act are long overdue.

- **Repealing Taft-Hartley.**

Organized labor appears to have given up on repealing Taft Hartley. It has also lost its focus on collective bargaining. It now seeks benefits for its members (and other working Americans) by lobbying the government for laws that are less favorable to corporations and more favorable to ordinary people. This is important and useful work, but it can only incrementally help the plight of ordinary working people and does nothing to restrain corporate abuses or reduce the excessive compensations of corporate managers. It is, no doubt, an honest policy arrived at only after long soul-searching by labor leaders. However, it is a policy labor would doubtless abandon if it could. A wiser long-term policy, I believe, would be to focus on (1) replacing Taft Hartley with a rational national labor law best accomplished by working toward a 2nd constitutional convention and (2) finding a way to attract new members from a radically changed (and changing) private sector workforce.

Repealing Taft-Hartley and replacing it with a progressive labor relations law would also be in the interests of activist churches and most member-funded NGO's. A coalition of unions, activist churches and member-funded NGO's could "new-model" our federal government. As suggested before, it is a coalition that could be inspired, triggered and energized by college and university students. As for attracting members in today's workforce, Labor should not respond to technological, workforce and industry changes by focusing its efforts on lobbying and thus turning its functions over to government. A more likely strategy would be for unions to ask themselves how they can "re-form" the house of labor in order to adjust to the changed priorities of a changed workforce.

• Decentralizing collective bargaining.

A strategy that deserves organized labor's consideration is the decentralization of collective bargaining. In fact, some labor leaders, chief among them Irving Bluestone, then V.P. of the UAW, did consider this strategy in the early 1970's. As a result, many unions experimented at the local level with different kinds of "participative" labor management relationships. These relationships, which focused on involving employees in the decision making process, were formed "outside the contract." This was done because labor leaders feared that they might replace collective bargaining contracts and develop the exploitive characteristics of "company unions." Typically, these experiments overcame the initial skepticism of workers and managements and, for brief periods of time, increased productivity and improved job satisfaction.

However, the cooperative agreements, being outside the contract, were not enforceable. They allowed either side to violate the agreements reached in participative committees and/or the provisions of the participative agreement itself. They also allowed either side to withdraw from the cooperative agreement completely—at any time for any reason. Both labor and management believed that cooperative agreements, by their very nature, could not and should not be enforceable. Ironically, this proved to be their fatal flaw. When managements changed in the experimenting workplaces, the new managers naturally canceled or rejected the cooperative agreements. When budget situations or other difficulties arose, managers reneged on their promises and commitments under the cooperative agreements. This made workers disenchanted with the cooperative agreements. Workers became even more dissatisfied when their involvement in decision making increased productivity, and management kept the increases.

Typically, labor and management both became less than satisfied. The participative relationships seemed a great deal of trouble for very little return. It would have been logical for labor and management to have commissioned a joint evaluation of the cooperative/participative approach. Such a commission might have identified flaws in the participative agreements and found ways to remedy them. This, however, did not happen. Participation programs are still undertaken—with mixed results. Some unions still support the cooperative/participative concept, notably the Service Employees International Union (SEIU).

However, unions still take it as an article of faith that employee participation should be kept separate from collective bargaining. This is a fundamental mistake. Instead, it is crucial that participation and collective bargaining be integrated—both for the success of participative experiments and for the rejuvenation of the labor movement. The rules of participation should be included in the labor contract, thus becoming enforceable. The labor contract should make agreements arrived at in participative committees enforceable. In this way participation and collective bargaining would be merged and, in part, decentralized to the shop floor level.

Those matters that could not be agreed to by both sides could be referred "up the line" until they were resolved or reached the bargaining unit level. There, they would become an item on the list taken to the existing bargaining table at the next bargaining session. This would democratize the union structure. Bargaining committees at every level of the organization would, on the union side, consist of elected union stewards.[153]   Both the democratization of the union and the opportunity to negotiate the quality of their work lives in small office and shop-floor units would be attractive to prospective members in both the private and public sectors. Integrating participation and collective bargaining would benefit both management and labor since participation, when properly designed, tends to increase productivity and to share any increased financial gains. This would benefit the economy as well as its institutions and the nation's workers.

REFORM AND FIVE OTHER US INSTITUTIONS

There are at least five other institutions that have positive roles to play in governmental reform: state legislatures, political parties, organized religion, education and member-funded NGO's.

• **Reform and our state legislatures.**

State legislatures can play a crucial role in reforming the federal government. First, Article V gives them the powers to require the calling of national constitutional conventions, to specify amendments for proposal by Congress, and to ratify proposed amendments or to call state conventions for this purpose. It is true that we do not need to act through our state legislatures in order to alter the Constitution.[154] For example, we might

---

[153] This approach to participation and collective bargaining is described in detail in my book, *Employee Participation and Joint-Management*, Jossey-Bass, 1990.

[154] Constitutional scholars tell us that Article V limits the government's power with regard to amendments, but does not detract from the people's power to alter the Constitution by other means than acting through their state legislatures. For example, see Akhil Amar, "The Supreme Court, 1999 Term-Foreword: The Document and the Doctrine" (2000). *Faculty Scholarship* Series, Paper 851.

choose to petition Congress directly for the calling of a convention or for the proposing of a specific amendment. However, the "road" laid out for us in Article V, while not clearly marked, has a number of advantages. For example, eventually the ratification of an altered Constitution must be done by state legislatures or conventions. This makes it advantageous for the states and the various organizations that have state-level structures to be involved in the amendment process from the very beginning.

Second, state legislators would benefit from federal reform and should be involved in developing its details. They would benefit because, in all probability, a genuine reform amendment would include a "term limits" provision for Congress. If, for example, this provision limited representatives and senators to a total of no more than six years of congressional service, five or six times as many Americans would have the privilege of serving in Congress than have that privilege now. Some of those additional Americans would no doubt come from state legislatures.

Finally, most state legislators would favor an honest federal government dedicated to serving the public over one unduly influenced by corporations and other special interest groups. Such a federal government would provide them and their constituents with a more just, equitable, and environmentally sound America. Many state legislators would also concede that our country is in a political, economic, moral and ecological decline. State legislators would very likely be influenced by their constituents' concerns with these crises.

• Reform and our political parties.

In a movement toward genuine government reform, our political parties would be split—not along party lines but according to income and wealth. The top ten percent of both political parties would no doubt fight any genuine reform movement with all the resources at their command. On the other hand, reform would be in the interests of the other ninety or so percent of both parties. This figure is probably much higher for "fledgling" parties like the Tea Party and Occupy.[155] Many of our 1,000 or so federal civil officers are either in the top ten percent or in the process of getting there. The interests of rank and file Democrats and Republicans, on the other hand, would lie with genuine reform. However, the top ten percent, supported by the military-corporate complex, would have the resources to outspend the ninety percent as regards TV time. This feature of present day political life makes even approximate democracy extremely difficult. In the election of delegates to state and national conventions, the candidates opposing genuine reform would, in the normal course of events, outspend the candidates from the ninety-nine percent. For this reason, we must find a way to prohibit the use of private money in the election of delegates to a 2nd constitutional convention. The Conclusions section of this book proposes approaches for dealing with this "Catch 22."

- **Reform and organized religion.**

The participation of organized religions, at both the grass-roots level and at higher levels in their denominations (or religions) is both appropriate and necessary. Political activism is not only consistent with religious principles. It is a means of spiritual expression for church members. Just as politically conservative Americans can agree with their liberal counterparts on the necessity for governmental reform, so can Christians, Muslims, Jews and persons of other faiths agree that a responsive, lawful government is far superior to a lawless government that is more responsive to money than to ordinary people. The higher levels

---

[155] Despite their fledging status these groups are extremely influential with the American public. Their commitment to a possible reform effort would be critical.

of denominations and religions could issue statements supporting the governmental reform effort. This would encourage their
individual churches to support the efforts of their members. In
the past, churches have been instrumental in stopping US
aggression. This was certainly true as regards the US intervention in Nicaragua during the 1980's. It would seem to be just as
spiritually sound to prevent wars as it is to stop them after they
have started.

The separation of church and state must, of course, be
maintained. We do not want our religions to be controlled by
the state. Neither do we want our government to be controlled
by religions. However, the participation of churches in anti-
war and anti-corruption efforts does not tend to concentrate
power in either institution. Instead, it tends to check the power
of government.

• **Reform and education.**

The participation of schools, universities and students would
be necessary both in carrying out a successful reform movement
and to educating us to assume a greater role in our federal government should the reform movement succeed. Just as the
"Greensboro Four" re-energized the civil rights movement in
1960, college and university students could trigger a responsible
governmental reform movement in present day America. Many
colleges and universities now encourage and assist their students
to become more active politically and in their communities.
They seem to be motivated by a desire to "channel" student
activism into positive activities. There could hardly be a more
positive activity than the reform of our federal government.
Colleges and universities could, for example, sponsor "moot"
constitutional conventions. These conventions could present
reports and proposals to their state legislatures. Presently, our
high schools, colleges and universities do very little in the way of

familiarizing students with the responsibilities assigned them by the Declaration of Independence and the Constitution.

It is reasonable to suppose that a successful reform movement would increase these responsibilities. To the extent that our federal government becomes more responsive to our views on policy matters, for example, it becomes more important that we inform ourselves with regard to these matters. In short, success would bring with it the necessity for us to adopt a view of government more consistent with the view expressed in our Declaration of Independence, our Constitution and the *Federalist Papers*. These documents place the responsibility for government squarely on our shoulders. This makes it senseless for us to complain to our government about our government. Our job is not to complain and protest. Our job is to take responsibility for our government and take whatever steps are necessary to improve it. We must both take this view and nurture it in our children and grandchildren if we expect them to perpetuate a reformed federal government. If our high schools, colleges and universities are to educate more active future voters and citizens, they must become involved now in our efforts to "new-model" a more responsive government.

It is never too early to start educating young people with regard to their government and the political duties the Constitution will call upon them to perform. This kind of nonpartisan political education is sadly lacking at all levels of our educational system. Yet one of the major purposes of education in our democracy should be to prepare our young people to participate actively in their government. James Iredell said, in the Philadelphia convention, "The only real security of liberty in any country is the jealousy and circumspection of the people themselves. Let them be watchful over their rulers."[156] Courses at every level of schooling that deepen our young people's under-

[156] James Iredell spoke these words in the North Carolina convention in July, 1788.

standing of the Declaration of Independence, the Constitution and the *Federalist Papers* would encourage them to keep jealous and informed eyes on their rulers. It is likely that, in using the word "jealousy" Iredell was referring to the constitutional fact that our leaders are also our servants and we should be jealous of our power and disinclined to give it up to our servants.

The best education is practical work with a clear object. "Moot" constitutional conventions could be effective at all levels of education. These moot conventions, whether held during class periods, weekends or for longer periods of time, would engage students in discussions of specific constitutional issues and require the older ones to write "federalist papers" and propose constitutional provisions of their own. This kind of practical experience might later become a regular part of every student's elementary, high school and university education. Its immediate value would be to prepare students to be delegates to future state and national constitutional conventions. It should be noted that this description of an "educational role" should include the possibility that some university and college students might ignite and energize a governmental reform movement— as four students from North Carolina A & T ignited the "sit-in" movement of the early 1960's.

- **Reform and our non-governmental organizations (NGO's).**

The participation of both liberal and conservative NGO's would be crucial in any governmental reform movement. It is in the interests of most member-funded NGO's to have a government that is m more responsive to the needs of their constituents and less responsive to "big money." They would bring to such a movement their valuable organizing skills and resources and, very possibly, the ability to coordinate (at the state and national levels) the activities of the major institutions that would participate in a reform movement. In a sense, such a reform movement would be an extension of their usual work. Their work often involves persuading governmental branches or departments to support their particular programs. A successful reform movement would result in the use of more national resources for the constructive ends pursued by most NGO's and fewer national resources for destructive ends such as spying drones, assassination, war and torture. De Tocqueville admired our "associations" for acting as a check on our federal government. They can deserve our admiration now by working for governmental reform.

It should be noted, however, that NGO's funded primarily by corporations and the top ten percent of the population will no doubt be opposed to any effort toward genuine reform. The probable position of "hybrid" NGO'S such as National Public Radio (which is funded in about equal shares by government, corporations and ordinary Americans) seems uncertain.

CHAPTER 8

TWO MAIN CAUSES OF GOVERNMENTAL LAWLESSNESS

If angels were to govern men, neither external nor internal controls on government would be necessary.
—James Madison, Father of the Constitution and our 4th President.

Our Constitution is sometimes called the most important political document of modern times. If this is the case, James Madison is one of the most important historical figures of modern times. One of his signal contributions to our Constitution was his recognition that our civil officers would not be "angels." He believed that, if we were to be truly self-governed, we needed some means of preventing our civil officers from pursuing their own self-interests at our expense. To this end, the Constitution provides us with the separation of powers, its system of checks and balances, the election provisions, the impeachment provisions and Article V. All these safeguards have contributed to America's political miracle. However, as Hamilton and Madison predicted, time has both revealed original flaws in our Constitution and created new ones. In large part due to these original and new shortcomings, our military-corporate complex has secured a disproportionate influence over the policies and operations of our government. The impeachment provisions and Article V have been mentioned in previous chapters. However, their centrality to reform and the fact that they contain original constitutional defects warrant the more detailed discussions below. At the same time, it should be emphasized that genuine reform will require a comprehensive review of the total Constitution and the altering of many existing provisions and the writing of some new ones.

THE FRAMERS' DREAMS AND INTENTIONS

The framers dreamed of forming a country in which those who governed would be honest and dedicated. They would be dedicated to the welfare of the people because this dedication would be in their own personal best interests. The framers dreamed of a country in which the final power would lie with the people. The people would control their civil officers (civil servants) and would, in this way, control their own destinies. The framers employed what Hamilton called the four "new discoveries" to turn their dreams into reality. These four new discoveries are: the separation of powers, a system of checks and balances, an independent judiciary and an elected legislature. Most of the framers regarded the presidency as simply the instrument of the legislature and the legislature as simply the instrument of the people.

To preserve the separation of powers over time and to help make honesty, lawfulness and dedication attractive to the civil officers of their new country, they wrote the impeachment provisions. To place the final power in the hands of the people instead of in the hands of the federal government, they wrote Article V. However, both the impeachment provisions and Article V were compromised and flawed from the beginning.

Their flaws weakened the four "new discoveries" and, therefore, are root causes of our present decline. Understanding these flaws is the first step toward correcting them.

Our founding fathers dreamed of creating a democracy that would be emulated by other countries. Hamilton wrote, in *Federalist 9*, "I trust that America will be the broad and solid foundation of other edifices, not less magnificent." They dreamed of America modeling an innovation that would "clog" wars and promote peace. This innovation was the assignment of the power to declare war away from the executive branch. Madison dreamed of a system of checks and balances that he believed would keep the war powers (and other powers of government) in their proper places.[157] The framers saw the necessity for rational design. They did not imagine that our civil officers would be honest and dedicated out of their love of virtue for its own sake. In *Federalist 53*, Madison wrote about supplying the "defect of better motives" (that is, about supplying the lack of a strong attraction to virtue for its own sake) by creating "opposite and rival interests . . . by which each (civil officer) may be a check upon the other." James Monroe and Patrick Henry did not subscribe to this theory. Henry alluded to the checks and balances as "rope-dancing"[158] and predicted their failure. The key check to lawlessness and corruption, in Monroe's view, would be supplied by the impeachment provisions.[159]

ROOT CAUSE NO. 1—
THE FLAWED IMPEACHMENT PROVISIONS

The (root) flaw in the impeachment provisions occurred when the framers, persuaded by Alexander Hamilton, abandoned

---

[157] He wrote, in *Federalist 51*, "If angels were to govern men, neither external nor internal controls on government would be needed."

[158] Henry used this term on June 5, 1788 while arguing against the proposed constitution at the Virginia Ratifying Convention.

[159] Monroe, *The People, the Sovereigns*, James River Press, p. 16

principle in favor of expediency. They abandoned the separation of powers principle because it was expedient to give the power of trying impeachments to the Senate rather than to the judiciary. This has proved to be a tragic error. Our fifth president, James Monroe, believed that, "if (the impeachment provisions) are preserved in full vigor, and exercised with perfect integrity, every branch will perform its duty, and the people be left to the performance of theirs . . ."[160] Unfortunately, due largely to these framers' "tragic error," the impeachment provisions have not been "preserved in full vigor." They have been tampered with, violated, ignored and misinterpreted. They are now worse than worthless. The framers thought they would make lawful and dedicated behavior on the parts of civil officers pleasant and lawlessness and the pursuit of personal self-interest painful. They believed that quick, certain and impartial impeachment justice would help create a dedicated and lawful corps of civil officers. However, the impeachment provisions did not produce quick, certain and impartial justice. They were slow and uncertain and promptly became politicized. Instead of creating an honest and dedicated group of civil officers, they made lawful and dedicated behavior irrational and were instrumental in making public service a haven for the pursuit of personal self-interest. How could the framers have designed a political system that produced results so diametrically opposed to the results they intended?

It was not that they were unaware of the necessity for arranging the powers of government in such a way that civil officers would see honest and dedicated behavior as being in their personal self-interests. It was not that they were unduly optimistic about human nature. It is not that they failed to see the centrality of this matter to their hopes for creating a viable democracy. Indeed, they expected the impeachment provisions to be the "pivot" of a viable and peaceful democracy that would be emu-

---

[160] Ibid.

lated by other countries and help make this a better world. Unfortunately, they were persuaded by Hamilton to violate the separation of powers principle by assigning the power to try impeachments to the Senate. This led, almost immediately, to the Senate's exempting itself (and, in effect the House as well) from impeachment. The pre-civil war politicization of the Senate further eroded the deterrent effect of the impeachment provisions. By the time Andrew Johnson was impeached in 1868, these provisions were virtually worthless. Much later, in 1999, the 106th Senate gave them a death blow when it acquitted then President Clinton.

An explanation for the flawed impeachment provisions

Hamilton almost single-handedly convinced his fellow framers that the power to try impeachments should be assigned to the Senate. It was admitted by all to be a judicial power. It was thought by many to be the most critical judicial power. The proposed constitutions submitted by the states assigned this critical power to the judiciary. The draft constitution assigned it to the judiciary. Yet Hamilton won the day. He devoted *Federalist 65* and *66* to arguing that the Supreme Court should not be given this power and that the Senate should. The framers agreed that this power could not be exercised impartially by an elected body—and these were the only two non-elected bodies available.[161] Hamilton's argument was essentially that the Senate would be capable of rendering impartial justice and the Supreme Court would not. The Senate would have the requisite strength, numbers and credibility. The Supreme Court would not. Hamilton conceded the weakness of his arguments (by implica-

---

[161] The Senate was originally selected by state legislatures. It became politicized in the mid-1800's and officially elective with the 17th Amendment in 1913.

tion) in *Federalist 65*. He wrote, "If mankind were to resolve to agree in no institution of government until every part of it had been adjusted to the most exact standard of perfection, society would soon become a general scene of anarchy . . ." This argument drew strength from Shays' rebellion, which had been put down in Massachusetts only four months prior to the Philadelphia convention. Hamilton further argued, in *Federalist 85*, "It appears to me to be susceptible of absolute demonstration that it will be far more easy to obtain subsequent than previous amendments to the Constitution." This did not prove to be the case. Many years have passed since Hamilton penned these words. The Senate has become elective and the Supreme Court has become powerful. The 17th Amendment would have been a convenient vehicle for correcting the error. Yet the power to try impeachment remains with the Senate. It seemed expedient to the framers to violate the separation of powers principle and leave it to us to "to obtain a subsequent amendment" correcting the flaw. This we have not done.

An approach to correcting the flaw in the impeachment provisions

The framers intended to achieve impartial justice by assigning the power to try impeachments to the Senate. Thinking it expedient, they approved this violation of the separation of powers principle in order to gain a slight benefit that soon turned into a serious flaw. The Senate became politicized and the judiciary became strong. Yet it never even occurred to the 20th century framers of the 17th Amendment to take account of these changes. They could easily have transferred the power to try impeachments to the judiciary in the same amendment that made the Senate elective. However, they were focused on one objective: making the Senate elective and thereby increasing the power of the people. They failed to notice their opportunity to more substantially increase the power of the people by transferring the power to try impeachments to the judiciary. This illustrates one of the dangers of amending the Constitution "bit by bit." The worthlessness of our existing impeachment provisions suggests that we take seriously Jefferson's suggestion. He proposed that we never allow twenty years to pass without a constitutional convention, during which the implications to other provisions of changing one provision could be discussed. Following Jefferson's advice would have enabled us to avoid unintended consequences such as the tendency of the 17th Amendment to support continued lawlessness on the parts of our civil officers.

ROOT CAUSE NO. 2—THE FLAWED ARTICLE V

Article V is flawed in that it does not provide a specific method for us, the people, to amend our Constitution. This flaw probably reflects, in part, the need in 1787 for the framers who favored a strong central government to satisfy those who wished to preserve the rights of the states. It is true that, despite Article V, we have the right to alter our Constitution whenever it seems to us to be necessary. The Declaration of Independence is explicit on this point. It gives us the "right to alter or abolish" (the Constitution) "and to institute new government." Hamilton alluded, in *Federalist 78*, to ". . . that fundamental principle of republican government which admits the right of the people to alter or abolish the established constitution whenever they find it inconsistent with their happiness." Madison echoed Hamilton in several *Federalist Papers*. The Declaration, the tenor of the Constitution and the text of the *Federalist Papers* declare us to be the supreme power. Further, Hamilton himself wrote, in *Federalist 80*, "There ought always to be a constitutional method of giving efficacy to constitutional provisions." If there ought to be a means of giving efficacy to constitutional provisions, there certainly ought to be a means of giving efficacy to the Declaration of Independence and to the tenor of our Constitution. Yet, there is still no *obvious* means of giving efficacy to what Hamilton calls the "fundamental principle" of our form of government. Our Constitution's Article V makes no mention of us, the people.[162] This is the flaw that, more than any other factor, has led to our country's present decline.

If, in fact, we had no right to alter our Constitution, we would not be living in a true democracy. We would, instead, be living in a benevolent oligarchy, a country run by a thousand or so civil officers who respond more to corporations and other special interests than to us. Because we have failed to create our own means of exercising this critical right, we do live under a form of government that is, in effect if not in theory, out of our control. We look for protection to our separation of powers, independent judiciary, elected legislature and system of checks and balances. Unfortunately, the force of these four "new discoveries" depends on the existence of a lawful and honest federal government that is impervious to the influence of "big money." In order to re-form our government so that it becomes lawful and honest, we must up-date our Constitution and correct its flaws. We must revise Article V so that it marks out for

---

162 Academics such as Akhil Reed Amar of the Yale Law School take a different view of the matter. They believe that Article V simply limits the role of the federal government in the amendment process. According to this view, the right of the people to amend the Constitution is a given. That is, it is implicit in the Constitution itself and explicit in the Declaration and in the writings of the Framers. Amar writes, in his landmark 1988 article (*Philadelphia Revisited: Amending the Constitution Outside Article V*, The University of Chicago Law Review, Vol. 55, No. 4) "Our failure to overcome inertia" (that is, our failure to propose a constitutional convention) "can plausibly be attributed to a basic (even if not perfect) contentment with, and consent to, the status quo." My own belief is that our failure can be attributed to the failure of Article V to provide us with a specific procedure for calling a convention.

future generations a clear "road to the people's decision." In order to do this, however, we must find our own way along the present unmarked and unclear "road" that is presently hidden among the Constitution's articles and amendments.

The down side to Article V:

Over and over in the *Federalist Papers*, Madison and Hamilton emphasized the power the people would have under the Constitution. In *Federalist 78*, Hamilton said we would be more powerful than Congress and the judiciary. In *Federalist 49*, Madison alluded to us as "the only legitimate fountain of power." Since, the only source of legitimate power in the US is its Constitution, we must consider what Article V (the amendment article) says. In summary, Article V says:

1. "Congress, whenever two thirds of both Houses shall deem it necessary, shall propose amendments.
2. On the application of the legislatures of two thirds of the states, Congress shall call a convention for proposing amendments.
3. Amendments shall be valid when ratified by the legislatures of three quarters of the states, or by state conventions, as the one or the other mode of ratification may be proposed by the Congress."

At first reading, Jefferson, Hamilton, Madison and the rest of our forefathers appear to have been "whistling in the wind." Their claims that, in the US the people would have the supreme power fall to the ground. In the "real world," the supreme power belongs to whoever has the ability to amend our Constitution. Article V does not even mention the people. Further, we have never exercised such a power. All of our twenty-seven amendments have been proposed by the federal government and all but one have been ratified by state legislatures. Congress has no power to call a convention unless the state legislatures request one. Congress can only "propose" amendments and can only "propose" whether they should be acted on by state legislatures or by state conventions.

Since the original Constitution was ratified by state conventions, Madison had a basis for his claim that it was "established" by the people. However, Madison also believed that it would be "alterable" by the people. Otherwise, his indication in *Federalist 53* that it would be "unalterable by the government" makes little sense. Despite Madison's claim, our Constitution has never been altered by the people. This explains, in large part, why it has been (illegally and routinely) altered by our federal government's three branches. Our neglect has created a vacuum and the federal government has (illegally) filled this vacuum. In doing so, it has controlled the amendment process, despite the clear intent of the framers that it not have the power to do so.

Despite our flawed Article V, our right to amend the Constitution is undeniable and we can create our own method for exercising this right. For example, we could require (by petition) thirty-four state legislatures to either require Congress to call a truly representative national convention or require Congress to propose (to all fifty states) an amendment to that effect. Alternatively, we could require Congress to place such an amendment on the national ballot. Either directly or acting through our state legislatures, we could rejuvenate our political system. It is true that, while the Declaration (taken with Article VII and the 1st, 9th and 10th amendments) clearly give us the right to amend the Constitution," the federal government would, no doubt, construct formidable road blocks. Should these road blocks be effective, the promises of our Declaration and Constitution would prove to be empty and our claim to have a government "of, by and for" the people would prove to be false.

The mystery of Article V:

We can only speculate as to why Madison and Hamilton wrote (in the *Federalist Papers*) as though the Constitution explicitly gives the power of amendment to the people—when, in fact, Article V doesn't even mention us. Perhaps they thought that, since the people's power to amend is explicit in the Declaration of Independence and implicit in the Constitution, we could find our own means of exercising it. Perhaps, since Article V was still being discussed as the convention was drawing to a close, time pressures caused them to lose track of it. Perhaps it was expedient to mention the state legislatures and to take the people's control over them as a given. In any case, our forefathers made a tragic error. For over two centuries we have neglected our most important duty as US voters. This has been largely due, to Article V's failure to provide us with a specific method for our use in performing this duty.

The up-side of Article V:

We should use the provisions of Article V as much as possible to avoid legal challenges. To support our specific approach (Part III suggests four possible approaches) we must look to the Declaration; the 1st, 9th and 10th Amendments; and to Article VII considered in the light of the *Federalist Papers*. The Declaration authorizes us to find a way. The 1st Amendment gives us the right to petition. The 9th and 10th Amendments give us the right to require compliance with our petitions. Article VII sets a precedent for an amendment specifying the method of its own ratification. These provisions of our supreme law guide us in mapping out our own road to a truly representative 2nd convention. This 2nd convention can give us the means for dealing with our present crises, and for mandating periodic conventions to avoid future crises. Once we bring about a truly representative convention, it could propose amendments that would lead to genuine governmental reform (See Chapter 10). The decision (as to whether ratification of the convention's proposals would be by state legislatures or state conventions) could be made by the delegates to the national convention.

The implied existence of potential "roads" to a people's decision is the upside to Article V. This genuine meaning of Article V can be determined by an examination of (1) the Declaration of Independence, (2) the tenor and structure of the Constitution, (3) the *Federalist Papers* and (4) the 1st, 9th and 10th amendments to the Constitution.

1. The Declaration of Independence gives us the right to "alter or abolish" the Constitution whenever a government "becomes destructive" of our "life, liberty and the pursuit of happiness.

2. The tenor and structure of the Constitution establish the people as the supreme power. I believe the tenor of our Constitution consists of two fundamental principles. First, our government is designed to protect the weak from the strong. Each of what Hamilton called the four "new discoveries" is aimed at providing this protection. The separation of powers seeks to prevent the strong from becoming all powerful. The checks and balances attempt to maintain the separation of powers. The independent judiciary should guarantee us impartial justice. The elected legislature should enable us to make our own laws. If these discoveries were vigorously enforced, the weak would be protected from the strong.

   The second fundamental principle is that the people, not the government, should possess the supreme power. The election provisions and the "new discoveries" seek to keep the government under our control. The Declaration of Independence itself gives us the right to alter our Constitution.

3. The *Federalist Papers*, which Jefferson said contained the "genuine meaning" of the Constitution, explicitly state that the people are our supreme power. In *Federalist 78*, Hamilton wrote, "The power of the people is superior to both" (the judiciary and the legislature). He added, "Where the will of the legislature, declared in its statutes, stands in opposition to that of the people, declared in the Constitution, the judges ought to be governed by the latter." This was very well for the original Constitution, since it was ratified by state conventions. Only one of our amendments to date, however, has been ratified in this way.[163] Even more important, not even one of our twenty-seven amendments was proposed by the people. Also in *Federalist 78*, Hamilton alludes to the "right of the decision of the people."

4. The 1st , 9th and 10th amendments give us the means to exercise our right to alter the Constitution. The 1st Amendment, among other things, gives us the right "to petition the government for a redress of grievances." This gives us the right to petition our state legislatures (or Congress) stating a grievance that our federal government is over-responsive to the influence of special interest groups and under-responsive to our needs. We could ask that the state legislatures (or Congress) assist us in bringing about a remedy by proposing to all the states a specific amendment calling for (among other things) a truly representative national constitutional convention. As to the

---

[163] This was the 21st Amendment (the repeal of prohibition). See: *The Declaration of Independence and Other Great Documents of American History*, John Grafton (ed.), Dover Publications, 2000, p. 31.

number of petitions required and the format etc. standards, we could rely on the precedent established by Sec. 3, Article XIV of the Illinois Constitution. This article states that amendments to the Constitution's legislative article may be proposed "by a petition signed by at least eight percent of the total votes cast for candidates for Governor in the preceding gubernatorial election."[164] As to the number of petitions required should we petition Congress instead of the state legislatures, Yale's Professor Amar suggests a number equal to a majority of US voters.[165] While a majority is certainly necessary to ratify an amendment, the 8% required by the Illinois Constitution would seem to be more appropriate for securing consideration of one. However, petitions are only effective if they are granted. The 9th and 10th Amendments solve this problem by making this particular kind of petition mandatory. This is so because the power granted us by the Declaration and Constitution and supported by the *Federalist Papers* would be meaningless if state legislatures (or Congress) could decline to comply with our petitions. The 9th Amendment reads, "The enumeration in the Constitution of certain rights shall not be construed to deny or disparage others retained by the people." The right to call a constitutional convention is certainly retained by a people who are the country's "only legitimate fountain of power."[166] The 10th

---

[164] Amar suggests a national petition signed by a majority of American voters (p. 1065). He bases this proposal on a provision of the 1777 Georgia Constitution. It is also worth noting that the Illinois Constitution also requires, in effect, a referendum at least once every twenty years to determine whether a state constitutional convention should be held." The people of Illinois, however, voted against a convention the last time it appeared on the ballot. Evidently, they believed that corruption can best be dealt with by "voting the rascals out" rather than by making constitutional changes.

[165] Ibid.

[166] Madison in *Federalist 49*.

Amendment reads, "The powers not delegated to the United States by the Constitution, nor prohibited by it to the States, are reserved to the States respectively, or to the people." The power to compel an application for a constitutional convention is neither delegated to the US by the Constitution nor prohibited to the States. Since by its nature it cannot be reserved to the states, it belongs to the people.

AN OBSTACLE TO DEALING WITH THESE (AND OTHER) CONSTITUTIONAL FLAWS

In order for a constitutional convention to produce genuine reform proposals, its delegates must be proportionately drawn from the population. That is, wealthy Americans should not be over represented. Allowing the use of private money in delegate elections would make a truly representative convention impossible. Until our Constitution prohibits the use of private money in delegate elections, candidates supported by corporations would win the majority of the delegate seats. Therefore, it would appear that, until we amend the Constitution we cannot amend the Constitution. One way out of this predicament might be to amend Article V without recourse to a constitutional convention.[167] Another way might be to include this "money-free" requirement in our petitions.

SUMMARY

Hamilton, had he lived longer, might have been disappoint-

---

[167] M. Farrand, The Records of the Federal Convention of 1787 (New Haven: rev. ed. 1939), 629-630. "Mr. Madison did not see any reason why Congress would not be as much bound to propose amendments applied for by two-thirds of the states as to call a convention on the like application." By the same token, the case could be made that an amendment should become law when proposed by three-quarters of the states.

ed that the people did not transfer the power to try most impeachments to the judiciary as soon as it became apparent that the Senate could not handle the job and that the judiciary could. He admitted, in *Federalist 81*, that the assignment of this key judicial power to the Senate "verged" on an absolute violation of the separation of powers and argued, that it would be much easier to amend the Constitution later than to get it right during the 1787 convention. He was right about the assignment of the power to try impeachments to the Senate being a violation. He was wrong, however, about it being easy to amend the Constitution. With one possible exception (the 21st Amendment), there has never been a genuine people's amendment to the Constitution. All the others have been proposed by the federal government and ratified by state legislatures. It is time we corrected the mistaken assignment of the power to try impeachments to the Senate. It is also time for a comprehensive review of our Constitution in the light of more than two centuries of experience.

Madison must certainly have been disappointed in the "road to the people's decision" that he believed "ought to be marked out and kept open."[168] The road is not marked out and has not been kept open. It is unmarked, overgrown and has been unused for over two centuries. However, our forefathers fought a desperate war to secure their (and our) freedom. It does not seem too much to ask of us that we find our own way along the admittedly difficult road to our "decision" in order to preserve our freedom. We and our descendants may pay a high price if we choose not to do so.

---

[168] See *Federalist 49*.

CHAPTER 9

REFORM ISSUES

While many of the issues discussed in this Chapter involve more than one branch of government, they are grouped with the branch which seems most nearly affected.

CONGRESSIONAL ISSUES

These are among the issues affecting Congress that merit discussion by a 2nd constitutional convention—should one be called. They are, first, the inaccessibility of the government to citizen suits; second, the tendency of Congress to abdicate its powers; and, third, Congress's failure to provide strict rules for the courts to follow. These strict rules are needed to protect the separation of powers, the checks and balances and the influence ordinary people can exert through elections.

The failure of Congress to mandate accessibility to the courts.

The most important of our civil rights is the right, when we are injured, to seek remedies in court.
—Chief Justice John Marshall in Marbury v. Madison (1803)

The accessibility of the courts to suits against our governments is treated here as a congressional issue since it should be remedied by law rather than by judicial action. Our right to seek redress in court is not only our most important civil right. It is one of the most important stabilizing elements in a democratic society. Let's assume that the people of a country have confidence in their courts' ability to render impartial justice and that they have access to their courts to challenge governmental actions. These people will be inclined to support their government and not inclined to rebellion or cynical indifference. In America, while most of us have had confidence in our courts in the past, our confidence is eroding. One reason for this erosion is that it is extremely difficult for us to use our judicial system to challenge governmental actions or inaction.

The erosion of our confidence in the courts:

We are becoming more and more skeptical of our judiciary's ability to render impartial justice. It is true that, compared to most of the countries of the world, America's courts are impartial. Yet we should be concerned about the erosion of their impartiality. *Gore v. Bush* (2000) dealt our faith a severe blow. While Republicans were happy with the result, even some Republicans were uneasy about the apparent partiality of the decision. The decision in *Citizens United v. FEC* has also been difficult for many of us to reconcile with the "tenor" of our Constitution.[169]

The blocking of other avenues for complaint:

Many Americans live in states with laws that fail to provide us with judicial means of securing remedies for our political

---

[169] Hamilton wrote, in *Federalist 78*, "Every act of a delegated authority, contrary to the tenor of the commission under which it is exercised, is void."

injuries. For example, Virginia has a law prohibiting referendums. Yet its state Constitution requires an opposing majority before its people can successfully challenge a governmental action. In order to show an opposing majority, a referendum is needed. Thus Virginia's referendum statute deprives Virginians of their constitutional rights. While referenda, initiative (the right of voters to propose legislation) and recall (the right of voters to remove an elected official) must be carefully designed in order to avoid negative effects, they are well worth the trouble.

The sovereignty principle:

America still clings to a principle we inherited from the old monarchies of Europe: sovereignty. This principle holds, in effect, that governments cannot be held financially accountable for their actions. This is an anachronism. It flies in the face of our constitutional principal that government exists for the good of the people, not for the benefit of its civil officers. It is true that we can file a complaint against a governing body and, so long as we seek an injunction rather than money, the sovereignty principle does not apply. But it is expensive to file and fight a case against the government. The ordinary citizen (or group of citizens) cannot afford to pay legal fees out of pocket. These fees must come on a contingency basis from money awarded the plaintiff by the court. Yet the sovereignty principle prevents such awards. This means that most Americans must "grin and bear it" when they are injured by our government.

Only those who don't need help can afford to take their grievances to court.

Finally, there are almost insurmountable difficulties with enjoining our government to take (or not to take) a given action. In theory, we can file a complaint against a state, federal or local government. However, to pursue a complaint through the trial process requires legal experience and large sums of money. This means that, as a practical matter, most Americans do not have access to the courts to seek redress for injuries inflicted on them by our governments. Ordinary people (or groups of people) have only one hope. This one hope is to secure legal and financial help from a non-governmental organization (NGO) devoted to fighting against the general abuse that has injured them. Environmental and governmental reform NGO'S, however, have their own agendas. They are not inclined to be responsive to members who are specifically threatened by the abuses of which, as a general thing, they disapprove.

What can we do to improve access to our courts?

One possible approach is to seek a constitutional right of access. Efficacy could be achieved by a clause providing for court-appointed counsel in cases charging a governmental agency with a specific injury or injuries. A special definition of standing would be required since the very nature of actions taken by the government is that they tend not to be particular to individuals or to classes of people. Since "particularity" is normally a requirement for "standing," many governmental offenses are insulated from judiciary action. Injuries inflicted by governments are often inflicted on all the people subject to the jurisdiction of the government being sued. As a result, none of these people have the "standing" required to bring an action in court.

The failure of Congress to protect its powers.

The policy of supplying, by opposite and rival interests, the defect of better motives, might be traced through the whole system of human affairs.
—James Madison, framer and 4th President in *Federalist 51*

Opposite and rival interests are certainly present in most facets of our lives. They sometimes do operate on each other in a positive way. While the "cold war" was not pleasant for the inhabitants of Korea and Vietnam, it is true that there was no world war during the time of the cold war. The governments involved acted, to an extent, as checks upon each other. Actually "supplying" these "opposite and rival interests" so that they operate upon each other in a positive way is, however, a tricky business. Madison and his fellow-framers attempted to supply them to the three branches of government in order to keep these branches separate over time. Their attempt was only partially successful. Circumstances have changed. Interdependent interests have replaced the rival interests of the three branches. The present situation features an underlying cooperation among the branches as regards the shifting of powers among them, much to the disadvantage of the "ninety percent."

Any "opposite and rival" interests in this case are between the two political parties rather than between Congress and the president. To the contrary, the interests of the president and about one half of the Members of Congress are more than similar; they are one and the same. The president can increase his personal power by assisting in the reelection of the Members of Congress who are also members of his political party. The Members of Congress themselves wish to be reelected in order to maintain their personal status and life style. This makes the prime interest of the president identical to the prime interest of about one half of Congress. This is an iron clad alliance rather than a set of opposite and rival interests. As regards the war powers, the alliance is even more strongly motivated. Far from contesting the presidential usurpation of the war powers, Congress has been and is only too happy to abdicate them. As for presidential "signing statements" that, in effect, alter bills, Congress has shown little interest in challenging them. Yet, in effect, signing statements take the final decisions on the making of laws away from the legislature and give them to the executive.

The Members of Congress and the justices of the US Supreme Court do appear to have "opposite and rival interests." In addition to being desirous of being reelected, Members of Congress want to be influential in deciding what legislation is good for the country and what is not. This is their constitutional job. They must temper their views, of course, by considering the views of their constituents. This is also both their job and a vital part of our system of government. On the other hand, it is not the job of judges and justices to consider what is good for the country. Actually, it is critical to the proper doing of their job that they not consider the good of the country. Their job is to apply the Constitution and the statutes to specific cases and controversies. We have attempted to assist them in the doing of their jobs by giving them life appointments subject to good behavior. This attempt to insulate them from outside pressures, however, has not been completely successful. While they may be free from political pressures, they are neither free from their own ideologies nor from an understandable desire to do what is best for the country. While it is Congress's job to give the courts "strict rules" which serve to "define and point out their duty in every particular case that comes before them,"[170] Congress has not seen fit to exercise this "check."

The venues of the judiciary and the president would seem, at first blush, to be so different that it would be easy to keep them apart. Yet this is not the case. While the judiciary has few resources with which to challenge the executive power, the executive head of our country has more resources at his command than any other person on earth. Assisted by their alliance with Congress, presidents are sometimes able to "pack" the courts

---

[170] See Hamilton in *Federalist 78* and *81*.

with judges and justices who are sympathetic to the executive ideology. Presidents are also able, through the issuance of policy-laden executive orders, to interpret the law—thus treading on the judiciary toe. Finally, the courts are reluctant to rule against the president on major issues. What can they do if the president ignores their decision—as Lincoln did in *Ex parte* Merryman (1861)?

Congress's abdication of the war powers:

The president wants the war powers because he can increase his personal power exponentially by exercising them.[171] To the Members of Congress, on the other hand, they are a liability. They rarely produce power or glory for individual Members of Congress. Rather, they sometimes produce blame and defeat at the polls. The congressional "solution" is obvious: simply transfer the war powers to the president. And that is exactly what Congress has done. With the War Powers Resolution of 1973, the Tonkin Gulf Resolution of 1964 and the Iraq Resolution of 2002, Congress has (illegally) negated what Madison called the "wisest" provision of the Constitution—the provision aimed at keeping the war powers out of the hands of the president.

Problems with abdication:

There are two problems with this solution however. First, it is unconstitutional. The power to declare war is a constitutional power and can be transferred only by constitutional amendment. Article V, in effect, prohibits the federal government from making constitutional amendments. To amend our supreme law is a function theoretically reserved to the people. Second, it hasn't

---

171 The framers believed and wrote that this was the case. History appears to support their views.

worked. The framers assigned the power to declare war away from the executive because they believed that anyone placed in that position would necessarily be war prone. Our wars against Korea, Vietnam, Cambodia, Nicaragua, Afghanistan and Iraq suggest that they were right.

The Members of Congress must be motivated to resume the powers they have abdicated and begin to perform the duties they have ignored.[172] Collective motivation would be extremely difficult and (experience with Congress suggests) would have little effect. Some individual Members of Congress are altruistically motivated to exercise their constitutional powers, but it takes a 2/3 majority to overrule the president on many issues. Further, Congress is unlikely to pass a bill instructing itself to take on a duty not presently being performed. A constitutional instruction from the people seems the only possibility. This instruction would give "efficacy" to Congress's existing power "to declare war."

The failure of Congress to instruct the courts:

To avoid an arbitrary discretion in the courts, it is indispensable that they should be bound down by strict rules and precedents which serve to define and point out their duty in every particular case that comes before them.
—Alexander Hamilton in *Federalist 78*

James Madison laid the philosophical groundwork for our Constitution in his *Federalist Papers*. He is rightly regarded as its father. Hamilton was also brilliant. He was able to imagine the actual implications of Madison's principles for the specific

---

[172] For example, Congress has the power (and the responsibility) to instruct the judiciary as to future guidelines where a case has been incorrectly decided. Hamilton alluded, in *Federalist 78* and *81*, to Congress's power to prescribe rules for the adjudication of cases.

arrangements required by our new republic. And we must keep in mind that the specific arrangements described by Hamilton in his *Federalist Papers* are the specific arrangements that the other framers and the ratifiers believed would take effect should the proposed constitution be approved. For this reason, they represent, (as Jefferson believed),[173] the genuine meaning of the Constitution. The above quote from Hamilton's *Federalist 78*, therefore, establishes a specific meaning for Article III. the judiciary should be "bound down by strict rules and precedents." The judiciary enjoys life tenure, but this does not mean that it can make arbitrary decisions and not be held accountable. It enjoys life tenure so that it can be free to render impartial justice—free from political pressures. However, it is not free to deviate from the people's will, as expressed by the Constitution.

Congress should make strict rules and precedents.

It is consistent with the tenor of the Constitution that Congress (the "people's branch") should make the rules that "bind" the judiciary. After all, the Constitution is America's Supreme law. And the *Federalist Papers* make it clear that the people are the "only fountain of legitimate power." Further, Hamilton is explicit in *Federalist 81*. He tells us that the legislature, "without exceeding its province, cannot reverse a determination made in a particular case; **though it may prescribe a new rule for future cases**." Congress generally includes these strict rules in the body of the specific statute concerned. As for precedents, in theory they do not threaten impartiality since they are (supposed to be) made in accordance with the people's strict rules, as expressed by Congress.

---

[173] See Jefferson's letter to Madison of Nov. 18, 1788.

Who has made strict rules in the past?

As regards constitutional cases, no one has made any rules, strict or otherwise. Therefore, it is difficult to say how it would work out in practice if strict rules were applied to the judiciary based on the genuine meaning of the Constitution. We do know that "not applying them" has not worked out well. With no strict rules to guide it, the judiciary has twisted and changed the genuine meaning of our Constitution. For example, it has condoned and participated in the illegal transfer of the power to declare war from Congress to the executive branch. Hamilton wrote, in *Federalist* 77, that the Constitution ". . . until the people have annulled or changed it . . . is binding . . . and cannot be changed by the people's representatives." It is reasonable to suppose that neither can it be changed by the judiciary, which is not elected by the people.

JUDICIAL ISSUES

Judges and justices are no less the servants of the people than are the president and the Members of Congress. It is true that they are independent in that they have life tenure. The purpose of life tenure, however, is to insulate them from political pressure. They are still bound to carry out the peoples' will as it is expressed in the Constitution and in instructions (strict rules) given them by Congress. This, at any rate, was the original intent of the framers. Jefferson, not a framer but influential nonetheless, believed that each generation should express its will by altering the Constitution (See Chapter 6). This has never happened and, partly because of the peoples' neglect, civil officers routinely violate the Constitution, justifying themselves with their "living constitution" slogan. Here two issues are suggested for the consideration of potential delegates to a second constitutional convention and by those who may be called upon to ratify a convention's proposals. The first issue is the tendency on the part of the judiciary to interpret the Constitution by giving weight to precedents in case law. The second issue is the failure of the courts to rule on the boundaries that define the powers of the three branches—when these boundaries bear on cases that come before them.

Constitutional cases and case law:

An irregular and mutable legislation is not more an evil in itself than it is odious to the people.
—James Madison in *Federalist 37*

It may be odious to Americans that the US government is prone to tamper with the Constitution, but it is not the government's fault. If each generation had held a convention and altered the Constitution as necessary, it is likely that our government would be less prone to tamper with it. The Constitution is US supreme law. Only statutes that are made pursuant to it are valid. Hamilton wrote in *Federalist 33* that the supremacy of federal statutes is "confined to laws made pursuant to the Constitution." The reason the Constitution is US supreme law in that it is (supposedly) made by the American people rather than by the government. This feature of the US governmental arrangements, the framers thought, would set America apart from other countries. It was to be the feature that would make the US truly a country governed by its people rather than by its civil officers. As events have shown, in order to turn these ideas into actual practice, the framers would have had to make Article V (the amendment article) more accessible to us. The US is lacking some of its original moral and political qualities due to the failure of Americans to hold periodic conventions.

What the *Federalist Papers* say about constitutional cases:

Hamilton wrote, in *Federalist 78*, ". . . where the will of the legislature, declared in its statutes, stands in opposition to that of the people, declared in the Constitution, the judges ought to be governed by the latter rather than the former." This statement was given effect in 1803 by the Supreme Court.[174] Hamilton also wrote, in *Federalist 78*, "the power of the people is superior to both . . ." (the power of the legislature and the power of the judiciary). It follows that where the will of the judiciary, declared in court decisions, stands in opposition to the will of the people, declared in the Constitution, the will of the people should prevail.

The problem with constitutional cases:

If the judiciary were to decide constitutional cases on the basis of the Constitution instead of citing case law, the problem would become manageable. Should a decision (or decisions) produce effects intolerable to the people, they would find their way through Article V to amend the offending part of the Constitution. This "thermostat" process might be slow, but would certainly be an improvement over the present state of chaos.

As it is, US courts often rely on case law, rather than on the Constitution, to adjudicate constitutional cases. They cite previous cases and base their arguments on them. In this way, court errors (perhaps small enough in and of themselves) lead to larger court errors. The effect is cumulative and, eventually, the

---

[174] Writing the decision in Marbury v. Madison, Chief Justice Marshall claimed for the Court the power to declare a federal statute unconstitutional. This established the principle of judicial review, which allows the judiciary to review an act or action by another branch and declare it unconstitutional.

Constitution's present day meaning is twisted and is, in some instances, contrary to the intent of the framers and ratifiers.

A case in point is *Doe v. Bush* (2003). As discussed before, the plaintiffs challenged the constitutionality of the Iraq Resolution and asked that Mr. Bush be enjoined from invading Iraq. The First Circuit dismissed the case and the Court of Appeals affirmed the dismissal. In doing so, it relied on a long list of precedents in case law. For example, it cited *Goldwater v. Carter* (1979)) in which "Justice Powell stated that courts should decline, on ripeness grounds, to decide issues affecting the allocation of power between the President and Congress until the political branches reach a constitutional impasse." This reliance on *Goldwater v. Carter* leaves the judiciary without the ability to find abdications unconstitutional. The First Circuit also cited Laird (451 F. 2d.) which held that "determining the scale and duration of hostilities" should be done "with the joint participation of the Congress and the executive." This holding is inconsistent with Madison's view that the "wisest" provision of the Constitution is the one that withholds the war powers from the executive. In short, US courts ignore their Constitution and rely, instead, on the possibly erroneous opinions of previous courts regarding its meaning.

This twisting of the Constitution as regards the war powers began with *Bas v. Tingy* (1800) in which Chief Justice Samuel Chase wrote, "Congress is empowered to declare a general war, or Congress may wage a limited war, limited in objects, in place and in time." This ruling was politically expedient at the time. However, it was used to allow Congress to authorize hostile actions without actually declaring war. This distinction led to Congress's authorizing small, undeclared wars. Eventually, a series of court rulings led, small step by small step, to Congress's authorization of limited wars with the president deciding when if and where to make use of the authorization. This delegation of the war powers to the presidency became total in the closing years of the 20th century. Our present-day courts appear to consider only previous cases (however mistaken), ignoring the explicit and substantive meaning of the Constitution. The framers explicitly expressed their desire that the power to "initiate, continue or cease" hostilities be kept out of the presidential hands.[175]

How can the problem with constitutional cases be resolved?

Congress has the power to instruct the judiciary to cite only the Declaration of Independence and the Constitution (as interpreted in the *Federalist Papers*) in considering and deciding constitutional cases. This would tend to make the operations of our government more consistent with the substantive intent of the Constitution. It would also have a positive side effect. It would create pressure for periodic constitutional conventions. The core proposal of this book (a 2nd constitutional convention) could also resolve this problem.

Cases Involving Boundaries:

Limitations of this kind (for example, the constitutional prohibition against ex post facto laws) can be preserved in practice no other way than through the medium of the courts of justice, whose duty it must be to declare all acts contrary to the manifest tenor of the Constitution void.

—Alexander Hamilton, Framer and one of the three authors of the *Federalist Papers* in *Federalist 78*

It is clearly the "manifest tenor" of the Constitution that the rule of law should be preserved by maintaining the separation of

---

[175] *The Writings of James Madison* 148, quoted by Louis Fisher, 1st.p. 11.

the three branches of government. Yet the courts have consistently declined to hear cases involving abdications and usurpations of power. Neither the Constitution nor the *Federalist Papers* are ambiguous on this matter. So how do we explain the judiciary's reluctance to do its duty? No doubt it is an onerous duty. However, it is part of the judiciary's job to stand firm in the face of criticism. It is possible that justices wonder what would happen if they ruled against the president and he ignored their ruling.[176] However, this is speculation.

How the judiciary justifies its neglect of boundary cases:

Of course, the courts give their reasons when they hand down their decisions (or refusals to decide). These reasons are startling. The courts do not justify their actions by quoting from Madison's notes of the 1787 debates, by citing the Constitution or by referring to its "genuine meaning" as expressed in the *Federalist Papers*. Instead, they cite cases in which judges or justices have expressed their opinions that boundary disputes among the branches should be left to the branches to resolve among themselves. This avenue of escape is made possible by the judiciary's power to decide what the Constitution means.[177] Thus, a court interpretation (or misinterpretation) of the Constitution is the final word unless and until the same (or a higher) court overturns it. Since the American people are the ones that are injured by these decisions and since they have no standing,[178] the decisions are rarely overturned.

---

[176] This has happened. See *Ex Parte* Merryman (1861).

[177] Hamilton wrote, in *Federalist 78*, that the Constitution "belongs to them (the courts) to ascertain its meaning."

[178] To gain standing in court, a plaintiff's (or plaintiffs') injury must be limited to the plaintiff(s) (or to a special group represented by the plaintiff(s). The injury cannot be general to the public.

Boundary cases commonly cited:

The most pernicious, destructive and irrational judicial doctrine of modern time was set forth by Justice Powell in the concurring opinion he wrote in *Goldwater v. Carter* (1979). The Powell doctrine holds that courts should decline to decide "issues affecting the allocation of power between the president and Congress until the political branches reach a constitutional impasse." It seems to have escaped Justice Powell's notice that one branch might be inclined to abdicate its powers and that another branch might to happy to "usurp" them, thus amending the Constitution without benefit of Article V. The two branches, acting in concert, would be usurping the people's exclusive power to amend the Constitution. Another commonly cited case is *Baker v. Carr* (1962). This case established the "political question" doctrine, which excuses the courts from deciding questions between two branches of government except under certain conditions.

Article III limitations on boundary cases:

Article III limits the power of the courts to "cases or controversies." The courts have assumed, for reasons unstated, that the controversy in war powers cases must be between the branches of government. For example, in *Doe v. Bush* (1973), the court found that the matter was not "ripe" because Congress and the president might yet resolve their controversy over whether or not we should invade Iraq. It ignored the fact that the plaintiffs who were members of Congress did not claim to represent Congress. They also ignored the fact that the plaintiffs included military personnel and the families of other military personnel. The controversy was not between Congress and the President. It was between the president and military personnel who did not wish to invade Iraq, the families of other military personnel who did not want their sons and daughters to die in Iraq and Members of Congress acting in their private capacities.

What can be done about boundary cases?

It seems that the courts have built a body of case law that justifies them in declining to decide boundary disputes. It also seems that they are unlikely to overturn this case law. It is possible (but unlikely) that Congress might set strict rules for the judiciary instructing it to do its duty and decide boundary disputes. It is also possible (and more likely) that the American people, might intervene by means of a constitutional convention.

EXECUTIVE ISSUES

Given the present US imbalance of powers, most executive issues involve the presidency exceeding its powers or usurping the powers of another branch. Of course, these are not solely executive issues. When Congress abdicates a power to the executive, it is also a congressional issue. The framers expected both Congress and the presidency to make attempts upon each other's powers. They staked the success of their experiment, in part, on the tendency of human beings to both covet the powers of others and to resist any attempts by others to wrest their own powers away. In that sense, executive problems are also congressional problems. They are also judicial problems since the courts do not resist executive encroachments. After all, US presidents are performing as expected, simply doing what comes naturally. Nevertheless, there is a benefit to be gotten from looking at the executive usurpations from a point of view that asks, "What is it that enables the executive to usurp powers that don't belong to it?" The following section looks at the president's dual role as both party head and president and at his increasing use of signing statements.

The President's dual role:

In order to lay a due foundation for that separate and distinct exercise of the different powers of government . . . the members of each (branch) should have as little agency as possible on the appointment of the members of the others.
　　　　　—James Madison, our fourth president, in *Federalist 51*

Madison exempted the judiciary from this general rule largely because "the permanent tenure by which appointments are held in that department must soon destroy all sense of dependence on the authority conferring them."[179] There is no reason to exempt the members of Congress from this rule—yet it would have amazed the framers had they been told that the presidency would come to exercise a considerable agency over the election of senators and house members.

The president's role in the beginning:

The framers and ratifiers understood that the Constitution they voted on did not intend the president to have any agency at all in the selection of senators and representatives. Senators, as a gesture towards "states rights," were to be appointed by state legislatures. House members were to be elected by their constituencies.[180] The House was to be the channel through which the people gave the president his "marching orders." The Senate

---

[179] See *Federalist 51*.
[180] This was in accordance with what Hamilton called the fourth "new discovery." The first three were the separation of powers, checks and balances, and the life tenures of judges and justices. See *Federalist 40*.

was to be a steadying influence on the people's "passions."[181]
To allow the presidency to exercise an "agency" on the election
of representatives and senators is an attack upon the separation
of powers. Further, every addition we allow to the powers of the
executive brings us a step closer to the concentration of governmental powers in one set of hands—Madison's definition of
tyranny.[182]

How the president's second role works:

The Constitution's pivotal[183] protection against tyranny
(impeachment, removal and disqualification) has failed. So, also,
has the check of "opposite and rival interests"[184] that the framers
assumed would motivate the members of Congress to resist any
executive encroachments. This motivation, the framers thought,
would arise from the members of Congress natural desires for
power, glory and wealth. As it happened, changes in circumstances turned the tables on the framers. While members of
Congress may have initially been able to secure power, glory and
wealth by resisting encroachments, the path to these pleasant
commodities now lies in a different direction. Now, if they
belong to the same party as the occupant of the White House,
members of Congress are well advised to keep in the president's
good graces.

---

[181] Madison, in *Federalist 63*, " . . . there are particular moments in public
affairs when the people, stimulated by some irregular passion . . . or misled
by the artful misrepresentations of interested men, may call for measures
which they themselves may be the most ready to lament and condemn."
[182] Madison, in *Federalist 47*, defined "tyranny" as the "accumulation of all
powers . . . in the same hands."
[183] James Monroe wrote this in *The People, the Sovereign*, James River Press,
p. 16.
[184] Madison used this phrase in *Federalist 51*.

How the presidency gained an agency in congressional elections:

While the two-party system established itself in the decades before the civil war, it wasn't until paid television began to dominate political campaigns that its effect on the separation of powers became so apparent. Even before robust campaign funding became so crucial to the reelection of representatives and senators, presidents had (in their capacities as chief executive officers) various tangible and intangible rewards and punishments at their disposal. When paid TV became important, presidents' control over party funds enabled them to exercise an even greater control over the political lives of their party's federal legislators. The executive is now in a position to bring considerable pressure to bear on his party's members in Congress.

The context of the "president's dual role" problem:

The president's agency in congressional appointments is not, unfortunately, the only increase that has occurred in presidential power. For example, he has become the dominant force in foreign policy and in the negotiation of treaties as well.[185] The framers intended that he do the "legwork" of treaty negotiation and leave the substantive work to the Senate. John Jay wrote, in *Federalist 64*, "Those matters which in negotiations usually require the most secrecy and dispatch are those preparatory and auxiliary measures which are otherwise not important in a national view, than as they tend to facilitate the object of the

---

[185] For another example, presidents have usurped (in effect) Congress's Article I legislative powers. Their ability to write "refusal to enforce" signing statements has given presidents the "final say" on federal legislation. George W. Bush did not veto one bill during his tenure. He found it far more effective to write signing statements.

negotiation. For these the president will find no difficulty to provide . . . Thus we see that the Constitution provides that our negotiations for treaties shall have every advantage which can be derived from talents, information, integrity and deliberate investigation, on the one hand, and from secrecy and dispatch on the other." Hamilton, who usually took the side of the executive in such matters, wrote, in *Federalist 75*, "The history of human conduct does not warrant that exalted opinion of human virtue which would make it wise in a nation to commit interests of so delicate and momentous a kind, as those which concern its intercourse with the rest of the world, to the sole disposal of a magistrate created and circumstanced as would be a President of the United States."

The greatest, and most tragic, increase in presidential power, however, has come with the illegal migration of the war powers from Congress to the executive. This increase alone gives urgency to the consideration of his dual role as both party head and head of the executive branch.

What can be done about the president's dual role?

In any rearrangement of our governmental powers, we should take into account the increased agency of the president in filling legislative positions. The increase in his agency with regard to the filling of congressional seats should be decreased or counterbalanced by checks to his other powers.

Signing Statements:

All legislative powers herein granted shall be vested in a Congress of the United States, which shall consist of a Senate and a House of Representatives.
—United States Constitution, Article I, Section I

A "signing statement" is a statement attached by a president to a bill he is signing into law. Until the 1980's, these statements were fairly innocuous. They sometimes expressed support for the bill concerned and sometimes disagreed with it. They did not, however, refuse to enforce any part of it. They understood that it is a president's job to carry out the law—not to make it. Ronald Reagan, however, changed this situation in two major respects. First, he usurped the power of Congress with signing statements that refused to carry out the law. Second, he usurped the powers of the judiciary as well by, in effect, declaring parts of bills unconstitutional in order to avoid enforcing those parts. His successors in the presidency followed suit.

The Constitution and signing statements:

Article I, Section 1 gives Congress "all legislative powers herein granted." Article I, Section 7 is specific about the process Congress must use in exercising this power. It is explicit with regard to the president's role in this process:

> "Every Bill which shall have passed the House of Representatives and the Senate shall, before it become a law, be presented to the president of the United States; if he approve he shall sign it, but if not he shall return it, with his objections to the House in which it shall have originated, who shall enter the objections at large in their Journal, and proceed to reconsider it."

If two thirds of each House approves the Bill, it becomes law despite the presidential veto. This seems clear enough. It gives Congress the final say over the making of law. When a president signs a statement saying he does not intend to enforce some certain provision(s) of a bill he is signing into law, he usurps the final say of Congress and commits an impeachable offense. That also seems clear.

Madison restates the "final say" principle established in the Constitution. He tells us, in *Federalist 48*, "It is . . . evident that none of them" (the branches of government) "ought to possess, directly or indirectly, an overruling influence over the others in the administration of their respective powers."

The argument for "refusal to enforce" signing statements:

Vetoing large and complex omnibus bills would have negative consequences for the people who would presumably be benefited by their passage into law. This means that a veto could have political costs for the president. George W. Bush solved this problem by making a record number of "refusal to enforce" signing statements. In this way he could rewrite bills without giving offence to his constituents by vetoing them. Mr. Obama, while he was critical of Mr. Bush's use of signing statements, is now using signing statements himself. Presidents often "rewrite" a bill on the grounds that certain portions of it are unconstitutional. Some academics suggest that presidents who believe a bill to be unconstitutionally encroaching on their powers should submit it for judicial scrutiny,[186] instead of attaching a "signing statement."

Congress and signing statements:

It is difficult to understand why Congress has not applied for a ruling on the constitutionality of "refusal to enforce" signing statements. This application could take the form of a complaint

---

[186] Brian Holbrook, "The constitutional significance of presidential signing statements," unpublished paper, 2008. In this paper, Holbrook cites Philip J. Cooper of the University of Kansas.

based on a number of such statements. The fact that Congress has not made an application to the Supreme Court on this matter suggests that it is not seriously interested in defending its constitutional boundaries. Madison's faith in "supplying by opposite and rival interests, the defect of better motives"[187] seems to be unfounded. It is evidently not in the personal interests of the members of Congress to defend congressional boundaries.

An example of a contested "refusal to perform" signing statement:

President Clinton exercised the authority granted him under the Line Item Veto Act. The US Supreme Court found (*Clinton v. City of New York* 524 U.S. 417, 1998) that this violated the Presentment Clause (Article I, Section 7) of the Constitution. This clause gave him only two options: either veto the bill or sign the bill. He signed the bill, but before signing it he deleted two provisions. Since the bill he made into law was not the bill passed by Congress, the Court found that he had encroached on congressional territory and that the Line Item Veto Act was unconstitutional.[188] Justice Breyer, in his dissent, cited the nondelegation doctrine. He argued that the Line Item Veto Act was legal and appropriate on both "practical" and "constitutional" grounds. Both sides cited case law to support their positions.

The American Bar Association (ABA) and signing statements:

An ABA task force report found that "signing statements" made by then President Bush (asserting his authority to disregard or decline to enforce laws adopted by Congress) under-

---

[187] He expressed this faith in *Federalist 51*.
[188] *Clinton v. City of New York*, 524 U.S. 417 (1998).

mined the rule of law and our constitutional separation of powers. The report recommended that Congress adopt legislation enabling its members to seek court review of such signing statements. It urged presidents to veto bills that they believe to be unconstitutional.[189] These recommendations do not appear to have had any effect on either Congress or the presidency.

What can be done about signing statements?

It would appear that the prescription of some rules by Congress in the matter of adjudicating "refusal to enforce" signing statements is needed. However, since Congress does not appear to be interested in protecting its boundaries, the "buck" stops with the US people. The issue of signing statements could be taken up by a 2nd constitutional convention.

[189] ABA Press Release dated July 24, 2006.

CHAPTER 10

CONSTITUTIONAL CHANGES NEEDED

Governmental reform presents a special problem in that genuine reform cannot be accomplished by statute. Statutes belong to Members of Congress: some of the very civil officers that need to be held accountable. At the same time, in order to be effective, reform provisions must be as explicit and specific as statutes. If it is left to Congress to write statutes interpreting constitutional generalities, we can be assured that no real reform will take place.[190] For this reason, our constitutional changes must be explicit and detailed. They must be very similar to statutes because they must do the same job that is done by those laws dealing with non-reform matters. That is, they must give efficacy to general principles. At this point, genuine reform cannot be accomplished by amending existing constitutional provisions one-by-one and hoping the amendments do not have neg-

---

[190] At least one of the framers agreed. James Madison's Notes of Debates in the Federal Convention of 1787 (for Sept. 15) read, in part, "Col. Mason thought the plan of amending the Constitution exceptionable and dangerous. As the proposing of amendments is in both the modes to depend, in the first immediately, in the second, ultimately, on Congress, no amendments of the proper kind would ever be obtained by the people, if the government should become oppressive, as he verily believed would be the case."

ative, unintended consequences—as did the 17th Amendment.[191] We must, instead, make a comprehensive review of the Constitution and propose a consistent set of interrelated amendments. The constitutional vehicle for doing this is, as indicated previously, is the constitutional convention.

This Chapter proposes language for use in amending some existing constitutional provisions in Articles I, II, III and V. It also proposes language for use in writing a badly needed impeachment article. These proposals are not based on a comprehensive review of the Constitution. They should be taken, along with the proposals of others,[192] as a starting point for such a review to be conducted by a 2 nd constitutional convention.

ARTICLE I—CONGRESS

Section 1:
NOTE: "All legislative powers herein granted shall be invested in a Congress of the United States, which shall consist of a Senate and House of Representatives."

Suggested additional language: "No Member of Congress shall serve for more than a total of six years, whether in the Senate or the House of Representatives, or in a combination of both."

Section 3—The Senate, Paragraph 6:
NOTE: "The Senate shall have the sole power to try impeachments. When sitting for that purpose they shall be on oath or affirmation. When the President of the United States is tried, the Chief Justice shall preside: And no person shall be convicted without the Concurrence of two thirds of the Members present."

---

[191] The 17th Amendment, by making the Senate elective, sounded the death knell to the impeachment provisions.

[192] For example, Larry Sabato's excellent book titled *A More Perfect Constitution* proposes possible constitutional changes—including a balanced budget amendment.

Suggested language: "The Senate shall have the power, subject to review by the Director of the General Accountability Office, to try all impeachments of the judiciary. When sitting for that purpose senators shall be on oath or affirmation to consider only the evidence and the law, giving no weight to their own opinions regarding the good of the Country, of their political Party, of the defendant or of themselves. And no person shall be convicted without the concurrence of two thirds of the Members present."

Section 3—The Senate, Paragraph 7:

NOTE: "Judgment in cases of impeachment shall not extend further than to removal from office and disqualification to hold and enjoy any office of honor, Trust of Profit under the United States, but the Party convicted shall nevertheless be liable and subject to Indictment, Trial, Judgment and Punishment according to Law."

Suggested language: "Judgment in cases of impeachment shall not extend further than to removal from office and disqualification to hold and enjoy any office of honor, Trust of Profit under the United States but the civil officer involved, whether or not impeached or tried or convicted, shall nevertheless be liable and subject to Indictment, Trial, Judgment and Punishment according to Law."

Section 4—Elections, Meetings:

NOTE: (There is no mention of funding in the existing Section 4).

Suggested language: "The election campaigns of senators and representatives shall be funded, in their entirety, by federal funds appropriated for that purpose. No other funding is permissible. The contribution, solicitation or use of private funds in federal elections shall be a felony."

Section 7, Paragraph 2, Sentence 1:
NOTE: "Every Bill which shall have passed the House of Representatives and the Senate, shall, before it becomes a Law, be presented to the President of the United States; if he approve he shall sign it, but if not he shall return it with his objections to that House in which it shall have originated, who shall enter the Objections at large on their journal and proceed to reconsider it."

Suggested language: "Every Bill which shall have passed the House of Representatives and the Senate, shall, before it becomes a Law, be presented to the President of the United States; if he approve he shall sign it, but if not he shall return it with his objections to that House in which it shall have originated, who shall enter the Objections at large on their journal and proceed to reconsider it. The President shall vigorously enforce every provision of every Bill that he or she signs. If the President doubts the constitutionality of any provision of a Bill, he or she shall refer the entire Bill to the Supreme Court for review." Any failure on the part of a president to observe this, or any other constitutional provision, shall be an impeachable offense.

Section 8, Powers of Congress, Paragraph 11:
NOTE: "To declare war, grant Letters of Marque and Reprisal, and make rules concerning Captures on Land and Water."

Suggested language: "To have the exclusive power to declare war and to order actions that might lead to war; to have the prime responsibility for avoiding war; to have the exclusive power of ordering by a specific date (not authorizing) all actions taken by US forces that might lead to war; and to establish (by transferring the CIA and other strategic intelligence services) a strategic intelligence capability in Congress's General Accountability Office thus enabling Congress to exercise the congressional powers herein granted."

Section 8, Powers of Congress, Paragraph 15:

These additional powers have to do with: "To provide for calling forth the Militia to execute the Laws of the Union, suppress Insurrections and repel Invasions."

Suggested language: "To order (not authorize) the calling forth of the Militia by a specific date to execute the Laws of the Union, suppress Insurrections and repel Invasions."

Section 8—Additional powers suggested for Congress:

NOTE: The funding of elections, the setting of judiciary standards, the balancing of the budget, global warming and the transfer of the strategic intelligence services are not mentioned.

Suggested language covering the setting of judiciary standards: "In order to avoid an arbitrary discretion in the courts, Congress shall set strict rules which serve to define and point out the judiciary's duty in every particular case that comes before a court. There shall be separate rules for constitutional cases assuring the immutability of the Constitution."

Suggested language covering the balancing of the budget: (No suggested language for this extremely complex change is included in this book. It is crucial to balance the budget, but it is also necessary to provide for some flexibility. A convention for governmental reform should consult with both conservative and liberal economists, debate the various approaches, and develop the constitutional language needed to meet both these needs).

Suggested language for global warming: "X percent of the annual budget shall be devoted to environmental research and experimentation (including, but not limited to, wind, wave, solar and geothermal energy) and to the application of research findings in the United States and abroad. The Senate shall set a high priority on entering into international global warming treaties."

Suggested language for the transfer of the strategic intelligence resources: "In accordance with the last paragraph of Article I, Section 8, Congress shall assign the necessary intelligence service resources, to support the making of all decisions on war and peace, to the legislative branch's General Accountability Office, including but not limited to the CIA and all other strategic intelligence services."

NOTE: No doubt, if a 2nd convention is called, the delegates will identify other areas for discussion (for example, health, the general environment, natural resource governance, etc.) and develop language dealing with them.

Section 9—Prohibitions:
NOTE: (There is presently no prohibition of torture)

Suggested language for the prohibition of torture: "Under no circumstances shall any person or part of the United States torture any human being as torture is defined by the Geneva Conventions. Neither shall any detainee or other human being be sent to a country where torture is allowed or may be practiced. Officers of the United States shall be legally responsible for any torture that occurs under them in the chain of command. The penalty for torture (or for the failure to prevent torture by subordinates within one's chain of command) shall be a minimum of 30 years in prison with no possibility of parole or early release."

ARTICLE II—THE EXECUTIVE

Section 1, Paragraph 1:

NOTE: "The executive power shall be invested in a President of the United States of America. He shall hold his office during the term of four years, and, together with the Vice-President chosen for the same Term, be elected, as follows:

Suggested language: "The executive power shall be invested in a President of the United States of America. This person shall hold his or her office during the term of four years. Campaign funds shall be granted all qualified candidates in the same amount; Standards for qualification shall be set by Congress. The Vice-President shall be chosen for the same Term. Election campaigns will use granted federal funds exclusively; the contribution, solicitation or use of private funds in any federal election, or in the ratification of constitutional proposals, shall be a felony. The candidate with the most individual votes shall be declared the winner."

Section 1, Paragraph 7:

NOTE: "Before he enters on the Execution of his Office, he shall take the following Oath or Affirmation: I do solemnly swear (or affirm) that I will faithfully execute the Office of President of the United States, and will to the best of my ability, preserve, protect and defend the Constitution of the United States."

Suggested language: "Before entering on the Execution of their Office, presidents shall take the following Oath or Affirmation: 'I do solemnly swear (or affirm) that I will faithfully execute the Office of President of the United States, and will to the best of my ability, preserve, protect and defend the Constitution of the

United States. I will not usurp, accept or exercise any power belonging to another branch. I understand that, if I violate this oath, I will be subject to impeachment, conviction and disqualification.'"

Section 2, Paragraph 1:

NOTE: "The President shall be Commander in Chief of the Army and Navy of the United States, and of the militia of the several states, when called into the actual service of the United States; he may require the opinion, in writing, of the principal officer in each of the executive Departments, upon any subject relating to the duties of their respective Offices, and he shall have Power to Grant Reprieves and Pardons for Offences against the United States, except in Cases of Impeachment."

Suggested language: "The President shall be Commander in Chief of the Army and Navy of the United States, and of the militia of the several states, when the militia is called by Congress into the actual service of the United States. Except where a war has been declared by Congress or where a military action has been specifically ordered to be taken by a given date (not authorized) by Congress, he or she shall take no military action (including the use of drones, missiles or air strikes), however small, that is hostile or may lead to hostilities; he or she may require the Opinion, in writing, of the principal officer in each of the executive Departments, upon any subject relating to the duties of their respective Offices, and he or she shall have Power to Grant Reprieves and Pardons for Offences against the United States, except in instances where the party has been impeached or Congress has considered impeachment and the party has resigned."

Section 4, Paragraph 1:

NOTE: "The President, Vice President and all civil officers of the United States, shall be removed from Office on Impeachment for, and Conviction of, Treason, Bribery or other high Crimes and Misdemeanors, ..."

Suggested language: "The President, Vice President and all civil officers of the United States, shall be removed from Office and disqualified to hold any Office of Honor, Trust or Profit under the United States upon Impeachment for, and Conviction of, Treason, Bribery or other high Crimes and Misdemeanors, including but not restricted to all felonies, actions that exceed constitutional powers, usurpations of power, constitutional violations and violations of oaths or affirmations. The long-term good of this country is always best served by vigorous enforcement of this provision."

ARTICLE III—THE JUDICIARY

Section 1—1st Sentence:
NOTE: "The judicial power of the United States, shall be vested in one Supreme Court, and in such inferior courts as the Congress may from time to time ordain and establish."

Suggested language: "The judicial power of the United States, with the exception of the power to try judicial impeachments, shall be vested in one Supreme Court, and in such inferior courts as the Congress may from time to time ordain and establish."

ARTICLE V—Lines 1-7:

NOTE: "The Congress, whenever two thirds of both Houses shall deem it necessary, shall propose Amendments to this Constitution, or, on the application of the legislatures of two thirds of the several states, shall call a Convention for proposing

Amendments, which, in either Case, shall be valid to all Intents and Purposes, as part of the Constitution, when ratified by the Legislatures of three fourths of the several states, or by conventions in three fourths thereof, as the one or the other Mode of Ratification may be proposed by the Congress."

Suggested language: "Section 1 The Congress, whenever so petitioned by a number of the nation's registered voters equal to or larger than eight percent of the number of voters casting ballots in the last presidential election, or when application is made by the legislatures of two thirds of the several states, shall (1) propose ratification by state conventions if a specific amendment is petitioned or applied for, or (2) call a convention for proposing amendments if such a convention is petitioned or applied for, or (3) place a proposition for recall, policy change or legislative initiative on the next national ballot if such a proposition is petitioned or applied for, or (4) place an advisory or binding referendum on the next national ballot if such a referendum is petitioned or applied for. The use of private money in all related elections, ratifications, petitioning drives, propositions, referendums and ballots is prohibited. The solicitation, use or acceptance of such funds shall be a felony."

"Section 2 State legislatures, whenever petitioned by a number of the state's registered voters equal to or greater than eight per cent of the voters in the state's last gubernatorial; election, shall make application for either the proposal by Congress of a specific amendment or specific amendments to the US Constitution for ratification or for the calling of a national constitutional convention—whichever is petitioned for. In the event nineteen years pass without either the people or the states calling for a national convention, Congress shall call such a convention itself. Each state shall be entitled to send one delegate from each of its congressional districts to each national proposing convention. Proposed amendments shall be valid to all intents and purposes when ratified by state conventions elected in three quarters of the states for the specific purpose of considering proposed amendments. Ratifying conventions in each state shall act upon proposed amendments within six months of the date the proposed amendments are received by the state legislature. Each state shall hold a ratifying convention within six months of receiving a proposed amendment. The election of delegates to federal and state conventions held to propose or ratify amendments to the US Constitution shall involve only public funds. The donation, solicitation or use of private funds in any federal election, to include all elections of delegates for the purpose of proposing or ratifying constitutional amendments, shall be a felony. The placing or accepting of political advertisements (in any form of media) that tend to support or oppose any candidate or issue involved in such elections shall be a felony. Congress shall call a constitutional convention for the purpose of proposing amendments within three months of the date this amendment becomes law. This amendment, unless proposed by three-quarters of the state legislatures (in which case it shall immediately become law) shall be considered and acted upon by state ratifying conventions elected for this purpose.

Constitutional conventions shall consist of one delegate from each congressional district. The seven delegates receiving the highest percentages of votes shall convene two weeks prior to the convention to prepare a proposed set of "rules of order" which, when convened, all delegates will vote on and abide by the approved rules during the convention."[193]

---

[193] A few days prior to the close of the 1787 convention, Madison attempted to delay approval of Article V until it was re-written to include the detail needed to give it what Hamilton called "efficacy." In the rush to sign the Constitution, Article V was approved by the convention without this necessary detail. We should be careful not to make this same grievous error a second time.

ARTICLE VIII—A NEW ARTICLE FOR IMPEACHMENT

NOTE: (There is no existing Article VIII)

Suggested Introductory Language: "Since impeachment is a crucial judiciary power and history has shown that it cannot be given its necessary vigor by statute, it is provided for here with specificity. The goal of this amendment is to assure the observance of our Constitution and statutes by our civil officers and assure their responsiveness to the needs and will of the people."

Section 1—The powers to investigate, impeach, prosecute and try cases of impeachments.

Suggested language: "The General Accountability Office shall have the power of investigating and prosecuting, where appropriate, the civil officers of all branches of government. The House of Representatives shall have the sole power to impeach civil officers of the judiciary and may appoint grand juries from among its members for this purpose. The US Supreme Court shall have the power to impeach civil officers of the executive and legislative branches and may appoint grand juries from among the justices of subordinate courts for this purpose. The Senate shall have the sole power to try all impeached civil officers of the judiciary and may appoint a court from among its members for this purpose. The term "sole" distinguishes the power of the House, (or other impeaching body) to determine the impeachability of alleged offenses and the adequacy of the evidence, from the power of the Senate (or other court of impeachment) to determine whether or not the defendant committed the alleged offense(s). Civil officers of the executive and legislative departments, including the president and vice-president, shall be impeached by grand jury. Civil officers of the executive and legislative departments, except for the president and vice-president, shall be tried in the appropriate district court. The Supreme Court shall try impeached presidents and vice-presidents. Neither impeachment decisions nor the decisions of impeachment juries or courts are subject to appeal. When sitting on grand juries or courts for the purpose off impeaching or trying civil officers, members of all such courts shall be on oath or affirmation to render impartial justice. Every impeaching body and court of impeachment shall be provided with a presiding officer from among the justices of the appropriate circuit court. This presiding officer shall have the power to make final rulings on all legal questions."

Section 2—Coverage
Suggested language: "Civil officers are all Members of Congress, the president, vice-president, and all presidential appointees of the executive and judiciary departments."

Section 3—Purposes and means of impeachment
Suggested language: "The purpose of judgments in cases of impeachment is to deter unconstitutional, lawless, corrupt and compromising acts on the parts of US civil officers. This shall be done by the rapid, routine and certain removal and mandatory disqualification of all officers who commit impeachable acts. No impeachment defendant shall be protected by any due process rule or technicality of the criminal law during any stage of impeachment proceedings, but shall be entitled to all the protections of criminal law, if indicted after resignation or removal under these provisions. The strict constitutional and statutory rules of impeachment shall be formed solely for the purposes of (a) deterring civil officers from committing impeachable misdeeds, and (b) assuring that all civil officers who commit such misdeeds are quickly removed and disqualified. Impeachment

defendants shall not be presumed innocent until proved guilty. To assume innocence would place the entire population at risk in order to protect one civil officer defendant appearing not as a person—but as a representative of the government."

Section 4—Separation of the impeachment powers

Suggested language: "The power to impeach consists of the sole power to determine whether or not alleged offenses are impeachable, the sole power to determine whether or not there is probable cause to believe the defendant committed them, and the sole power to determine whether the evidence is adequate to justify a trial. The power to try is the power to determine whether or not the defendant committed the act charged and, if so, to remove the defendant and disqualify him or her from any future position of honor and trust and from any privileges, protections and entitlements associated with retired civil officers of his or her rank. Removal and disqualification are mandatory upon conviction. The exercise of these powers is final and is not subject to any review either administrative or judicial. All impeached civil officers must be tried; whether or not they have resigned."

Section 5—Impeachment criteria

Suggested language: "The President, Vice-President and all civil officers of the United States shall be removed from office and permanently disqualified from any civil officer position (and from any honors, privileges and entitlements that might otherwise be due, including diplomatic assignments or other recognitions that might detract from the deterrent effects of his or her impeachment) upon a judgment that they have committed: any act that (a) oversteps the bounds of their constitutional powers, (b) usurps the power of another branch or body, (c) abdicates any of their constitutional powers, (d) violates an oath or affirmation (including oaths of office and the oath or affirmation sworn to by grand juries and courts of impeachment), (d) interferes with the rendering of impartial justice in the United States, (e) interferes with the administration or enforcement of a law of the United States, (f) accepts or solicits from any source money, favors, travel tickets or expenses, tickets to events, accommodations, meals or any other item of value, (g) commits any felonious act [194] or (h) engages habitually in behavior that insulates the civil office from a knowledge of the concerns and circumstances of ordinary Americans (for example, the use of business or first class air travel while traveling on government-related business). The Supreme Court will have original jurisdiction over presidential and vice-presidential trials. The grand jury for presidential and vice-presidential impeachments shall consist of randomly selected appellate justices."

Section 6—Resignations
Suggested language: "Civil officers who resign their positions are nevertheless subject to impeachment, trial, conviction and disqualification. No civil officer may be pardoned for an alleged or actual impeachable offense, either before or after impeachment, resignation or conviction. Civil officers who resign after an impeachment vote has been scheduled but before being impeached are automatically disqualified for life from service in any civil officer position or other position of honor and trust."

Section 7—Special oaths
In the Clinton trial, the senators and presiding officer took the following oath or affirmation: "Do you solemnly swear that in all things pertaining to the trial of the impeachment of William Jefferson Clinton, President of the United States, now pending,

---

[194] Offering a civil officer of the United States any of these items, or any other item of value, is a felony.

you will do impartial justice according to the Constitution and laws so help you God?" This oath (or affirmation) did not prevent some senators from voting to acquit because they thought it would be best for the country. These votes suggest that their oaths were not sufficiently explicit.[195]

Suggested language: "Do you solemnly swear that, in the impeachment proceeding of John Doe, now pending, you will find only with regard to the defendant's guilt or innocence of the acts alleged, taking into consideration only the evidence and the law, and disregarding public opinion, your own opinion as to whether or not the alleged offenses are impeachable, and your own opinions concerning what outcome might be good for the country, good for your party, good for your constituents, or good for your own personal interests, so help you God?"

Section 8—Congressional rules governing impeachment and trial

Suggested language: "Congress shall establish by statute strict rules covering, but not limited to, (a) the relationship between criminal and impeachment law, (b) criteria for impeachable behavior, (c) oaths for impeachment courts and grand juries, (d) criminal penalties for communications to impeachment courts, grand juries and congressional bodies appointed to serve in these capacities, (e) criteria for the recusal of impeachment court members, (f) the nature of due process as it applies and does not apply to impeachment proceedings, (g) standards of proof and evidence for impeachment trials, (h) impartiality, and (i) two-issue voting. Congress shall establish strict rules triggering the impeachment of presidents violating the constitutional assignment of the war powers. These rules shall limit the ability of a

---

[195] See Chapter 11 of my 2009 book, *After Patrick Henry*, for a discussion of the Clinton impeachment and trial.

president to use force to (a) cases where US air or ground space has been violated or will be violated immediately if no action is taken, (b) cases where Congress has explicitly ordered the president to use force immediately upon a specific target (authorizations constitute impermissible delegations of constitutional power), and (c) cases where Congress has formally declared war.

ARTICLE IX—AN ADDITION TO THE BILL OF RIGHTS

NOTE: (There is no existing amendment establishing the right to organize)

Suggested language: "The right of the people to organize or join trade unions and student unions shall not be infringed. Such trade and student unions being consistent with the people's well being and life satisfaction, the organization of and membership in them shall not be impeded either by management intervention, by any fear of retaliation, or by the imposition of voting procedures that discourage the formation or continuance of trade or student unions."

PART III

SUMMARY AND NEXT STEPS

The only real security of liberty in any country is the jealousy and circumspection of the people themselves. Let them be watchful over their rulers. . . . Should the government, on trial, be found to want amendments, these amendments can be made in a regular method, in a manner prescribed by the Constitution itself.
—James Iredell speaking to the NC convention on July 28, 1788

CONCLUSIONS, STRATEGIES AND ROLES

Events of the past half-century have borne out Iredell's belief that Americans cannot rely upon their government to secure their liberty. He was certainly correct in thinking that we should be "watchful over our rulers." He was optimistic; however, in thinking that, when future generations found their government to require reform, they would make the necessary constitutional amendments, "in a manner prescribed by the Constitution itself."

What has gone wrong? In short, Americans and their activist organizations (such as Public Citizen, Common Cause, Move on, the Tea Party and Occupy) have adopted unworkable reform strategies. They seek to reform their government by criticizing it, protesting, marching, petitioning it and occupying it. This is nonsensical for several reasons. First, genuine reform requires the altering of government powers and the 1,000 or so civil officers of the US government are employees of the people and cannot alter their own powers. As Madison put it, the US Constitution is "unalterable" by the government. Secondly, genuine reform is contrary to the personal interests of these civil officers. Why should rational human beings be expected to deprive themselves of their, incomes, opportunities for wealth, elitist life styles and celebrity status—even if they had the power to do so? Thirdly, the American people and their activist organizations have the motivation, the power, the means and the duty to reform their government. It is past time for us (and our activist organizations) to stop complaining and begin acting. All that is needed to wrest control of the US away from special interest groups, corporations and big money is the joining together of the rank-and-file Republicans and Democrats who make up ninety percent of America's population.

It is true that the "regular method" prescribed by the Constitution for its own alteration has so far been inaccessible to ordinary Americans. All 27 constitutional amendments have been proposed by the federal government and all but one have been ratified by state legislatures rather than state conventions.[196] The framers thought, perhaps, that they were giving future generations a workable method to use when the Constitution "wants amendments." No doubt the method given us is workable in theory. It is also vague and inexplicit. But this does not excuse our negligence. The Declaration of Independence gives us the power and it is up to us to devise a procedure. America will continue to decline in terms of democracy, competitiveness, prosperity and morality if a procedure consistent with Article V and with the tenor of the Constitution is not developed and used.

Chapter 8 proposes a possible procedure. It now remains to summarize some of the specific conclusions that can be drawn from the historical material presented in Parts I and II of this book—and to propose a Jeffersonian approach to reversing America's decline. For the reader's convenience, Section A of this Part re-states these specific conclusions. Section B summarizes a strategy for bringing about a "money-free" "proposing" convention. Section C comments on the "roles" that must be played by various societal groups in order to organize and carry out a successful reform movement.

A. REFORM CONCLUSIONS

Here are twenty-one specific conclusions that bear on governmental reform. They are based on material presented and discussed in previous chapters of this book.

---

[196] Congress "proposes" (in effect, decides) whether a proposed amendment will be ratified by state legislatures or by state conventions. Congress can also propose amendments and call conventions. It has never called a national convention and has only once chosen to have a proposed amendment ratified by state conventions rather than be state legislatures.

1. OUR FEDERAL GOVERNMENT IS LAWLESS, CORRUPT AND UNRESPONSIVE.

Our executive branch has usurped the war powers. It has also usurped Congress's legislative powers. It now writes laws by attaching "signing statements" to congressional bills. Our Congress abdicates some of its powers and fails to exercise others. Our judiciary makes decisions that seem to be far from impartial. Congress fails to impeach members who are blatantly dishonest. Members of Congress write laws that give them access to corporate money. Congress fails to regulate industries that can (and do) inflict catastrophic damage on our finances and our environment. Our election system no longer serves as a check on lawless, corrupt and unresponsive behavior on the parts of Members of Congress. Candidates are dependent on corporate money for their election campaigns and are therefore more responsive to corporations than to their constituents. Since corporate short-term interests are often in conflict with the people's long-term interests, public policies are in a state of disrepair.

2. OUR COUNTRY IS DECLINING IN TERMS OF COMPETITIVENESS, PROSPERITY AND MORALITY.

Within the past decade our country has fallen from its number one rankings in "world competitiveness" and "prosperity." It is now ranked fourth in competitiveness and tenth in prosperity. If the way we distribute our national income and the way we use our military forces are indications of national morality, our decline is even more marked in these respects. We are ranked 73rd among the nations of the world on the Gini index of income equality. The people who do our undeniably useful work (such as picking up our trash, protecting us from crime and educating our children) receive a tiny fraction of the compensation gathered in by people who provide no useful product or service but, instead, cost us trillions of dollars through their financial escapades. Our military adventures cost money and inflict death and debilitating injuries on both military personnel and innocent civilians. We are losing our international reputation for democracy and a respect for human rights. We are now regarded in some parts of the world as militaristic, brutal, environmentally indifferent, and inclined to torture.

3. SOMETHING MUST BE DONE.

In addition to the short-term damage being done by our defective political system, it is leading us into tyranny. Our government's lawlessness, corruption and lack of responsiveness are not only inflicting immediate injuries on us and on the people of other countries. They are also leading us down the path away from our remnants of self-government toward elective tyranny. War is as dangerous to our personal liberties as it is to the lives and the bodies of those who are killed or maimed by it. It is used, for example, to justify wire tapping and violations of *habeas corpus*. A perpetual state of war, such as our "war" against terrorists, presents a cumulative threat to our freedom. Just as serious, a perpetual war concentrates more and more power in the executive branch. As Madison remarked in *Federalist 47*, "The accumulation of all powers . . . in the same hands . . . may justly be pronounced the very definition of tyranny."

4. THE PROBLEM DOES NOT LIE WITH OUR CIVIL OFFICERS.

Blaming our civil officers for our present predicament makes no more sense than blaming water for running downhill.

Rational people do what brings them pleasure and avoid doing what causes them pain. Our civil officers are rational people. We have so arranged the checks and balances of our government that it is pleasant for them to favor corporations and other special interest groups and unpleasant for them to favor us. It is true that some people are so constituted that they receive their main pleasure from honest, unselfish behavior. However, they are in the minority. Further, it is not the responsibility of our civil officers to "new model" government. They are servants not masters. Their job is to follow our instructions. They have no power to effect genuine reform.

5. THE PROBLEM LIES WITH OUR POLITICAL SYSTEM.

Our civil officers' behavior is determined by the rewards and punishments integral to our political system. If our political system were to make it more pleasurable and less painful for federal civil officers to devote themselves to our interests and needs, they would do so. In effect, our interests and needs would become their interests and needs. Our political system, however, makes it pleasurable for them to favor special interest groups over ordinary people—and, of course, that is what they do. There are many ways by which our political system could have made (and still could make) it pleasant for our civil officers to adopt lawful, honest and responsive behaviors. There are also many ways our political system could make lawless, corrupt and unresponsive behavior unpleasant. For example, vigorous impeachment provisions would make impeachable behavior extremely unpleasant. They would quickly humiliate and disqualify miscreants—as well as removing them. It is our duty—not the duty of government—to establish our political system.

6. THE CONSTITUTION IS NOT THE PROVINCE OF GOVERNMENT.

Our political arrangements are in no way the responsibility of our civil officers. The Constitution is not the province of government. As Madison wrote in *Federalist 53*, it is "unalterable" by government. Madison and his fellow framers regarded this fact as a critical and (at the time) unique feature of our form of government. It is the feature without which our civil officers are our masters—rather than our servants.

7. WE, THE PEOPLE, ARE RESPONSIBLE FOR REJUVENATING OUR GOVERNMENT.

Our Declaration of Independence gives us the right to "alter or abolish" our government when it becomes "destructive" of our "life, liberty and the pursuit of happiness." The nature of our government is determined by our Constitution. Madison wrote, in *Federalist 53*, that we (the people) have the power to "establish" the Constitution and that our government does not have this power to alter it. Hamilton wrote, in *Federalist 78* that "it is the right of the people to alter or abolish the established constitution whenever they find it inconsistent with their happiness." Every right, of course, has its concomitant responsibility. Our responsibility in this case is to alter the Constitution so that it makes efforts on behalf of the people in the self-interests of our civil officers. We owe this to future generations as well as to ourselves. Hamilton wrote "The security of the society must depend on the care which is taken to confide the trust to proper hands, to make it in their interest to execute it with fidelity, and to make it as difficult as possible for them to combine in any interest opposite to that of the public good." It makes little sense for us to complain about our federal government to our civil officers—when the responsibility for altering it is our own.

8. A CONSTITUTIONAL CONVENTION IS REQUIRED.

A constitutional convention is required for two major reasons. First, the only alternative would be to call upon Congress to pass reform statutes or to propose constitutional amendments. Since genuine reform is not in the best interests of the Members of Congress, the results would be "dishwater" statutes. Passing ineffectual laws would have disastrous consequences. Not only would these laws be worthless themselves. Their passage would take the energy out of any effort at genuine reform. The futility of calling upon Congress to propose a constitutional amendment or amendments is discussed under "Strategies for Reform" (Section B). Second, a number of amendments are required and each one needs to take into account all the others —along with the existing provisions of the Constitution. We have seen the result when an amendment is crafted without this comprehensive analysis: the 17th Amendment perpetuated the most serious weakness of the impeachment provisions. A 2nd convention should be representative of ordinary Americans (and not of the "one percent."). Otherwise, it would simply perpetuate our present difficulties.

9. INCREMENTAL REFORM IS NOT ENOUGH.

We are in a state of crisis. Incremental improvements in the way our government is organized are not a sufficient remedy for its many weaknesses. Further, time is not on our side. We are deteriorating rapidly and bold steps are necessary to stop this deterioration. The original framers were in a similar situation.

The Confederation of States was deteriorating rapidly. The Articles of Confederation were inadequate to the task. They were causes of the crisis—not remedies for it. The delegates to the Philadelphia convention realized this and, rather than make incremental improvements in the Articles, wrote a new Constitution. We do not need a new Constitution. But we need to correct a large number of closely related ills that afflict us because we have failed to follow Jefferson's advice. He believed we should give our Constitution a comprehensive review at least once each twenty years. In this way we could both correct its flaws and bring it up-to-date. We need to rewrite our impeachment provisions, our electoral provisions and our amendment provisions. They need to be made explicit and strong. They need to give "efficacy" to the implicit intent of the existing Constitution: that ours is a government of, by and for the people. This requires, not a set of statutes, but a comprehensive overhaul of the Constitution. There is a particular urgency to rewriting the impeachment provisions and Article V. There is also a particular urgency to writing provisions governing election funding, setting term limits and balancing our national budget. The impeachment provisions must be re-written so as to make it extremely unpleasant for a civil officer to violate a clear set of easily enforceable rules. The power of the people rests on Article V. It must be re-written to explicitly define a clearly marked and accessible road to our decision on major policy issues.

10. THE CONVENTION SHOULD BAR FEDERAL CIVIL OFFICERS FROM PARTICIPATION.

The civil officers of the federal government have managed to usurp the power of the states and of the people by controlling the amendment process. Congress proposes amendments and also "proposes" the body to ratify them. If the federal government is allowed to set the agenda and propose amendments at a convention to reform government, its "reforms" will be worthless. Madison in *Federalist 10* and Hamilton in *Federalist 80* remind us that "no man should be judge in his own cause." Federal civil officers should not be allowed to participate in designing the checks that would make the pleasures they now enjoy unlawful. Their position as the representatives of the only body in a central position at a national convention would give them *de facto* control of the agenda. On the other hand, if the federal government were not represented, the states could develop their own coordinating body with the single purpose of presiding over the convention. In this way a set of genuine reform proposals could be developed.

11. PRIVATE MONEY MUST BE PROHIBITED IN THE ELECTION OF DELEGATES.

This means that the state legislatures should be petitioned to require Congress either to call a "money free" convention or to propose to the 50 states an amendment that would not only require Congress to call a convention, but would includes prohibiting the use of private money in electing delegates to the convention. The former method would be quicker. The latter method, by avoiding legal "nit-picking," would be more certain.

12. A COALITION OF LIBERALS AND CONSERVATIVES IS NEEDED.

Whether we are conservative or liberal, our futures (and the futures of our children, grand children and great grandchildren) depend on our doing our duty as Americans. Our principal duty, at this point in our history, is to stop our country's economic, political and moral decline. In order to perform this duty we must first take the control of our government away from the military-corporate complex and return it to the people. This requires a 2nd constitutional convention at which the views of both conservatives and liberals would be taken into account. In order to bring about such a convention, as well as to assure its success, rank-and-file liberals and rank-and-file conservatives need to join forces. We are not in disagreement with each other about the need for a lawful federal government that responds to the needs of its people. Any petitions submitted should ask for a convention limited to proposing amendments aimed at governmental reform. Social issues would be out-of-bounds. While their self-interest prevents the leaders of our political parties from joining forces to bring about genuine reform, our self-interest should motivate us ordinary American liberals and conservatives to join together to bring about a truly representative 2nd constitutional convention.

13. THE SUPPORT OF UNIONS, CHURCHES AND OTHER NGO'S IS CRUCIAL.

Bringing about a constitutional convention for genuine governmental reform requires central planning and organization. This kind of central planning is generally carried on by the federal government. Yet any involvement of the federal government in this reform movement (aside from carrying out the instructions of the state legislatures) would compromise a 2nd convention from the start. Therefore, a coalition of activist political groups (such as the Tea Party and Occupy), trade unions, student unions, churches and NGO's is required. Without such a coalition, success would be problematical. The first need is for a council of representatives from these groups and organizations to coordinate a campaign petitioning the fifty state legislatures to apply for a 2nd constitutional convention.

14. IT WOULD BE WELL TO INVOLVE OUR STATE LEGISLATURES.

Our state legislatures have the power, collectively, to call a national convention. They also have the power to make the proposals of the convention into federal law.[197] Further, should we persuade Congress, rather than our state legislatures, to call a convention; it would be difficult to prevent Congress from controlling its agenda and finding other ways to forestall any genuine reform proposals. In order to bring about genuine governmental reform, a convention must be free of any federal or corporate control.

15. THE PROPOSALS MADE BY A NATIONAL CONVENTION SHOULD BE RATIFIED BY STATE CONVENTIONS.

The delegates to a national convention should propose, among other things, that Article V be amended to require the ratification of future proposed amendments by state conventions elected specifically for this purpose in elections that prohibit the use of private funds. It is clear from the Constitution and the *Federalist Papers* that the "people" of 1787-1791 wanted to have the final say on all matters involving the re-arranging of governmental powers. State conventions ratified the Constitution itself. Why should we not have the right to ratify proposed

---

[197] Congress "proposes" either the state legislatures or state conventions as the ratifiers of proposed amendments. The fact that the Constitution says that Congress "proposes" the method for ratification (rather than "decides" or "determines") suggests that state legislatures have the discretion to delegate or not to delegate this power. In any event, one of the changes needed in Article V is a provision making state conventions mandatory. They were mandatory for the ratification of the original constitution and there is no reason they should not be mandatory for amendments.

amendments in state conventions rather than state legislatures? Article VII provides a precedent for proposing conventions to require that their proposals be ratified by "money-free" ratifying conventions rather than by state legislatures.

16. ARTICLE V SHOULD BE MADE EXPLICIT ABOUT OUR POWER TO CALL A CONVENTION.

Article V's failure to explicitly give us the means of proposing amendments (and to give state conventions the sole power to ratify them) can, perhaps, be explained partially by the need of the 1787 federalists to make concessions to the "states rights" delegates.[198] In any event, these failures have obscured the "road to a people's decision" on constitutional matters. We have never called for a convention or proposed an amendment. We made the final decision in only one instance.[199] Nevertheless, Madison's promise of a road to the people's decision was kept, however obscurely. This road is not as well "marked" as Madison would have liked. In fact, it is so poorly marked that it has never been traveled. Yet the road does exist and it is our task to find our way through the underbrush despite the poor markings. Our first signpost is the 1st Amendment, which gives us the right to petition. But what if our state legislatures fail to act on our petitions? We may, perhaps, submit a number of signatures equal to eight percent of the voters in 34 states—yet the legisla-

[198] It should also be noted that the text of the amendment was decided in the rush of bringing the convention to a close. Article V was still being discussed on Sept. 10 and 15, 1787 (just a few days before the convention completed its work. Hamilton wanted Congress to be given the power to call a convention. Madison objected to the vagueness of the Article. Col. Mason objected on the grounds that the draft gave Congress too much power. He said that, if we depended o Congress for amendments, "No amendment of the proper kind would ever be obtained by the people."

[199] The single exception is the 21st Amendment, which repealed prohibition. Congress proposed that this one amendment be ratified by state conventions.

tures in these states may not apply for a national convention. What then? The next signposts are the Declaration of Independence and the 9th and 10th Amendments. The Declaration gives us the unequivocal right to alter the Constitution. The 9th Amendment says that we have rights in addition to those "enumerated" in the Constitution. The 10th Amendment, says that powers, not delegated to the US or prohibited to the states, "are reserved to the states, respectively, or to the people." The power to compel compliance with a petition calling for a legislature to apply for a convention (or for the proposal of specific amendments) is neither delegated to the US nor prohibited to the states. Therefore, it is reserved to either the state or to the people. It is absurd to believe that the state legislatures should be made judges in their own cases. Therefore, the power to make their petitions mandatory in this case must be reserved to the people. These signposts, while not explicit, can be used to give efficacy to the right granted us by our Declaration of Independence.

17. DIRECT DEMOCRACY IS NEEDED AT THE NATIONAL LEVEL.

Direct democracy is not an alternative to representative democracy. It is a necessary component of representative democracy. This is so for two reasons. First, it is a "fall-back" right (explicit in our Declaration and implicit in our Constitution) for us to use when the representative component of our political system breaks down. Madison expressed this view of direct democracy when he wrote, in *Federalist 49*, ". . . a constitutional road to the decision of the people ought to be marked out and kept open, for certain great and extraordinary occasions." Second, the availability of direct democracy would tend to make representatives more responsive to the people's will. However, our "right" to a people's decision is not enough in and of itself. We need to exercise this right occasionally if we want our representatives to take it seriously.

In a sense this book is about our implicit right to include some elements of direct democracy in our system of representative democracy. It is also about our need to make this right explicit in our Constitution. This book is intended, among other things, to contribute to a public discussion of the various forms of direct democracy and how some of them might serve a constructive purpose as a component of our national representative system.

Article V needs to be revised to include some explicit elements of direct democracy if future generations are to fulfill their responsibilities for improving and updating the Constitution. Indeed, the sad state of the US strongly suggests a need for supplementing our system of representative democracy with some explicit elements of direct democracy. These elements are stated in the Declaration and implied in the Constitution. However, "efficacy" (as Hamilton expressed it) has not been given to these general provisions. Methods and procedures need to be made explicit in order to transform democratic principles into an effective and genuinely democratic political system.

Many of the countries ranking high on international measures of democracy, honest government, prosperity and other aspects of national life have adopted some of the forms of direct democracy at the national level. Why not study their systems of "initiative," "referendum," and "recall" and consider tailoring them to the US situation and needs? Just as Americans' access to the courts is limited, so is their ability to affect national policy. In a time of ever-increasing constituencies for members of Congress and of ordinary Americans' ever-decreasing influence over government through the election process, it is appropriate to consider other means of bolstering our democracy. A national provision for citizen "initiatives" might put citizen-friendly policies, statutes and constitutional amendments on the national ballot. Also, the threat of recall might restrain presidents from encroaching on the powers of Congress and the judiciary.

18. REFORMING GOVERNMENT WILL REQUIRE POLITICAL EDUCATION.

Over the years Americans have come to believe that the civil officers of our federal government are our masters and we are their servants. The Declaration of Independence, the Constitution and the *Federalist Papers* disagree. US schools and universities, however, do not insist that students read and understand these documents. The resultant general misunderstanding of the US political system has led to the making of federal civil officers into a "nobility" of celebrities. They set their own compensation, fly first or business class (insulated from their constituents) and are soon infected by a congressional culture that places them above the law and, even more serious, allows them to make laws that support their elitist life styles. Ordinary Americans have become their servants and they have become the servants of "big money." We Americans are so manipulated that, when we feel outraged and injured, instead of exercising our constitutional power to reform our government, we go to our civil officers as complainers and supplicants. We somehow believe that, once we have told them about the reforms we would like to see, they will be happy to destroy their elite lifestyles by acceding to our wishes. This expectation, of course, is unrealistic. Our federal government has neither the motivation nor the duty nor the power to reform itself. Ironically, we (the people) do have the requisite motivation, duty and power. A part of this "American tragedy" can be attributed to a public educational system that leaves Americans unfamiliar with the Declaration of Independence, Constitution and *Federalist Papers*. Americans can hardly be expected to perform the duties of citizenship when they have never read and discussed their "job descriptions." One of the most important duties of citizenship is to keep a "jealous" eye on civil officers and "new model" government when they get out of control.[200]

The need for political education would become even greater should we be successful in reforming our government. At present, we take an essentially complaining and passive role in governmental affairs. We are upset when we read in the newspapers about the exotic trips taken by Members of Congress and their families at the expense of special interest groups. We groan when we read of the first class airline tickets they buy at our expense. But we accept corruption as an inevitable by-product of government. It never occurs to us that we, not our civil officers, are responsible for these abuses. Such constitutional reforms as six-year term limits, a balanced budget amendment, enforceable impeachment provisions, periodic constitutional conventions and a prohibition of any private funding in federal elections—would put an end to such abuses. These reforms would make it in the best interests of our civil officers to mend their ways. They require alterations in our Constitution, however, and only we have the motivation, duty and power to make these alterations.

An effective first step toward adequate political education would be for our high schools and universities to sponsor "moot" constitutional conventions. These "moot" conventions could provide future voters with the understanding and experience needed to serve as delegates to national (proposing) conventions and to state (ratifying) conventions—or to participate in the election of others to serve as delegates to these conventions.

[200] See Madison in *Federalist 49* and James Iredell speaking at the North Carolina ratifying convention on July 28, 1788.

19. STATE ELECTIONS ARE PIVOTAL.

The election of state legislators who favor prohibiting the use of private money in delegate elections and who also favor the calling of a national "proposing" convention is central to the re-forming of the US government. Ironically, votes in state elections can have more influence on the quality of the federal government than can votes in national elections. Votes in state elections and signatures on petitions presented to state legislatures are two means of bringing about a national convention. Votes in national elections may change the cast of characters in Washington, but the quality of our federal government can be changed only by altering the Constitution. This is the province of state governments and conventions.

20. "WE THE PEOPLE" MUST DEVELOP OUR OWN REFORM PROCEDURES.

Perhaps the most important lesson to be learned from our first two centuries of existence is that the "people's right" involving the reform (and continuing citizen control) is worthless without methods and procedures to give it "efficacy." [201] Further, in the case of government reform, we cannot expect Congress to provide us with methods and procedures. We must provide our own.

For example, we have the right to alter our Constitution—but we have never done so. We have never done so because Congress has not given our right to do so "efficacy" by statute. Why should it do something so adverse to its members' self interests? The Framers also failed to provide methods and procedures. They were evidently so caught up in the necessity for agreeing on a Constitution promptly that they ignored Madison's plea for Article V methods and, procedures. Instead,

---

[201] Hamilton wrote, in the *Federalist Papers*, that every constitutional provision should be given "efficacy."

they listened to Hamilton's argument that any imperfections in the Constitution could easily be corrected later by amendment.

This may have been true for many constitutional imperfections. It did not, however, apply to imperfections that encouraged lawlessness on the part of our civil officers and discouraged them from placing the needs of the people above their own short-term self interests. We had no methods given us for exercising our power to correct these imperfections and—for over two centuries—have failed to create our own. The needed checks to self-interested civil officer behavior (for example, money-free federal elections, term limits and strong impeachment provisions) have never been instituted. Our failure to create our own methods has, quite naturally, turned our civil servants into celebrities with elite life styles. If we are to encourage them to abandon their elite life styles and become civil servants again, we must alter the Constitution itself. We must alter it to specify checks presently required (such as money-free federal elections) and to further specify methods and procedures we (and future generations) can use to create any additional checks to improper civil officer behavior that become necessary in the future. In short, since the only means we have of mending civil officer behavior is to amend the Constitution, we must treat it, as regards civil officer behavior, as though it were a statute. We must be detailed and explicit.

21. OUR SECOND CONVENTION MUST BE LIMITED TO REFORM ISSUES.

We ordinary Americans must put aside our legitimate disagreements on social issues in order to bring about a 2nd constitutional convention. Further, in order to be successful the convention itself must be limited to the discussion of governmental reform proposals. As regards to social issues, we "rank and filers" from different political parties have differences of opinion. As regards to governmental reform, the interests of the "ninety per cent" (whether Democrats of Republicans) conflict with the interests of their civil officers and party leaders, but are shared by the rank-and-file of all political parties. On this issue, we are in harmony with each other. Americans from all our political parties want a more honest, responsive and effective federal government. Further, we have the power, the motivation and the means to reform our government. We must bring about a "money-free" convention and limit that convention to making proposals only for governmental reform—the issue on which we have general agreement. On this issue, we need only discuss and develop specific proposals for achieving our shared goals. This discussion cannot take place in the atmosphere of conflict and antagonism that would be created by discussing those matters on which we disagree. No general issue (for example, Article V, campaign finance reform, term limits etc.) should be placed on the convention agenda without being approved for discussion by a two-thirds vote of the delegates. Our failure to maintain control of our federal government has been due, in large part, to the failure of ordinary Americans from all parties to join forces and pursue shared interests.

B. REFORM STRATEGY AND APPROACHES

This Section first makes some general comments regarding a reform strategy. Then it suggests a number of possible "first steps" that might be taken by a people's reform movement. Political philosopher Dick Howard once wrote, "It is one thing to think up a Constitution, or to imagine remedies for defects in such an instrument; it is another to think through the political conditions in which such a framework could actually work."[202] I would suggest that, among the conditions under which govern-

---

[202] Letter to the author of Sept. 5, 2006.

mental reform is possible, discontent with the existing political system is prominent. It appears that this condition exists in our country at present. The formation of the "Tea Party" on the right and the "Occupy" movement on the left testify to this discontent. As for the political conditions in which a reformed "framework could actually work," I think some of these conditions can be built into both our strategy and into the alterations themselves. For example, petitioning drives at the state level would create a politically educated core group in every state. Since people tend to become committed to a system they helped create, this strategy would help us meet one of these political conditions—the existence of an educated, politically active citizenry.

Some needed political conditions could be created by the constitutional amendments themselves For example, these amendments could create improved systems for impeachment, election and judicial control. Further, an initial alternation of Article V as a starting point in a reform movement could provide a training ground for us to become more involved in the management of our country. A comprehensive alteration of the same article by a 2 nd constitutional convention could create political conditions favorable to maintaining a culture of good citizenship.

The flaws in our sub-systems are fundamental. Yet they are themselves products of a deeper failure. This deeper failure is the failure of Article V to provide us ordinary Americans with the means to perform our most important civic duty: the correction of both original constitutional flaws and subsequent flaws that have been created by changing circumstances. In short, an inadequate Article V is the underlying reason for our national distress. If Article V had included the "marked out road to the people's decision" promised by James Madison, we would have called frequent constitutional conventions and—over time—legally maintained and improved our supreme law.

Because we failed in this principal duty, Congress, the executive and the judiciary have felt it necessary to alter the Constitution in whatever ways expediency and their ideologies have suggested.

Article V is not only the key to our failure to improve and maintain our Constitution. It may also be the key to our success in devising a reform strategy. That is, our reform strategy must find ways to overcome the difficulties raised by the flaws of Article V. In order to hold a truly representative "proposing" convention, we must remedy the most serious flaw in Article V —its failure to provide a "road to the people's decision." That is, the Constitution fails to provide us with a procedure for us, the people, to use in amending it. A second difficulty arises from the ability of Congress to "propose"[203] the method to be used in ratifying proposed amendments. A third difficulty is posed by the seeming "Catch 22" that can be expressed as follows: "We cannot prohibit the use of private funds in elections until we can elect a representative proposing convention and representative ratifying conventions. Yet we cannot elect representative proposing and ratifying conventions until we pass an amendment taking special interest money bout of these election processes."

The first difficulty can be overcome by constructing our own road. The second difficulty can be overcome by specifying in our proposed amendment (if we choose option 2) that it be ratified either by state conventions or by a national referendum. The third barrier can be overcome by citing our present Article VII. This Article established the precedent that proposed constitutional provisions can specify their own methods of ratification. Language for a "first step" amendment is suggested in the Appendix to this book. Language for a comprehensive re-write of Article V by a 2 nd constitutional convention is suggested in Chapter 10.

---

[203] State legislatures have taken the word "propose" to mean "specify."

1. OUR CURRENT REFORM STRATEGY:

At present, we have a "Tea Party" movement on the right and an "Occupy" movement on the left. In addition, "Public Citizen" is gathering signatures for a petition asking the federal government to propose a constitutional amendment reversing the *Citizens United v. FEC* decision. Our present efforts are divided and, for this reason alone, are probably futile. Here, I will comment on several approaches to reform that are now being pursued and several other approaches that would be available to a "shadow government" (should one form itself).

2. OUR CURRENT REFORM APPROACHES:

The strategy adopted by the groups currently "in the field" accepts the current governmental arrangements and provisions. These groups seek to improve government within the context of these present arrangements and provisions.

a. The "Tea Party" approach is based on the assumption that our national problems are being caused by faulty civil officers pursuing faulty policies. Its aim, therefore, is to replace the present incompetent civil officers with competent, dedicated people who will pursue effective policies.

b. The "Occupy" approach assumes that we can solve our problems by listing the reforms that need to be made and petitioning the three branches of the federal government to carry them out.

c. The "Public Citizen" approach responds to *Citizens United v. FEC* by leading an effort aimed at overturning the Supreme Court decision. It is gathering signatures on a petition urging

Congress to support "its" (Public Citizen's) proposed amendment overturning Citizen's United.

3. AN ALTERNATIVE REFORM STRATEGY:

An alternative strategy would aim at correcting the flaws in our present governmental arrangements. It would pursue this goal by bringing about a representative constitutional convention to review our supreme law and identify its flaws. This convention would then propose amendments to state conventions correcting these flaws. This "convention strategy" would involve either (1) petitioning the state legislatures to apply for a constitutional convention, or (2) petitioning the state legislatures to apply for an amendment to be proposed to the state legislatures, such amendment requiring periodic constitutional conventions. The language for these petitions is suggested in Appendix B.

It is essential that these petitions be recognized as having the force of law. This is so because, unlike other petitions, they are necessary to our only constitutional method of exercising a fundamental right - the right to alter our Constitution. This right is granted by our Declaration of Independence and given "efficacy" by our Constitution. A necessary step toward our exercising it is the calling of a constitutional convention. A necessary step toward the calling of a convention is that two-thirds of our state legislatures apply for one. A necessary step toward this collective application is the recognition of our "petitions to apply" as having the force of law. Should a state legislature ignore or deny such petitions, it would constitute a governmental usurpation of our (the people's) most fundamental right. It would invalidate America's claim to be a democratic state.

C. REFORM ROLES:

Unity, comprehensiveness, energy, idealism, moral authority, strength, resources and education are not the only ingredients for genuine reform.[204] They are singled out for discussion here because they involve groups or institutions that must work together to achieve reform.

1. PROVIDING UNITY AND COMPREHENSIVENESS?

Unity is an essential ingredient for a successful effort to reform our federal government. Different strategies pursued by different groups of people are doomed to failure. Piecemeal amendments, however critical, are not enough. We need a comprehensive review limited, however to reform issues and alteration of our Constitution. We have let too many years go by without a constitutional convention. No single amendment can reverse our decline. The word "coalition" is in bad-repute of late because it is commonly used to describe groups of nations that join together to fight wars. It is also true that a permanent coalition of NGO's could conceivable turn into little more than another political party. However, a natural commonality of interest exists among unions, churches and many activist NGO's and ordinary people of both conservative and liberal beliefs. We all desire a more lawful and responsive federal government. Making our government more lawful and responsive would help all of us pursue our separate and different interests. It would be worthwhile for each of our NGO's to allocate some small percentage of its budget and time to support a genuine reform movement. Such a unified movement could attack the root cause

---

[204] See the Afterword in *After Patrick Henry* for a fuller discussion of ingredients.

of our country's problems with a substantial force. At present we are divided and easily dealt with by the civil officers of our government. We can only make incremental improvements in our various areas of interest.

Most of our NGO's, both on the right and on the left, are disposed to work for governmental reform. A movement for the genuine reform of the federal government would be both difficult to organize and unlikely to succeed without these NGO's uniting to play a key role in its formation and programs. They are familiar with the terrain and know how to organize constituencies. The participation of organizations like Common Cause, Public Citizen, Move On and Credo is not just important. It is necessary. The first institutional step in a reform movement might be a meeting of the heads of the four or five leading NGO's from both sides of the political spectrum.

These organizations would benefit institutionally. Joining one or more of them would be a natural first step that could be taken by students and others who decide to support a reform movement. Member-funded NGO's might well be able to contribute to the movement's coordinating budget out of increased revenues from the dues of new members. There are many signs that Americans are ripe for participation in an effort to reform our federal government. Political parties, of course, are unlikely to join forces however urgent the need. Yet individuals from the right and the left might well form temporary alliances and work toward a common goal.

2. PROVIDING ACTIVISM, IDEALISM AND ENERGY?

Pearl S. Buck, author of *The Good Earth*, once wrote, "The young do not know enough to be prudent, and, therefore, they attempt the impossible, and achieve it, generation after generation." On Feb. 1, 1960, Franklin McCain, Ezell Blair, Joe

McNeil and David Richmond took their seats at a Greensboro Woolworth's lunch counter. Within weeks a "sit in" movement was sweeping the upper south and a flagging civil rights movement was reenergized (See Chapter 3). American students have been consistently influential in movements aimed at improving the human condition.

a. Activism

The late 1960's are generally considered to have been the period in America when student activism was at its highest level. However, this may not actually be the case. Noam Chomsky said in a 2009 interview, "I think it's grown since the 1960's" Chomsky then cited the feminist, environmental and global justice movements as examples.[205] Diana Alvarado agrees with Chomsky. She writes, "The reality is that students are as active as ever. In fact, a survey conducted by Levine and Cureton suggests that today's students may be the most socially active generation since the late 1930's."[206] Student activism now deals with a more fragmented set of issues. Alvarado adds, "Unlike the civil rights movement and the Vietnam War activism of the sixties, no single compelling issue today mobilizes students."

Student activism has become institutionalized. UC Berkley, for example, has a special assistant to the chancellor with "the specific charter of helping foster initiatives on the edge of multiple academic disciplines.[207] This institutionalizing of student activism has enabled students to adopt business strategies and use institutional resources. Karl Brooks, assistant professor of history at the University of Kansas, said that "student activism today is a world away from the angry protests of the 1960's and

---

[205] Gabriel Schivone. University of *Arizona Daily Wildcat*, Sept. 14, 2009.
[206] "Student activism today," Office of Education and Diversity Initiatives, AAC&U, accessed May 30, 2011.
[207] John Hagel and John S. Brown, "Student activism can change the world," *Bloomsberg Businessweek*, accessed May 30, 2011.

1970's."[208] The growing student union movement may help moderate this co-option of student activism.

Noam Chomsky said in a 2009 interview that student activism has "grown since the 1960's." That is no doubt true, but its diversity is more a weakness than a strength. Today's activists are taught "to transform the core, start at the edge."[209] Unfortunately; there are hundreds of different "edges." For student activists to divide their considerable strength among these hundreds of different edges (or causes) is to resign themselves to incrementalism. What is most needed today is a single underlying cause around which all student activists can rally.

Such a cause lies ready at hand: "students for a responsive government." Our government's responsiveness to money and lack of responsiveness to its people lie at the heart of most of the problems to which students now devote their energy and their idealism. Their increasing sophistication and use of the media are great assets. But they are assets devoted to losing causes. If student activists were to unite against the root cause of most of our difficulties, they could take a giant step toward solving many of the problems they are now fighting in a fragmented fashion. This root cause could be the need to reform our federal government.

The institutionalizing of dissent by universities and foundations has its down side. On the plus side of the ledger, it improves the quality of dissent and guides the dissenting energy of students into constructive channels. On the minus side, each university and each foundation has its own areas of concentration. This makes it difficult to interest students in solving the mega-problem that underlies most of the projects undertaken. While "studies suggest that students are highly skeptical of pol-

[208] David Linhardt, "Student activism becomes more media-savvy," *New York Times*, May 10, 2006.
[209] Hagel and Brown.

itics, politicians and government . . . they tend to focus on local problems and community issues, seeing them as more manageable and subject to real intervention."[210]

This, in a nutshell, is our mega-problem. How can the energies of students (and the energies of the rest of us—including our NGO's) be focused on the root cause of our distress: a government that responds to money more than to people? Students are dissatisfied with government. They have the energy, the idealism and the ability to initiate a genuine reform movement. It would seem that, since universities and other non-governmental organizations have become involved in the channeling of activist energies, they have a responsibility to channel a portion of these energies toward solving the root problem. This requires far more than one or two universities and institutes adopting "governmental reform" as their special area of interest. It requires a coalition of all universities and other non-governmental organizations.

b. Idealism

During their early teens, young people are focused on becoming familiar with whatever portion of the world they were born into. By their mid- to late-twenties, many have married and, perhaps, had children. For the next twenty to twenty-five years, their focus is, very rightly, on providing security, education and love for their children. This is no doubt the greatest contribution they can make—not only to their children—but to their country and to human progress. However, a modest investment of time spent in voting, signing petitions, and writing an occasional letter to their representatives in Congress would not detract from their major purpose in life (the care and education of their children). This is especially true since the example set by parents is a major part of a child's education. After our child-

---

[210] Diana Alvarado, Student activism today."

rearing days are over, while our idealism may have been moderated by our life experiences, many of us, nevertheless, can still summon the energy to vote, to carry an occasional petition ands to write an occasional letter.

c. Energy

The initiation of a reform movement also requires a high level of energy that is rarely available during the middle, career building and child raising stages of our lives and is rarely present when our child rearing days are over. The high level of energy required to initiate a movement toward genuine governmental reform in a climate of disillusion and apathy is most likely to come from young adults 18-25. Pearl Buck's point is also important. The natural reaction of older folks, even those of us who work for or volunteer in NGO's, is predictable. It goes something like this: "Major reform is an impractical dream; incremental reform is the wiser course. Make your donations, but leave the actual reform to those who know what they are about." This reaction, however, is counter-productive. We should not leave reform to the NGO's. They "know enough" to be prudent and do not have the kind of energy needed for genuine reform. Their business is to work for incremental improvements. Our government is too lawless and unresponsive for the "incremental improvements" strategy to be a valid option. Nevertheless, we need the organization and the continuity of the NGO's. But the initial energy needed to take on "impossible" jobs can best come from our colleges and universities. As soon as students have organized petition drives or student conventions in one or two states, the NGO's will be convinced that genuine reform is not impossible and will put their organizational ability and their resources to work supporting the students. For the long haul of course, we must count on all Americans, young and old, to bring about genuine government reform.

3. PROVIDING THE MORAL AUTHORITY FOR REFORM?

Our churches should provide the moral authority for reform. Their support would greatly improve a reform movement's chances of success. They were the driving force behind the movement to end our war in Nicaragua during the 1980's. During those years, as many as forty thousand Americans traveled to Nicaragua and went to the countryside to protest the attacks of our Contra mercenaries upon the population. In 1987 the churches led an attempt to defeat a bill providing funds to pay and supply the Contra Army. While the end of the war in 1990 was probably due in large part to the collapse of the USSR, the churches had fought an admirable fight for ten years in an attempt to stop the bloodshed. These same churches would be doing equally beneficial work if they joined a coalition for the specific purpose of making our federal government more lawful and more responsive to our wishes and our will. We can help stop a war by protesting against the actions of our lawless government. But the only way we can prevent wars is by reforming our government so that it is lawful and responsive to our will.

Joining a coalition for lawful and responsible government would be, in effect, joining a coalition for peace. It would be joining a movement for peace based on a logical analysis of the US political system. Our government is dominated by the executive branch and the executive branch, as our forefathers understood very well, is prone to war. For this reason, the framers gave the power to declare war to our legislative branch (an innovative approach to keeping the peace). Madison called this innovation the "wisest" part of the Constitution. For reasons discussed elsewhere in this book, the innovation failed. One of the consequences of genuine government reform would be to return the power of war and peace to its rightful place in the legislative branch. This is a far more logical approach and would probably be far more effective—than attempting to persuade Congress to stand up to the presidency and attempting to persuade the presidency to become an emissary of peace. Persuasion isn't going to work. We should learn from history that elections and a "parchment" separation of powers are not enough. A recent historical event teaches this lesson. We were sure we were electing a "peace president" in 2008. Before the first year of his presidency was up, he escalated the war in Afghanistan.

4. PROVIDING THE STRENGTH TO GET THE JOB DONE?

The participation of organized labor is also necessary for genuine reform. Until its membership eroded, labor was perhaps our main check against irresponsiveness and lawlessness in government. It is still a force to be reckoned with. While it cannot compete with corporate donations, it does have some influence with Congress. More important, just as labor can "get out the vote," it could also be the backbone of a campaign to petition state legislatures to apply for the calling of a national convention. It is possible that the growing student union movement might adopt governmental reform as a priority. If this were to happen, it would both strengthen the student union movement and increase the chances for success of a government reform effort. It should be noted that anti student union legislation (such as that being proposed in Wisconsin) could be prohibited by a "right-to-organize" amendment (See Chapter 10).

Genuine reform is in the interest of organized labor for several reasons. First, it would benefit labor's institutional interests. A federal government more responsive to the people and less responsive to corporations would be more likely to repeal the Taft-Hartley Act of 1947 and pass a genuine labor reform bill. A strong labor law is needed. Such a law would enable unions to strengthen their collective bargaining position and increase their membership. Genuine reform would also produce a Congress more friendly to organized labor's legislative efforts to help working people.

5. PROVIDING THE RESOURCES?

Participating NGO's, unions and church organizations could among them support a coordinating function (perhaps performed by an existing NGO) at a very modest per-member cost.

6. PROVIDING THE EDUCATION?

We do not educate our students at any level for performing the duties and assuming the responsibilities of US citizens. It is not improbable that many US citizens are unaware that they—not our federal civil officers—are responsible for maintaining the effectiveness, honesty and morality of our federal government. It is also not improbable that many more do not realize that they have the power to bring about genuine structural reform and that the federal government does not. Upon graduation from high school, all students should have spent a substantial amount of time with our Declaration of Independence and our Constitution. Our lack of awareness is at least partially due to the failure of our educational system to emphasize civic responsibility. This should be done in elementary schools, secondary schools and universities. It is conceivable that, had we been more aware of our duties to our country, our country would not now be in its political, economic and moral decline. We should look to our long term quality of life and add more courses in civic responsibility to all levels of our educational system. We are now expending our resources on the teaching of many courses of far lesser importance. Citizenship courses could be mandatory in our public schools. In the meantime, we need to educate our present-day students of voting age in their civic responsibilities so that they can better participate in a movement to reform our federal government. This might be done by the funding of "moot" constitutional conventions to be held by colleges and universities. The funding for these "moot" conventions might be provided by private foundations.

If the institutions of our society—and, most important, the American people (young and old) commit themselves to bringing about a 2nd constitutional convention, we can rejuvenate our country. We owe this commitment to ourselves and to future generations.

APPENDIX A
Data sources for international measures

The rankings shown in Tables 1-3 of Chapter 7 are based on the sources shown below. In the cases of union density and life satisfaction, the rankings are shown for only those OECD countries that reported union density percentages as recently as 2008 or 2009. All other OECD ranking shown in Tables 1-3 are based on world rankings for 2011 or 2012.

1. Union Density
This measure is published by the Organization for Economic Cooperation and Development (OECD) in its statistical extracts for union density. The data used as the basis for the Chapter 7 rankings is for 2009, except in the cases of France, Greece, Hungary, Iceland and the Slovak Republic. The data for these five countries is for 2008. The percentage figure shown for each country indicates the percent of the country's workforce that belongs to unions.

2. Democracy
The OECD rankings are based on the Economist Intelligence Unit's 2011 Democracy Index. This Index is based on sixty indicators covering five areas of government: elections, civil liberties, effective government, political participation and political culture.

3. Corruption
In Chapter 7 the Corruption Perceptions Index is referred to as the "honest government" index, since it gives the least corrupt country the number one ranking and the most corrupt country the lowest ranking. It is published by Transparency International and ranks 178 countries. The rankings in Tables 1-

3 are based on the Corruption Perceptions Index of 2011. This index defines corruption as "the misuse of public power for private benefit."

4. Competitiveness

Tables 1-3 are based on the rankings shown in the Global Competitiveness Index of 2012-2013. This Index is produced by the World Economic Forum and defines competitiveness as "the set of institutions, policies and factors that determine the level of the productivity of a country."

5. Prosperity

The OECD rankings in Chapter 7 are based on the 2011 Legatum Prosperity Index. This Index ranks 110 countries on their ability to prosper. It uses eight criteria: the economy, entrepreneurship, governance, education, health, safety and security, personal freedom and social capital.

6. Life satisfaction

OECD's Better Life project asked a sample of the people in each OECD member country if they were satisfied with their lives in general. Tables 1-3 use the 2011 OECD data since this question was not asked in the 2012 survey. In Chapter 7, the percentages of people in each country answering "Yes" to this question are used as indicators of the extent to which the country's political and economic systems are doing their job.

APPENDIX B
Suggested petition and amendment language

The "convention strategy" approaches to reform outlined in Part III of this book all aim at the calling of a "money-free" constitutional convention. State legislatures and the two approaches petition Congress. Both of the two approaches involve amendments to the Constitution prior to the actual calling of a convention. The other two go directly to the convention. This Appendix suggests language for each of the four possible petitions and for the prior amendment.

1. Petition the states to apply to Congress to call a constitutional convention.

In accordance with the rights provided me by the Declaration of Independence and the 1st, 9th and 10th Amendments, I hereby petition the state legislature of the State of (name of state) to immediately apply to Congress to call a constitutional convention limited to making proposals to reform the federal government of the US. I further petition the state legislature of the State of (name of state) to instruct Congress that one delegate to this convention be elected from each congressional district in the state and that the use of private money to promote in any way any candidate be prohibited and any solicitation, acceptance or offering of such money be treated as a felony.

2. Petition the states to apply to Congress to propose a specific constitutional amendment to the 50 state legislatures.

In accordance with the rights provided me by the Declaration of Independence and the 1st, 9th and 10th Amendments, I hereby petition the state legislature of the state of (specify state name) to apply to Congress that it propose the following amendment to the fifty states. "Congress shall call a convention limited to making proposals to reform the federal government of the US within three months of the effective date of this amendment. It shall call a constitutional convention at least once each twenty years thereafter. The amendments proposed by these conventions shall be acted upon by state ratifying conventions within six months of the date the convention proposals are received by the state legislatures or they will be treated as approved. The elections of one delegate from each of our 435 congressional districts to the proposing convention and the elections of delegates to the state ratifying conventions shall be conducted solely with public funds. The solicitation, acceptance, offering or use of private funds in campaigns for the election of delegates to proposing or ratifying conventions shall be a felony."

Both of the above petitions would have the same two purposes: (1) to bring about a constitutional convention and (2) to assure that this convention would be representative of all the people and limited to government reform. Both of the approaches to the "convention strategy" are aimed at calling a convention that would, among other things, construct a clear, well-marked "road to the people's decision" in matters of major import such as the reform of the federal government. All of the proposals contained in Part III rely on the wisdom and judgment of all of us ordinary Americans, conservatives and liberals alike, to reverse the political, economic and moral decline of our country.

CASES

Baker v. Carr, 369 U.S. (186) 1962

Bas v. Tingy, 4 Dall, (4 U.S.) 37, 401800)

Bush v. Gore, 531 U.S. 98 (2000)

Citizens United v. Federal Election Commission, 558 U.S. 08-205 (2010)

Clinton v. City of New York 524 U.S. 417 (1998)

Doe v. Bush, 323 F. 3d 133 (1st Cir. 2000)

El-Shifa v. United States, 506 U.S. 224, 228-36 (1993)

Ex parte Merryman, 17 F. Cas. 144 (1861)

Ex parte Milligan, 71 U.S. 2 (1866)

Feagan et als. v. Hudgins et als. Case No. CL08-6016

Goldwater v. Carter, 444 U.S. 996 (1979)

Laird 451 F. 2d. 26 (1st cir. 1971)

Marbury v. Madison, 5 U.S. (1 Cranch) 137 (1803)

Schlesinger v. Holtzman, 414 U.S. 1321, (1973)

REFERENCES

Amar, Akhil Reed. "Philadelphia Revisited: Amending the Constitution Outside Article V" (1988) *Faculty Scholarship Series.* Paper 1023...

Amar, Akhil Reed. "The Supreme Court, 1999 Term-Foreword: The Document and the Doctrine" (2000), *Faculty Scholarship Series*, Paper 851.

Bacevich, Andrew J. *The Limits of Power*, Metropolitan Books, 2008.

Bentham, Jeremy. *A Fragment on Government*, T. Payne, London, 1776.

Berger, Raoul. Impeachment: *The Constitutional Problems*, Harvard University Press, 1973.

Bowen, Catherine Drinker. *Miracle at Philadelphia*, Back Bay Books, 1966.

Brier, Stephan (Ed.). *Who Built America?* Volumes I and II, Pantheon Books, 1992.

Douglas, Paul H. *Ethics in Government*, Harvard University Press, 1952.

Bugliosi, Vincent. *The Betrayal of America*, Thunders Mouth Press, Nation Books, 2001.

de Tocqueville, Alexis. *Democracy in America*, Signet Classics, 2001.

Farrand, M., *The Records of the Federal Convention of 1787* (New Haven: rev. ed., 1937).

Ferguson, Niall. Colossus: *The Rise and Fall of the American Empire*, Penguin Books, 2004.

Fisher, Louis. *Presidential War Power*, University Press of Kansas, 1995.

Henry, Patrick. *The Anti-Federalist Selected Writings and Speeches*, Classic Books America, 2009.

Herrick, Neal Q. *After Patrick Henry: A Second American Revolution*, Black Rose Books, 2009.

Herrick, Neal Q. *Joint Management and Employee Participation: Labor and Management at the Crossroads*, Jossey-Bass, 1990.

Ketchum, Ralph (ed.). *The Anti-Federalist Papers and the Constitutional Convention Debates*, A Mentor Book, 1986.

Lane, Eric and Michael Ogresses, *The Genius of America: How the Constitution Saved Our Country and Why It Can Again*, Bloomsbury; 2000.

Melton, Buckner F. *The First Impeachment*, Mercer University Press, 1998.

Monroe, James. *The People, The Sovereigns*, James River Press, 1987.

Obama, Barack. *Audacity of Hope: Thoughts on Reclaiming the American Dream*, Crown Publishers, 2006.

Paul, Ron. *The Revolution: A Manifesto*, Grand Central Publishing, 2008.

Posner, Richard A. *An Affair of State*, Harvard University Press, 1999.

Rakove, Jack N.(ed.). *James Madison's Writings*, The Library of America, 1999.

Richards, Leonard L. *Shays' Rebellion*, Penn. Press, 2002.

Rossiter, Clinton (ed.). *The Federalist Papers*, Signet Classics, 2003.

Ryan, Allan (ed.). *J. S. Mill and Jeremy Bentham. Utilitarianism and Other Essays*, Penguin Classics.

Sabato, Larry J. *A More Perfect Constitution*, Walker & Co., 2007.

Index